PITCHING
AGAINST
MYSELF

To ADAM JAAFAR,
I AM SO PROUD OF THE MAN YOU ARE
BECOMING. YOU ARE GOING TO LEAVE
BEHIND QUITE THE LEGACY.

WITH INFINITE LOVE & GRATITUDE,

PITCHING AGAINST
MYSELF

IT IS MORE THAN A GAME

RILEY TINCHER

TINCHER ENTERPRISES, LLC
www.RileyTincher.com

Pitching Against Myself

Requests for information should be addressed to:
Tincher Enterprises, LLC
P.O. Box 366
Jenks, OK 74037
Or electronically addressed to: riley@rileytincher.com

ISBN 978-0-9990259-0-1 (Paperback Edition)
ISBN 978-0-9990259-1-8 (eBook)
ISBN 978-0-9990259-2-5 (Audio Book)

Riley Tincher is represented by Guy A. Fortney, Attorney at Law of the Law Offices of Brewster & De Angelis, P.L.L.C., in Tulsa, Oklahoma.

Written & Edited by *Riley Tincher*
Book Jacket & Cover Design by *Riley Tincher*
Photograph on Front Cover by *Allie A. Klawitter | Allie Klawitter Photography*
Photograph on Back Cover by *Dan Lassiter | GazetteXtra*
"Broken Baseball" Drawing on Book Spine created by *Jonathan Hood*
Book Interior Design by *Riley Tincher*

First printing on May 29th, 2017 | Printed in the United States of America

DEDICATION

To John, Mary Lynn, Nigel, Hans, Josh, & Senna Saurino - Thank you is not enough for coming into my life, at the *perfect* time, when I *desperately* needed a family like yours. Thank you for welcoming me into your home, & treating me like one of your own. Thank you for continually showing me a love & generosity I have *never* experienced before. I will never be able to repay you for all you have done for me.

To Dad & Mom - You helped raise a great man, & you should be proud of that. Every good & bad thing that happened during my childhood, has made me who I am. I know you tried your best, the only way you knew how to, & I am grateful for that. I still love you, & I *always* will.

To Coach Darin Everson - Thank you for believing in me when no one else did. Thank you for not allowing me to quit, & encouraging me to *get back up there*. Thank you for getting me opportunities I did not deserve. I would not have accomplished the things I did, if it was not for you. I cannot wait to see you in a Major League uniform.

To Coach John Vodenlich - What you taught me goes *far* beyond baseball; you taught me how to be a better man. Thank you for demanding so much from me. You showed me what I was capable of accomplishing, & you showed me who I was capable of being.

To Matt Millar – You led me to the best decision of my life, & dropped a Rock in my pond. You were a *constant* bright light in my very dark life. Thank you for *being* my introduction to the *real* Jesus Christ.

CONTENTS

FIRST PITCH

The most crucial pitch, for every pitcher, in all of baseball, is the *first pitch*. Every at-bat is like a chess game between the pitcher & the hitter. The best pitchers pitch to their strengths. The best hitters hit to their strengths. Both have a job to do. To put it simply, the hitter's job is to get on base, & the pitcher's job is not to let that happen.

The first pitch sets the tone for the rest of the at-bat. If the pitcher throws a strike, it *significantly* increases the chances of getting the hitter out – which, again, is the pitcher's job. Statistically speaking, less than ten-percent of first-pitch strikes turn into base hits. After the first-pitch strike, batting averages significantly decrease, & the number of walks significantly decreases, as well. Most importantly, pitchers who throw the most first-pitch strikes, win the most games.

This introduction chapter is the first pitch of this book. As an author, I fully realize that if I do not grab your attention in this chapter, & captivate you in one way or another, you are less likely going to finish this book; which, defeats the whole purpose of a book.

I want to be completely honest with you: I initially did not write this book for you to read. I started writing this book for therapy purposes, to help me get through a *very* dark time. *It did.* I also wrote this book to help me remember all the great things I accomplished & all the wonderful people I met throughout my baseball career.

To be even more honest with you, I am amazed that you are even reading this right now. A couple of months before I started writing this book, I planned on committing suicide. When I say I planned, I mean I literally planned it out – I knew the date I was going to do it, I knew how I was going to do it, & I even had the suicide note written. Thank

God for one of my mentors (whom, I had not heard from in over a year) calling me out of the blue on *the* day I planned on killing myself. I was reluctant to answer his call, but I am so grateful I did. He refused to accept the answer I gave him when he asked me how I was doing. When he finally got me to tell him that I was planning on committing suicide, he would not hang up the phone until I promised him that I would not do it. Then, he proceeded to call me every hour on the hour, for the next several days, to make sure I was *ok*. He saved my life.

Throughout our several phone conversations, he loved on me, encouraged me, & poured out the truth to me. He helped me change my perspective by showing me that there was purpose in my pain. He told me that "we do not go through what we go through for ourselves, we go through what we go through to help someone else who is going to go through the same thing." He also told me that I have a story to share, & that there is something greater for me other than playing baseball. The problem was, we did not know what that was yet.

We talked about my childhood, & my years in school. He asked me what I enjoyed, & what I was passionate about while I was in school, & I told him about the time I made a presentation in graduate school about "teaching life lessons through sports." He asked me to go into more detail about the presentation, so I explained to him that I interviewed some of my former teammates, & other athletes I had coached throughout my coaching career. I also explained that in these interviews, I asked the athletes questions about what their respective sport taught them about life, & how they applied what they had learned to their life after their athletic career was over. He stopped me in the middle of my explanation, & asked me if I had interviewed myself. Since I did not, I responded, "no." Then, he told me that I needed to ask myself the same questions I asked the athletes I interviewed for my presentation, & write down every answer I could possibly come up with. He encouraged me to start from the beginning, when my baseball career started in eighth grade, & write about *everything* that happened – on & off the field - all the way up to the final out that was made in the last game I ever played.

This was an enormous task he was requesting me to do. The sheer amount of writing seemed impossible for a dyslexic kid like me, so I laughed at it, & he quickly responded, "I'm *serious*." I confoundedly asked him "how am I going to do that?" & his response was, "I do not know, but I will do whatever I can to help you figure it out."

Over the next couple of months, we came up with a plan to start writing. We also came up with ideas on how I was going to write. We decided that it would be best if I wrote it in a book format - each chapter being a game, or a season I pitched in, followed by a life lesson I learned from that game, or season. We also came up with two standards for the writing process: one, I would not hold *anything* back (no secrets, or hidden details – all real, authentic, genuine stories; no matter how bad, or how foolish they may make me look), & two, I would write at least one page per day, until I was done with the book. We did that because how do you write a book? One page at a time. When we finalized our plans, we came up with a date to start writing.

On January 1st, 2014, I started writing this book. I eagerly went to a local bagel shop in Tulsa, Oklahoma. I ordered a coffee, sat down at a table, set up my laptop, opened up Microsoft Word, & stared blankly at my computer… for *two* hours. No words. No sentences. *Nothing*. Just a blank page. It was not necessarily writer's block; I just did not know how to start. As time went on, I became increasingly frustrated. Negative thoughts began to swirl around in my mind:
"What is the point of this?"
"This is just a *huge* waste of time."
"I have nothing good to write about."
"I should just give up."

The moment I thought that – "I should just give up" - I was instantly reminded of what my eighth-grade coach told me at the end of the season, & an hour later, the first chapter was written.

Not every day was like the first day. There were days where I struggled to write just one page, & on some of those days, I did not even use the page I wrote for the book. There were also days where it was amazingly easy to write, & words were flowing out of me faster than I could type. These were the days where it felt like I could not stop writing, & I ended up writing multiple pages, & on very rare occasions, even entire chapters. There were days when I got done writing, I felt elated & overjoyed. Then, there were also days that were unbearably emotional, where tears filled my eyes, & were rolling down my face as I was trying to write.

Were there days where I did not want to show up to write? *Of course, there were.* However, that same mentor that saved my life, did not allow me to not write. He texted me *every* morning at 8:00 AM to make sure that I wrote. At first, the text message he sent me was a simple question: "Did you write your page?" Then, over time, the daily text message changed, because the purpose of the book changed.

As the writing process unfolded, & I got deeper & deeper into the book, I started meeting more & more former athletes who were struggling with the same things I was struggling with – identity crisis, & figuring out what to do with life after sports. The number of former athletes I met who were also struggling was overwhelming. I heard so many (*too* many) heart-wrenching stories about depression, drug & alcohol abuse, & suicide. It became obvious that transitioning out of sports was not just a struggle for me, but for the majority of athletes. I was so discontented by all that I heard, that I became angry. I started thinking, "somebody has to *do something* about this."

I told my mentor about all of the former athletes I was meeting who were struggling with the same things I was struggling with, & I expressed my anger & frustrations to him. He reminded me about the conversation we had about there being purpose in my pain. Then, he told me "the things we are most discontented about, are God's way of pulling on our heart, & telling us that we are supposed to be the ones to change it." I asked him "how can I change this?" To which, he responded, "through this book." He continued with, "you have an incredible story to share, that people need to read, & it would be selfish of you not to share it." He then asked me if I could think of any other books that were teaching athletes how to transition out of sports, & I could not think of any, so I responded "no." He followed up my response with another question, "don't you wish you had a book like this that you could have read when you were playing?" I emphatically said, *"absolutely!"* Then, he said, "this is your chance to be the voice you needed to hear back when you were playing. This is your chance to create what you wish existed."

His daily 8:00 AM text changed to: "create what you wish existed." The purpose of this book changed, as well. It was no longer about me anymore. It was no longer *only* for me to read. It was for every former athlete who is struggling with life after sports, & trying to figure out what to do next. It was for every current athlete who is hoping to one day play professional sports, despite getting overlooked & written off, & being told that they will never amount to anything. It was for every coach who has forgotten about the power & impact their influence has on all of their athletes. It was for every parent who fails to realize that their children are watching *everything* they do, & are listening to *everything* they say. It was for every child who is living in a broken home that is trying to escape. It was for every adult who is wanting to break free from the cycle of addiction & oppression that has kept their family in bondage for generations. It was for anyone who is going through an identity crisis. It was for anyone who feels undervalued & unappreciated. It was for anyone who feels forgotten, or like they do not belong. It was for anyone who is struggling with depression & suicidal thoughts. It was for anyone wanting to restore their hope. It was for anyone needing a reason to believe again.

As you are reading this book, you will find two books within it. The first book is about my baseball career & *everything* that was happening to me on & off the field throughout it. It is about how I went from sitting on the bench to becoming an All-American. It is also about the internal struggles I was having throughout the process; most of these struggles have been kept hidden up until now. In this book, I invite you into places I have never let *anyone* into before. I share stories I have *never* shared before. It is very vulnerable. It is extremely emotional. It is incredibly inspiring. It is as raw, real, & uncut as I could write. It is not a sob story. It is a victory story. It is *my* story.

The second book is the book I wish I would have read when I was playing baseball. This book is the "knowledge applied" section in every chapter. These sections are not just filled with quotes & clichés, they are filled with tried & *true* principles that apply to *everyone* – no matter if they are an athlete, or not – in *every* situation, & circumstance. There are a few redundancies in these sections, because I had to learn some of these principles multiple times... some, the easy way & *most*, the hard way. The reason why these sections are called "knowledge applied" is because wisdom – the *greatest* treasure we could ever ask for, or receive – is simply defined as "knowledge *applied*." With that being said, the only way these principles will work for you, is if you *apply* them. As John C. Maxwell, a world-renowned speaker, a best-selling author, & one of the world's greatest leadership teachers, says, "knowledge without application is *useless*."

You will also find two common themes in this book. The first common theme is that the most difficult paths lead to the most beautiful rewards – the harder the struggle, the sweeter the victory. The second common theme is that anything (& I mean, *anything*) is possible for those who believe... & persevere.

I have held on to this book for *far* too long. I finished writing it in November of 2014, & then I put it away. I came up with every excuse not to edit it. Then, when I finally started editing it, I came up with even more excuses not to finalize it – one of the main excuses being, "it needs to be *perfect*," even though perfect does not exist. While this was going on, more & more people kept asking me when my book was going to be finished, & all I could tell them was "it will be released soon." "Soon" turned into over two years later.

The truth is, this book scares the hell out of me. There is nothing more vulnerable than writing down *every* insecurity, weakness, wrongdoing, & shortcoming of my life... for *everyone* to be able to read. On the other hand, the quote - "Our deepest fear is not that we are inadequate. Our deepest fear is that we are powerful beyond measure." - from *Return to Love* by Marianne Williamson is absolutely, positively, one-hundred-percent true. I can feel the power & magnitude that this book has, & it *terrifies* me.

A year ago, in June of 2016, all of my excuses quickly disappeared as I was painfully reminded of the purpose of this book, & why it is not about me. I was on vacation in Los Angeles, California, & I met an older woman whose son *was* a professional baseball player. After telling her about this book, my baseball career, & my struggles with depression & suicidal thoughts after my career ended, she revealed to me that her son had recently committed suicide. He was a pitcher in the Minor Leagues, & was released shortly after injuring his shoulder. Soon after his release, he decided to kill himself. He wrote a suicide note, & in this note, he said: "I dedicated my whole life to baseball. All I know is baseball. All I am is a baseball player. I do not know how to be anyone else, & I do not want to be anyone else."

At the end of our tear-filled conversation, we hugged, & just as we began to part ways, she turned back to me & told me something that I will *never* forget. She said, "my son *needed* to read your book."

The time has *finally* arrived. It is now time for *you* to read this book. The first pitch has been thrown, & the game is underway. There are going to be a lot of strike outs. There are going to be a lot of homeruns. There are going to be some errors. There are going to be some groundballs hit into double plays. All of which, make the game of baseball, my life, & this book, *perfectly* beautiful.

"Anything (& I mean *anything*) is possible for those who believe... & persevere."

"Wisdom - the *greatest* treasure we could ever ask for, or recieve - is simply defined as 'knowledge applied'"

@RileyTincher | #PitchingAgainstMyself

CHAPTER 1

YOU SHOULD QUIT

I loved baseball. I loved baseball before I even started playing it. Words cannot even begin to describe the love I had for baseball. It was an obsession. It was all I thought about. It was all I talked about. It was all I dreamed about. I devoted my life to it. A professional baseball player was all I wanted to be, & I was willing to do *anything* to ensure I became one.

I was in eighth grade when I decided to start playing baseball, competitive. It has been one of the best decisions of my life. Who knew a 14-year-old boy could make such a great decision on his own?

Before making the decision to play baseball, competitively, I played whiffle ball with all the neighborhood kids in the backyard of one of their houses, pretty much, every day (sometimes, twice per day). I would have played it from sunrise to sunset, if I was allowed to... & if they wanted to.

Every once in a while, if we had enough kids, instead of playing whiffle ball, we would all go down to the little league fields, which were a block away from the neighborhood, & we would play homerun derby. There would be one hitter, one pitcher, & everyone else would be in the outfield, with their gloves, trying to catch all of the baseballs that did not make it over the fence; just like it is done during the Major League Baseball Homerun Derby at the All-Star break.

We would rotate pitchers & hitters. Everyone would have ten outs to see how many baseballs they could hit over the fence. We would play several rounds (if time allowed), & the hitters with the fewest homeruns were eliminated each round, until the one with the most homeruns was left standing - the Homerun Derby Champion.

I was *always* crowned the Homerun Derby Champion. The reason why I always won was because, for quite some time, no one ever hit a homerun... except for me. I was the *only* kid in the neighborhood who could hit the baseball over the 260-foot center field fence at the fields. I *thoroughly* enjoyed always winning.

If I was not playing whiffle ball, or down at the little league fields playing homerun derby, I would *try* to play catch with my dad in our backyard. Unfortunately, this did not happen very much.

My dad worked nights driving a semi-truck from Madison to Chicago & back, or from Madison to Minneapolis & back, every Monday through Friday night. When I would get home from school, he would be getting ready to leave for work. On the weekends, he would *always* be busy doing work around the house; mainly, in the garage. Often times, the only chance I could get to play catch with him, was right before dinner on Sunday nights. Even though these chances were *rare*, & despite the fact that we would only be able to throw the baseball back & forth a couple of times (because it was too dark to see the baseball) when we did get the chance, I *loved* playing catch with my dad.

My dad was the main reason why I loved baseball. I loved baseball because he *loved* baseball, or I should say, he *loved* the Milwaukee Brewers. It seemed like every time I went out into the garage, there was a Brewers game playing on the television, & Bob Uecker, the Hall of Fame announcer for the Brewers (best known for his role in the movie, *Major League*), was playing through the radio speakers. To this day, I have yet to meet a more passionate Brewers fan than my dad. Every run that was scored, every homerun that was hit, & every strikeout that was thrown, I could hear my dad's voice echoing throughout the house I grew up in. To him, every game they won, was as if they won the World Series.

My dad was the reason why I decided to start playing baseball. He was the one that encouraged me to try out for the eighth-grade team.

He was the one that drove me to the sporting goods store & bought me a glove, a bat, a pair of cleats, & catcher's gear. Yes, you read that correctly... *catcher's gear.* In eighth grade, I wanted to be a catcher - not *all* of my decisions were great when I was 14 years old.

For those who know nothing about me, I am left-handed. If you do not know anything about baseball, there has *never* been a left-handed catcher, & there probably never will be. At the time, I did not know that. Either that, or I was determined to prove everyone wrong; which, you will *quickly* find out has been a common theme of my life.

The decision to try out for the baseball team was not an easy decision. None of my friends played baseball, & none of the neighborhood kids played baseball, competitively. As a matter of fact, I did not know *anyone* that were on the baseball teams.

When the day of the tryouts came, I went *alone.* Just as any 14-year-old kid would be (& *should* be), I was nervous. I did not know what to expect, because I had never experienced anything like it before. It was my first tryout for any sport, *ever.* I did not know what I was going to do that day. I did not know how the tryout was going to be run. I did not know how long the tryout was going to be. I did not know who was going to be at the tryout. I did not even know who the coaches were, who were the ones leading the tryout.

I had to walk to the tryout with all my catcher's gear. The tryout was held at the high school, which was a little over a mile away from the house I grew up in. As I got closer to the high school, my nervousness got worse. I actually started to walk slower; the closer I got, the slower I walked. Fear & doubt began to consume. I started to question my decision to tryout for the baseball team. I wanted to turn around, but I could not. I did not want to let my parents down. More importantly, I did not want to let my dad down. He spent *a lot* of money (money, we barely had) on my baseball equipment, & I could not go back home & tell him that I decided not to try out for the baseball team. He would have been so disappointed in me.

When I walked into the high school, I pretended to be lost, even though there were signs pointing to where the baseball tryout was being held. I started roaming the hallways of the school to stall for more time, until one of the coaches saw me. He approached me & asked me if I was there for the baseball tryout, & I said "yes." He told me to follow him, & we walked together to the fieldhouse, where the tryout was being held.

The tryout had already begun. I was late. I was immediately overwhelmed. There were *a lot* of other baseball players there; at least fifty of them (all of whom I did not know). They were warming up. As I was trying to find a place to set down my bag, one of the coaches began to yell at me to hustle up & join them. When I finally found a spot to set my bag down, I reached in & grabbed my bat & my glove, & off I went. The next hour of my life was *chaos.*

When the tryout was over, I had a very long walk home… *alone.* As I was walking home, questions & doubts began to arise in my mind:
"What just happened?"
"What happens next?"
"How did I perform?"
"Did they like me?"
"Do they even know my name?"
"Did I make the team?"

Several days after the tryout passed, & the team rosters still had yet to be announced. The more weeks that passed (it felt more like months), & the further it got away from the tryout, the more doubt began to consume my mind, & the negative self-talk became worse:
"I won't make the team."
"Nobody liked me."
"I made so many errors."
"All of the other players were so much better than me."

Then, the day *finally* came. The rosters & schedules were announced. They posted the roster on the community pool's front door on a Sunday night. As soon as I found out, I rushed out of my front door, got on my bike, & rode over to the pool, which was right next to the little league fields where we would play homerun derby.

When I got to the pool, I ditched my bike, & I ran up the stairs to the front door of the pool, where the rosters & schedules were posted; I probably skipped three or four steps with each stride. When I got to the door, I was so nervous, I covered my eyes with my hands. I *slowly* separated my fingers to peak through, so I could read the rosters.

There were two rosters for two teams, & guess what? *I made one of the teams!* I was so excited to see my name on the roster, that I did not even look at the schedule to see when the first practice was. It was one of the *best* feelings of my life. I ran down the steps, got on my bike, & road home the fastest I had ever ridden my bike before. I was so proud. All those doubts I had quickly vanished. *I made the team!*

This was the first team I had been on since I played basketball, a few years prior. This was the first *real* baseball team I had ever been on. I did not know about practice. I did not know the rules to follow. I did not know how long the base paths were, or how far away the pitcher's mound was from home plate. I did not even know where all the positions on the baseball field were; I always mixed up left field & right field, & shortstop & second base. All I knew was that I *loved* baseball, & I could *finally* say "I am a baseball player."

When I got home, I ran inside to look for my parents to tell them the good news that I made the team. As always, they were in the garage. When I told them, they were excited for me; however, not as excited as I was. The excitement did not last long because it was time to get ready for dinner, which we always ate late. As my dad came in from the garage to take a shower & get ready for dinner, I snuck down to the basement to watch some baseball on the television. I always looked forward to every Sunday night, because that meant Sunday Night Baseball was on ESPN. I *loved* listening to the legendary voices of Jon Miller & Joe Morgan talk about baseball.

PLAY BALL!

Fast forward a month later, & I am in left field, playing my first official baseball game. As you can imagine, I was *beyond* excited. I was so excited, that I actually showed up to the baseball field two hours early; an hour before anyone else showed up, including the coach. When the coach finally showed up to the field, he told me that I would be starting in left field & batting ninth in the lineup. I was overwhelmed with joy.

When the game started, I sprinted out to my position; just as every baseball player *should* do. I sprinted out to the field every single inning... for the rest of my career. It was not until the top of the third inning, when I finally got some action. A hard-hit ground ball was hit between the third baseman & the shortstop & was headed directly towards me. It was my job to field the ground ball & throw it into the cut-off man as quickly as possible, to make sure the baserunners did not advance. Unfortunately, things did not go as planned.

Since it was early May in Wisconsin, the snow had just finally melted a few short weeks before the game. The grass was still brown & dry, & the ground was hard, so that groundball that was hit towards me *never* slowed down.

I got into my fielding position that my coach had been teaching me for the past couple of weeks. By the time I got into position, it was too late. The groundball had already gone between my legs. I had to turn around & sprint after the baseball.

Because of my error, two runs scored. All of that pre-game excitement instantly disappeared. All of the joy I had when I was told that I was starting in left field quickly faded away. All of the pride I felt when I saw I made the team was immediately forgotten. *I was embarrassed.* I made a fool of myself in front of *everyone*. I let myself down. I let our fans down. I let my team down. I let my coach down.

As I stood in left field, *desperately* wanting the inning to end, the same doubts I had before making the team came back:

"I am not good enough to play baseball."

"What a stupid mistake! *No one* makes that error."

"I do not deserve to be on this team."

"Why am I even here?"

To make matters worse, when I got back to the dugout after the inning was over, I was not greeted by my teammates; no pats on the back to let me know everything was going to be *ok*, & no words of encouragement to keep my head up. I was not greeted by any of my coaches to tell me what I did wrong, how I could fix it, & what I need to do the next time I got a groundball hit to me. Instead, I was told by the *assistant* coach that I was out of the game. I sat on the bench for the rest of the game. I did not even get a chance to hit.

CHIP ON MY SHOULDER

As the season went on, things did not get better, they got worse. I rarely saw the field *at all*, & there was no explanation for it. Was it because of the one error I made in the first game? I *never* knew. There was a point in the season where I went an *entire* month without having an at-bat. It did not matter anyway, because every at-bat I did have, I struck out. You can add "hitless season" to the long list of embarrassments during my baseball career.

Whenever I got the opportunity to have an at-bat, I tried *everything* to get a hit; this is where my baseball superstition began. I would go up to the plate with a different bat. I would wear a different batting helmet. I would wear batting gloves, then I would wear one batting glove, & then, I would not wear any batting gloves at all. I would wear high socks, then I would wear low socks. I actually started putting pennies that I found on the ground, in my cup (yes... the cup in my jock strap), for "good luck." *Nothing* worked.

The season was hard for everyone in my family. My mom eventually stopped going to my games. Luckily for my dad, he could not go, because of work. One time, I forgot to take the pennies out of my cup before laundry, & my mom found them, & brought them to me bawling her eyes out. My mom hated seeing me hurt & frustrated. She would try to talk me out of going to the games, or she would tell me I needed to ask my teammates if they could give me a ride, hoping I would not ask. When I did, I always felt *terrible*, because whoever gave me a ride would travel an hour, sometimes, two hours, to a game, just for me to sit on the bench.

Every practice we had, *every* time it was my turn to hit in batting practice, & *every* time it was my turn to field ground balls, or catch pop-flies, it seemed like the coach would just wait for me to get done, so he could move on to his next player.

I found out years later, that sometimes the coach would not call to let me, or my parents know that the team was having practice. Worse yet, he would reschedule rained-out games, or he would schedule new games, & he would purposely not tell me, so he could invite players from the other eighth grade team to play for him, in my place.

My attitude continued to decline, as the confusion & doubt continued to increase. I had never felt so unwanted before in my life. No one on the team would talk to me, not even the coaches. It was almost like they would hope that I did not show up, & they acted so disappointed when I did.

My second & final start of the year came at the end of the season, on the second to last game of the season. I started only because the coach went on vacation. It was my first time playing first base. The coach's son was our starting first baseman, & since he was also on vacation, we needed someone to fill his spot. So, I did.

We played Monroe that game, & to say they were bad would be an understatement. They made *a lot* of errors, & they had the worst pitching we faced all year. I made contact with the baseball (my bat touched the ball when I swung it) for the first time all season, that game; I did not hit into fair territory, but I made contact. I got walked for the first time all season, that game... & walked again, my next at-bat. I scored a run for the first time all season, that game. I had my first stolen base of the season, that game (it may have been a passed ball, but I am going to call it a stolen base). I played great, defensively, that game. I played so well that when the coach came back from vacation for the final game of the season, he asked me to play first base, when his son went in to pitch.

I was excited to do so, because it meant I would be guaranteed to have one more at-bat to finish the season; one more chance to get my first hit. Before I walked up to home plate, the coach called me over to meet with him in the third-base coach's box. He put his arm around my shoulders, leaned in, & told me, "you & I both know you are *not* going to get a hit, so I want you to get as close to the plate as possible & take one for the team." Of course, I did what he asked. I stood so close to the plate, that my toes were probably on the plate. I got hit by the first pitch in my left ankle (I *still* have the markings of baseball laces on my ankle). I limped my way to first base, & later in the inning, I scored what would be the winning run.

At the end of the game, we all met in left field; the same spot I made the error in the first game of the season. The coach gave his "end of the year speech" & handed out awards. At that point, I did not care how many games we won, or lost. I did not care who the most valuable player was (which, of course, was *his* son). I did not care who the best pitcher was (again, *his* son). I did not care who the most improved player was. I did not care how well we played as a team. I did not care how "proud" the coach was of us, because to me, it was all *lies*. All I cared about was that it was over, & I was glad that it was.

After the speech, after all the awards were handed out, & after we broke out of the huddle for the last time as a team, the coach pulled me aside & asked me to stay back with him. As the rest of my teammates started walking back towards the dugout, he turned to me & told me something that I will *never* forget. The words that came out of his mouth would lay the foundation of my baseball career, & would form *the biggest* chip on my shoulder that I would play with for the rest of my career. He looked down at me, & he said: "Riley, I don't think you have a future in baseball, *you should quit* & find something else to do." Then, he walked away.

As I watched him walk away from me, I felt the most defeated I have ever felt before in my life. What I thought was my lowest point, became even lower. Shortly after, my sorrow transformed into anger. I did not know I was capable of such *hatred* towards someone as I had towards my eighth-grade coach. I sat in left field with my head buried in my glove to hide my tears.

When everyone left, I finally stood up & walked back to the dugout. As soon as I got back to the dugout, I fell to my knees, & I began to cry even more. I was completely distraught.

How could he say that? How could a grown man tell a 14-year-old kid such *defeating* words? How could a coach tell one of his athletes to quit the sport they loved? The athlete he volunteered to take care of. The athlete he was responsible for. The athlete he was supposed to teach how to play the game. How could this grown man even be allowed to coach kids? I looked up to him. I showed up to every game, & to every practice, because of *him*. I did everything he ever told me to do, & I never once complained about it... or him. I hung on to *every* word he said. How could he do this? He had *no idea* what I was capable of. But, he was about to find out.

Fortunately, my love for the game exceeded anything negative he could ever do or say to me. That season, I got a taste of what it was like to be a baseball player. I got a taste of what it was like to play for something bigger than myself. I *needed* more of it. On that day, when I was told that *I should quit*, I had to make a decision - to give up, or to move forward. I got up on my feet, wiped my tears away, & I decided that I was going to prove him wrong. My mindset quickly changed from trying to impress him to making sure he would *never* forget my name.

I *SHOULD* HAVE QUIT

He was right. I should have quit. I should have quit when I made that error in left field. I should have quit when I did not get a single hit in the season. I should have quit when I continually sat on the bench. I should have quit when he lied to me & my parents about the schedule, just so I would not show up. I should have quit when he told me that I did not have a future in baseball.

Unfortunately... *for him*... I did not quit.

Since I was a little boy (as young as I can remember), I felt like I was *destined* for something greater. I never knew what it was, until I started playing baseball.

In the beginning, no matter how terrible I was, & no matter what everyone else around me told me, I held on to that greater belief. I always saw something great in myself, even when the coach & my teammates did not see it. I believed in myself, even when the coach & my teammates did not believe in me. I knew I was significant, even when the coach & my teammates thought I was insignificant. I knew I was valuable & I had something to offer, even though I was overlooked, & the coach thought I was *worthless*. There was no possible way that I was going to quit *just* because he told me to.

This was my chance to make a name for myself, & for my family. This was my opportunity to pursue something I *always* wanted to be. There was absolutely no way I was going to just let go of it. Besides, it is way too easy to quit. I prefer doing things the hard way; which, you will also *quickly* find out is another common theme of my life.

KNOWLEDGE APPLIED

I firmly believe, deep-down inside of all of us, is an innate desire to want more for our lives. There is absolutely no way to ignore it. It is *hard-wired* in all of us. We can put it away for a while. We can try to cover it up. We can even try to hide from it, but it will *always* resurface & come back to the forefront of our minds.

We all yearn for our lives to be better. That is why we read the books we read. That is why we watch the videos & shows we watch. That is why we listen to the music & podcasts we listen to. We all want to be inspired - inspired to know better, do better, & ultimately, *be* better. If not for the sake of our own lives, but for the sake of our loved one's lives.

When we are kids, we are told to dream big, & that we can become anything we want to become. Then, when we get older, we are told that our dreams are unrealistic.

Some of you reading this right now have a dream - a dream that has yet to be pursued. Unfortunately, some of you reading this have given up on your dream, completely. *Why?* Trust me when I say I know just how hard it is to take action & pursue your dream, but it is an absolute tragedy not to.

Let me tell something that you may not fully understand, yet: There is no occupation without opposition. There is no dream without disapproval. There is no purpose without problems. There is no calling without calamity.

There are *always* going to be people in your life that are going to tell you that you are not good enough, smart enough, strong enough, talented enough, etc. There are *always* going to be people in your life that tell what you should & should not do. There are *always* going to be people in your life that think they know what is best for you. There are *always* going to be people in your life that tell you that *you should quit.* It is *your choice* to listen to them, or ignore them. Choose *wisely.*

They may not understand your passion. They may not agree with your intentions. They may not approve of your decisions. They may not believe in your dream, but *you* do, & that is all that matters. It is *your* life, not theirs. It is *your* dream, not theirs. Never justify *your* life. Never justify *your* dream.

There are two types of people who are going to tell you that your dream will never come true – one, the people who are afraid to try to pursue their own dream, & two, the people who are afraid you will succeed at your dream.

Their projections should not determine your decisions. Their dream may not have come true, but that does not mean your dream will not come true. They may have given up on their dream, but that does not mean that you should give up on your dream.

Too often, these projections come from the people who are closest to you. They may not mean to crush your spirit, or destroy your dream, but that is exactly what they are doing. They may think they are protecting you, but really, they are holding you back. These people are not your family, they are not your friends, they are not your coaches, they are not your teammates, they are cancers, & they are killing you. Hold onto your dream. *Never* give it up.

Other's inability to see our worth, does not change it.

If you think my eighth-grade coach telling me that I should quit was the worst thing that I have ever been told by someone who was closest to me, you are *wrong*. About a year after my baseball career was over, my mom signed me up for a life insurance policy, & made herself & my dad the beneficiaries, so they could pay off my student loans that they were co-signed on, in case something happened to me, & I died before them. As we were driving back to the house I grew up in from the insurance agency, my mom turned me with a straight face, & said, "this life insurance policy does not cover suicide, so do not go & kill yourself." She may have meant it in a joking manner, but it was the worst thing she could have possibly said to me at that time, because I was in the middle of the *deepest, darkest* depression of my life.

There are not many things worse than when the people closest to you do not believe in you. It is hard to pursue *anything* without support from people who *should* be in your corner.

On the other hand, sometimes, it is not even them, it is *us*. It is *our* assumption of what we think people may think of us, that keeps us from pursuing our dream. Especially, what we think people who are closest to us, & people we care about the most, may think of us. We are afraid of what they may say. We are afraid of what they may think. We are afraid that they may be disappointed in us if we fail. We are afraid of embarrassing ourselves in front of them. The possibility of those things happening – which is slim, to none - is paralyzing us.

Think about how ridiculous that sounds: "I am afraid to pursue my dream because I am afraid of what the people who are *supposed to* love me & support me *unconditionally* are going to think of me if I *hypothetically* fail." Pretty ridiculous, right?

Quite frankly, we are lying to ourselves, in order to protect ourselves from things that may not even exist. Why do we do this to ourselves? Why do we get in our own way? I believe it is because we are constantly seeking the approval of others, & we care way too much about what other people think of us.

The truth is, it is nearly impossible to not care what other people think – especially, the people who are closest to us, & we care about the most. The people who say they do not care what other people think are lying. *Everybody cares.* Regardless, we need to be aware of the harmful side effects this is causing us, like, not pursuing our dreams. *What is the point of living, if you are not living out your dream.*

"It is *your* life, not theirs. It is *your* dream, not theirs. Never justify *your* life. Never justify *your* dream."

"What is the point of living, if you are not living out your dream?"

@RileyTincher | #PitchingAgainstMyself

CHAPTER 2

GET BACK UP THERE!

Answer this question for me: Have you ever met someone who *immediately* had an impact on your life? The moment you crossed paths with them, or the instant you were introduced to them, you knew, *without a doubt*, that they were going to significantly change the direction of your life.

My freshman year of high school, I was fortunate enough to meet not just one of those instantly influential people, but *two* of them – Mark Diercks & Darin Everson.

Mark Diercks was my freshman baseball coach. At the time, he was finishing Graduate School at the University of Wisconsin in Madison (the town of Oregon that I grew up in, was a suburb of Madison, about ten miles away from the University). In order to complete his Master's Degree in Kinesiology, he had to complete an internship in student-teaching at a high school, so he choice my school to student-teach physical education. He also chose to volunteer to coach the freshman baseball team, & I am *beyond* grateful that he did.

Mark Diercks, or Coach Diercks, was the epitome of passion. It poured out of every pore he had in his 6'4" body. He would stare into my eyes when he was talking to me, & I swear I could see fire in his eyes. *He was an anomaly.* There was no other coach like him... well, maybe one, or two others.

The moment he introduced himself to me at our first practice, I knew *instantly* that he cared more about me & my teammates, more than he did about himself. From that moment on, he *always* showed up early to practice. He was *always* prepared, & he would *always* stay after practice, in case any of us wanted extra work... & I *always* did.

One day after practice, he hit me groundballs at first base for so long, that we had to stop, because it was too dark to see the baseball. If we had lights at our field, I *guarantee* he would have kept hitting me groundballs, for as long as I wanted him to.

Coach Diercks was not even the head coach. He was an assistant coach. Actually, he was a *volunteer* assistant coach. Yet, we all respected him as if he was the head coach; quite frankly, he should have been the head coach. He devoted his time, *for free*, to all of us, & he never once made us feel like he did not want to be there, or that he had something better to do; which, he probably did, because at the time, he was newly married.

Everything Coach Diercks did, he did with excellence, & he expected us to do the same. He was hard on us, physically. He demanded a lot out of us, & we - or I should say, *I* - was better because of him. We would do some workouts that were so hard, that a lot of my teammates considered quitting, & unfortunately, some of them did. Those that quit did not understand that there was a reason for everything he made us do. They did not understand that all of it was for the betterment of the team; he wanted us to become better than we wanted to, & he was our biggest fan when we did. They did not understand that the harder we worked, the harder it would be for us to quit... *at anything.* They did not understand that the more difficult the struggle is, the sweeter the victory *will* be. They did not understand that the coach who is the hardest on them, is usually the coach who cares the most about them... *But, I understood.*

I would have never tried out for the ninth-grade baseball team if it was not for Coach Diercks. As much as I wanted to prove the coach I had in eighth-grade wrong, I *still* had a lot of doubts, & I did not want to go through what I went through my eighth-grade season, again. It was difficult to recover from.

To make matters worse, the coach I had in eighth grade was not the only person who thought I should quit playing baseball. For the next four years (my *entire* high school baseball career), I would *constantly* battle my mom about whether I should continue playing baseball, or not. She would try her best to convince me that I needed to do something else besides playing baseball. It was either in the form of "you need to get a job" or "you need to focus on school."

Maybe, she was trying to protect me from the inevitable heartbreak that baseball would give me, or maybe, she was doing it for her own benefit. I do not know. However, I do know it is hard to fight for anything, when you have no one in your corner supporting you. It is even harder to keep fighting, when you do not have the support from your own parents. This is why I was instantly drawn to Coach Diercks, & leaned on him as much as I possibly could.

When I pitched for the first time ever, my freshman year, I ended up walking the *entire* lineup, & giving up eight runs in the first inning. When I was finally pulled from the game, I did not seek the comfort of my mom, I sought out Coach Diercks. He was quick to let me know that "one game does not define you," & "you are going to get another opportunity." He believed in me way more than I believed in myself. He did not give up on me, when everyone else did. He gave me a chance, when no one else would... & then, he gave me a *second* chance. He did not allow my doubts to stop me from trying. He did not allow my feelings to stop me from taking action. Most importantly, he did allow me to quit... even when I failed over & over again.

When I think about the success of my baseball career, I *immediately* think of Coach Mark Diercks. He kick-started my high school career, & he revitalized my college career (I will tell you about that later in the book). He put lighter fluid to my fire, & re-ignited my passion. He challenged me more than I have *ever* been challenged before. He showed me that I was capable of way more than I thought I was. He forced me to grow; I had no other choice with him as my coach. Of all the things he showed me & gave to me, the one I am most grateful for is how *significant* he made me feel; which, is one of the most important things – if not, *the* most important thing - every parent, teacher, coach, & leader should ever make a child feel.

DON'T HANG THE SPLITTY!

There is no amount of words I could ever write or say that would rightfully honor Coach Darin Everson, the way he deserves to be honored. To put it simply, he was *the greatest* coach I have ever had.

I will *never* forget the day I met him. I was a freshman in high school, & I was in a room full of high school baseball players. We were all there for the preseason meeting that was being held by the newly-hired varsity head coach, which was Coach Everson.

The moment he walked into the room, the whole room went silent; that is when I knew how respected he was. As he began his speech, it felt like he was making eye contact with *everyone* in the room... all at once. There was a presence about him that cannot be explained. He was boisterous. He was charismatic. He was confident. He was a visionary. He spoke with so much certainty, that he made everyone in the room believe in the future he was talking about.

To be honest, I did not hear a word he said the entire speech, because I was too busy being in awe of him. He was a *giant*. I had never met anyone as big as him. Not only was his physical stature dominating, but he also had a deep, thunderous voice that echoed around the room as if he was speaking through a microphone.

At the end of the meeting, he stood by the door & shook everyone's hand as we were leaving the room. I have yet to meet someone with bigger hands than Coach Everson - *They were bear paws.* Not only were they big in size, but they were *hard as bricks.* When I shook his hand, it did not even budge, & I could barely fit my fingers around his palm, & my hands are bigger than the average person's hands.

What a *great* first impression. I left that meeting hopeful & excited; even though, I had no idea what he just said. I felt something

I had not felt in a while, & I knew, right then & there, that I wanted to play baseball for *that* man.

Coach Everson was a former professional baseball player. He had a great Minor League career as a catcher & first baseman in the Boston Red Sox & Montreal Expos (now known as the Washington Nationals) organizations. He had an even better career playing Independent League baseball, which landed him in Madison, Wisconsin playing for the Madison Black Wolf. As soon as he retired playing baseball, he became an assistant coach for the Madison College Wolfpack (a division II junior college in Madison), & he became a scout for the Baltimore Orioles. He also started teaching Physical Education at Oregon High School; the high school I went to.

I had no idea who the varsity coach was before Coach Everson, & truth be told, I did not care, because Coach Everson was *my* coach now, & I was so proud of that.

To say he came in & changed the baseball program, would be an understatement. He *completely* changed it, almost immediately. He raised the standards, & he got rid of everything & everyone who did not meet those standards, & did not deserve to be there anymore. For the first time, Oregon had a varsity coach who did not politic, & did not have favorites. Unfortunately, many people did *not* like that – especially, my eighth-grade coach. He set strict boundaries, & he protected his players, & we won because of it. He took a below .500 team to the State Championship within two seasons.

If you wanted play for him on his team, you had to meet certain expectations. There were no exceptions. If you missed practice, you did not play. If you were late to practice, you did not play. If you missed school, you did not play – there was no such thing as "Senior Skip Day," if you played for Coach Everson. The school required a "C-Average" to play sports. He did not allow any C's at all.

He had a grade report that we had to fill out, get signed by our teachers, & give to him every other week. One time, my junior year, he found one of the grade reports in the garbage, so, he called a meeting after school that day.

My teammates & I sat in the room he told us to meet him in, & we waited for him to enter. When he finally did, he did not say a word. He *slammed* the wrinkled-up grade report on the table in the front of the room, & he kicked the table half way across the room, that forced the two front rows of players to slide back in their seats. Then, he went off. He scared the crap out of all of us (almost, literally).

After that meeting, we made sure *no one* threw their grade report away in the garbage *ever* again.

He ran his program like an *elite* college team runs their program. We had structured practices. We had practice uniforms. We had to wear our uniforms & hat (*never* backwards) a certain way. We had the best equipment. We had great assistant coaches, & he made sure we called them "coach" & respected them as much as we respected him. We had to dress a certain way to class; more specifically, on game day. We had to sit in the front row of the class.

What he taught us goes *far* beyond baseball. He taught us character. *He taught us how to be better men.*

I thought I could not love baseball any more than I did, until I met Coach Everson. As structured & as disciplined as he ran his program, it was equally as fun. We had homerun derbies (which, are my favorite). We had a Blackhawk Helicopter flown in during practice, just so we could take pictures with it for our schedule posters. We went to a Milwaukee Brewers' game as a team (which, was my Dad's favorite). We were always the loudest team; constantly yelling in the dugout. We went to a few movies together as a team. We also won *a lot* of games, which, to me… is the *definition* of fun.

The second greatest memory I have of playing for Coach Everson, was the opportunity he gave us to play in the Metrodome – the former stadium of the Minnesota Twins. The memory I have was not even playing in the game; it was the ride to & from the Metrodome. On the bus ride there, we watched highlight tapes of him playing. He replayed (*several* times) a homerun he hit against former Major League pitcher Jack Morris, & every time he would replay his home run, he would yell, "don't hang the splitty!"

He exemplified the principle, *attitude reflects leadership.* The habits we developed were a reflection of his coaching. He overflowed with confidence & it poured out into all of us, & we became more confident. His fire & passion for baseball lit a fire inside of all of us. He was so competitive that it forced us to be competitive just to keep up with him. More importantly, he loved us, so we loved him.

My junior year, we had an inter-squad scrimmage during practice, & I was pitching. To put it lightly, I was *dominating,* & I made sure everyone knew it. I got out almost every hitter that stepped up to the plate, until he decided to step up to the plate. He did not have a batting helmet on. He did not wear any batting gloves. He stood in the batter's box, took two pitches (one for a strike, & one for a ball), & on the third pitch of the at-bat, he hit one of the farthest home runs off me I have *ever* given up. He hit the ball into the practice football field, which was a little less than two-hundred feet behind the right field fence. He did not hold back on celebrating.

As he jogged (quite slowly) around the bases, he asked every player he passed "did you see *how far* that went?" When he *finally* touched home plate, he turned to me & said, "Tinch, that will not be the last homerun you give up, but it is never about the homeruns you give up, it is about how you *respond* to them."

He was as superstitious as they come; which, only made me more superstitious than I already was (I will tell you about my pre-game "routines" later in the book). He *always* wore the same jersey number; #20. He *always* wore the same long-sleeve shirt under his jersey; he *still* does. He *always* had the same ritual between innings as he went out to the third-base coaching box; he *still* does. He *always* stood, or sat in the same spot in the dugout; he *still* does.

During my junior year, we lost three games in a row; which, was unheard of. We lost a close game to a conference rival, Madison Edgewood, & then, we were swept in a Saturday doubleheader against Deforest. After the doubleheader, Coach Everson had us go all the way out to centerfield, as far away from the parents as we could get, for our postgame meeting. We all were all *terrified*. We did not know what he was going to say, so we assumed the worst. Losing was not acceptable in our program, so we were anticipating a tongue-lashing, but to our surprise, he did not give it to us. Instead, he told us to look over at the Deforest team as they were celebrating, & he said, "they are celebrating like they won the State Championship, because these games were their State Championship." He then told us to soak it all in, because the same feeling they had, we were going to have when we would win the State Championship.

To showcase his superstition, after we left the field, & returned to the locker room, he had us all throw our jerseys in a dirty laundry bin, & one by one, we spit on them, to symbolize our disgust towards the losing streak we were on. Now, I am not going to give credit to his superstition by saying it was because of us spitting on the jerseys, but we won the next game, & we never went on a losing streak again. Is that a coincidence? I will let you decide.

NO RHYTHM

If you were paying attention earlier, I shared with you my *second* greatest memory I have of playing for Coach Everson, *not* my greatest memory. The greatest memory I have of playing for him was the reason why I wrote this chapter.

My first varsity high school baseball start as a pitcher was my junior year. It was the second game of the season, & we were set to play Monroe; who was in our conference.

Our Ace, who was one of my best friends at the time, & is now a Navy SEAL, threw a *gem* the first game. He pitched exactly how you think a Navy SEAL would pitch. He had great poise. He pitched with attitude. He threw with conviction. He was fearless. Best of all, he had a *phenomenal* leg kick – just like Charlie Sheen's leg kick in the movie, *Major League*. For a long time, I wanted to be *just* like him. He is the reason why I have tattoo sleeves, & why I wear my watches with the face on the bottom of my wrist. He taught me how to *compete* on the mound, & in life. He taught me how to make it through *anything*. He showed me how to *truly* work hard for what I want.

On a side note, I still have the picture his mom gave me that was taken of him right after he survived "Hell Week" in BUD/S training to become a Navy SEAL. In the picture, you can barely recognize him – he has bandages all over him, & he is swollen & bruised. The picture has always been on my nightstand, to make it is the first thing I see when I wake up, & the last thing I see when I go to bed. It constantly reminds me that whatever I am going through, no matter how bad it may seem, is not even close to as bad as what he has gone through. It also reminds that no matter how hard I think I am working, there is always someone working harder, & that someone is him.

There was a certain *buzz* in the air on the bus ride to Monroe. The team knew this matchup was *highly* in our favor, & it was our chance to put ourselves in the headlines as a "shoe in" for a State Championship. A lot of my teammates were also excited to see me pitch. I had earned the respect of most of them because of the amount of work I put in, in the offseason. I attended every pitching & hitting camp, I was at every open gym we had in the winter, & I made sure I was the hardest worker at every single practice. Every chance I had to get better, *I took*. Plus, I was a quiet kid. I was not one to brag, or boast. I let my work do the talking for me.

I was probably the most anxious person on the bus. The pressure I put on myself was *enormous;* which, you will *quickly* find out has been another common theme of my life. This was my chance to finally make a name for myself & put my name in the headlines, as well. This was my chance to prove my eighth-grade coach, & all my other doubters, wrong. This was my chance to prove to everyone (especially, the pitchers who wanted to take my spot) that I deserved to be the number two pitcher. This was my chance to carry on the legacy of the number I was wearing, #16, which was worn by one of the best pitchers to ever pitch at Oregon High School, who was selected in the MLB Draft the year before, & was now playing Division I baseball. He was living out the dream I wanted to live out.

I had my headphones on, & my music was *blaring*; I was listening to Atreyu's Album, *The Curse*, at maximum volume on my Discman. I could not stop moving; I was either rocking back & forth in my seat, or I was knocking my knees together. My heart rate was through the roof. I was so tense, that my shoulders started to spasm. There was a lump in my throat so big, that I could barely talk.

When we finally got to the field, it got *worse*. My mind was racing so fast, I forgot what I was supposed to do to warmup for the game. I went through a bunch of random stretches (which, were completely unnecessary), & started playing catch with our catcher. When we got to the bullpen, I was all over the place. I did not know where anything I was throwing was going. Of the 30+ pitches I threw in the bullpen, I do not think I threw even one strike. When it was time for me to go out to the mound to start the game, the game was already over for me. I walked every hitter I faced, I threw a few wild pitches & I gave up five runs before Coach Everson finally relieved me of my misery.

As soon as I got to the dugout, I put a towel over my face to hide my tears. The same feelings & doubts I had when I was told that I should quit baseball came rushing back. "That's it," I thought to myself. "That's the end of my baseball career."

I was so embarrassed, yet again, because I not only let my teammates down, I let Coach Everson down. I had come so far in my career, only to fail yet again. To make matters worse, my eighth-grade coach was at the game, because his son was also on the team. When I saw him, my heart dropped. "He was right, I *should* have quit" I said to myself as I assumed he was so happy to see me fail.

Luckily, we had a great team, full of a lot of great hitters, & we came back & won that game. Our ace – the Navy SEAL I spoke about earlier – came in & relieved me, & he shut down the Monroe offense for the rest of the game, which, gave us the chance we needed to comeback & win. As sad & embarrassed as I felt about my performance, I was also happy that it was redeemed & that we won. As we were celebrating the comeback, & the victory, on the bus ride home, I could not help but think about my chances of ever pitching again; which were *zero…* Or, so I thought.

When we got back to the high school, Coach Everson had me stay behind with him. I assumed he was going to tell me how disappointed he was in me; guilt & shame was used a lot to get things done around the house I grew up in. Instead, he had me follow him into the field house (the same field house where the tryout was for the eighth-grade baseball teams). When we walked in, our catcher, Brian Zimmerman (also known as "Zimm"), was standing there, fully-equipped in all his catcher's gear, & he already had a mound set up for me to throw on.

Since I had only thrown about fifty pitches total that day, Coach Everson wanted me to get more work in. I thought to myself, "*why?*" I had already proven to him that I do not have what it took to pitch at the varsity level, but he did not think so.

After I got done warming up, I stepped up on the mound to start my bullpen, & he stopped me, & he said, "Riley, I know what your problem is. You have no rhythm." I thought he was referring to my dance moves, & I was confused, because that is *far* from the truth. *I can dance.* He continued to say:

"Watching you pitch today, was like watching paint dry… You took forever in between pitches. You would throw the ball, get the ball back from the catcher, walk around the mound, shake your head, adjust your clothes, & then *finally* get back on the mound to pitch again. I timed you one time – it almost took you a full minute to deliver the next pitch. It is impossible to get into a rhythm if you are taking that much time in between pitches. Plus, the more time you had to think, the worse you got. The focus of this bullpen is to show you what getting into a rhythm is like."

Every pitch I threw that bullpen was followed by Coach Everson standing behind me yelling *"go!"* as soon as I got the ball back from Zimm. I threw about forty pitches – all fastballs – until he shut it down by saying, "that's it. I want to save the rest for Saturday" (we had a doubleheader scheduled against Mt. Horeb that day). As we were walking out of the fieldhouse, he put his arm around my shoulders (the same way my eighth-grade coach did), leaned in towards me, & said: "I am going to give you a second chance this Saturday, Riley, & I want you to pitch the way you just pitched that bullpen - The way I, Zimm, & everyone else on the team *believes* you can pitch."

Saturday came, & I had the same feelings & doubts I had before the Monroe game. Except, this time, Coach Everson was there for me *every* step along the way. He stood by my side as I warmed up. He stood by my side when I was throwing my bullpen. After the bullpen, he walked me back to the dugout to start the game. Then, he did the unexpected. After the first pitch I threw (which was a strike), he yelled *"get back up there!"* It echoed across the field, & it caught me off guard. I rushed to get back up on the mound to deliver the next pitch, & after I threw it, he yelled it again… & again, the next pitch… & again, the next pitch… & again, the next pitch. He yelled *"get back up there!"* after *every* pitch I threw that day. I *never* took my time in between pitches again. I was pitching at such a fast tempo that I had no time to think; it was almost like I was in shock… & so were the Mt. Horeb hitters.

I struck out fourteen batters that game (a seven-inning game); which, almost broke the school record for strikeouts in a game set by the player who wore #16 before me (he struck out sixteen). What a difference one bullpen, a few days, & a head coach who believes in his players can make.

That game catapulted my baseball career. That game put my name in the headlines. That game completely changed my confidence on the field. That game was the "defining moment" that showed me what I was capable of, & that I *actually* do have a future in baseball. That game made me so happy that I did not quit.

ONE PUSHUP FOR BEING LEFT-HANDED

I owe Coach Everson *a lot* more than words could ever describe. He took a *well below-average* baseball player & developed me into an All-American. He gave me a second chance, when no other coaches would have. He completely changed the way I pitched, & I have a room full of awards & trophies because of it. He is the reason why I committed myself to becoming a professional baseball player. He is the reason why I got a full scholarship to play baseball in college. He is the reason why I even had a chance to play professional baseball. Without him, there was no baseball for me.

This may come as a surprise, but I resented him for a long time. My senior year, he left me & my team a few months before our season started, to take a job as a Minor League manager in the Florida Marlins organization. I thought he was selfish for doing so.

We were supposed to win a State Championship together. I worked so hard for him. I did *everything* he told me to do – I lost forty pounds my senior year because he said I should. I spent an enormous amount of time with him. I looked up to him. He was like a father to me. How could he just leave me like that? I felt betrayed, & rejected.

The truth is, I was the selfish one for wanting him to stay. He once told me, "if I do not make it to the Majors as a player, I will make it as a coach." This was his chance to do just that. This was his chance to make his dream come true. This was his chance to make a better life for his family. Who am I to tell him that he cannot do that?

He did not completely vanish, & he did not forget me either. In fact, he did the opposite. He pretty much orchestrated my entire baseball career after high school. He was the one that persuaded the Wausau Woodchucks manager to take a huge risk by taking in a high school baseball player; the first high school baseball player in Northwoods League history. He showed up to my first start as a pitcher in college, during spring training in Florida, when I was at North Iowa Area Community College (NIACC) – I will never forget the joy I felt when I heard him say "hey lefty" through the fence when I was warming up to start the game. During that same spring training, he gave me & my dad tickets to the Florida Marlins spring training game against the St. Louis Cardinals. Plus, he allowed me to come in to the Florida Marlins spring training facility & meet some of the Florida Marlins. He hired me to work at some of his hitting & pitching camps. He always texted me after *every* start I had at the University of Wisconsin – Whitewater. He was the first person to call me when my baseball career was over, to let me know how proud he was of me.

Even though, he always made me do one pushup for "being left-handed," I still loved him. I loved him like a son loves his father. Like I said before, he was the *greatest* coach I have ever had. More than that, he was the greatest mentor I have ever had. However, I did not realize this until well after playing for him. It was not until I went to Baylor University for Graduate School to become a coach, that I started studying coaching, & some of the all-time great coaches, & I realized "Oh… Coach Everson did that."

A BOY & HIS DOG

During the offseason before my senior season in high school, I went to one of Coach Everson's pitching camps. For this camp, he brought in a special guest speaker, Steve Foster, who was a relief pitcher for the Cincinnati Reds in the early 90's, & is now the pitching coach for the Colorado Rockies.

During his speech, he talked about the mentality every pitcher should have on the day of their start. He said, "when you are a pitcher, you are a king." This immediately sparked my interest, because my dog's name was King, & he was my *best* friend.

He continued his speech by saying:

"As a King, on the days that you start, you put on your crown. When you are a King, & you are wearing your crown, you need to carry yourself a certain way – with class, confidence, & consistency – because everyone is watching you, & you lead the way. The thing we need to understand is, we are not just wearing our crowns when we step onto the field, & run out to the mound. We are wearing our crowns the moment our feet hit the floor in the morning. We are wearing our crowns when we go to school. We are wearing our crowns when we go out to eat. We are wearing our crowns when we are hanging out with our friends. We are wearing our crowns *all of the time.* We need to remind ourselves of that *every* day."

I *needed* to hear that speech.

I struggled *a lot* with confidence (not just on the mound), & I needed the reminder that I am a King, & that I do wear a crown.

On my drive home from camp, I was consumed with the thought of being a King, & I tried thinking of ways that I could remind myself of this truth every day. When I got home, I was immediately greeted by my dog, King. As always, he was so happy to see me; he had a unexplainable way of always making me feel so loved & appreciated. As he came running up to me, I bent down to hug him, & pet him. I told him that I loved him, & the moment that "love" came out of my mouth, an idea popped up in my mind of writing "King" on my chest, where my heart is, because heart & love are synonymous.

Before the next game that I started, I put this idea to the test. During my pre-game "routine," I wrote "King" on my chest in *big* letters with black permanent marker.

I threw a no-hitter that game.

I wrote "King" on my chest in black permanent marker again before the next start I had, & I threw *another* no-hitter.

A few months later, I decided to make it *actually* permanent, & I went & got my first ever tattoo – which, was "King" in black lettering, on my chest, right where my heart is, & right where I would write it in black permanent marker. It (obviously) stayed with me for the remainder of my baseball career, & it served as a reminder to me that King was always with me, & that always gave me the confidence I needed to compete on the mound.

KNOWLEDGE APPLIED

Everyone needs a coach. Coaches are not just for sports, & they are not just for athletes. They are for *everyone*. I need a coach. You need a coach. We all *need* coaches.

Do not get it confused – when I refer to the word "coach," I am also referring to the words "leader" & "mentor."

We live in a society that is obsessed with *self*. There is an illusion that society has created & glorified called the "self-made man." We all have been led to believe that when times get tough, we must "pull *ourselves* up by our boot straps" & figure things out on our own; which, is one of the biggest lies we have ever been taught, & have been led to believe.

We did not get to where we are on our own, & we will not get to where we want to go on our own, either. We *need* help!

Some of you reading this have an idea of what you think it takes to succeed at the level you are at (because you were taught that), but *none* of you know what it takes to get to (let alone, succeed at) the level where you want to be. *A coach knows.*

Success leaves clues. We need to find someone who is where we want to be, & then, learn as much as we can from them. Often times, that requires us to set aside our ego. We must not become jealous of those we could be learning from. We must allow other people's accomplishments to serve as inspiration, not as a grievance. We must have the courage to ask for help.

Our lives *never* get better on accident. Not even experience makes us better, but evaluated experience does. We are all subjective when it comes to ourselves. We all see ourselves a certain way. The only way to remove that bias is to request & *accept* outside, professional opinions. We cannot change what we do not acknowledge. There are things we cannot see, that a coach will be able to see. We *need* feedback. We *need* evaluation, & the evaluation must be unfiltered. If we cannot talk about it, or criticize it, we cannot make it better.

We need a coach to show us why what we are doing is working. Anyone who is winning, *consistently,* has extraordinary *clarity* about what they are doing, & why they are doing it. They know this because a coach showed them how.

We need a coach to show us what adjustments we need to make. Otherwise, we are going to keep making the same mistakes over & over again, expecting different results, & that is *insanity*.

We need a coach to push us farther than we will ever push ourselves. We need a coach to hold us accountable to things we do not want to hold ourselves accountable to. We need a coach to tell us what we need to hear, not what we want to hear. We need a coach who believes in us more than we believe in ourselves. We need a coach to show us what we are capable of. We need a coach who is going to encourage us to take action, especially, when we do not feel like it. We need a coach who is going to tell us to "get back up there!" when we fall down. We need a coach to give us second chances, just like Coach Everson & Coach Diercks gave me. We need a coach who is not going to let us quit, even though we want to. We need coach who is going to give us opportunities, even if we do not deserve them. We need a coach... *period.*

You may be one coach away from completely changing your destiny.

"We did not get to where we are on our own, & we will not get to where we want to go on our own, either. We *need* help!"

"You may be one coach away from completely changing your destiny."

@RileyTincher | #PitchingAgainstMyself

CHAPTER 3

OPPORTUNITY COSTS

M y success from my junior season, made me think my senior season was going to be *easy*. I thought every game was going to be a fourteen-strikeout game. I thought every Division I school in the country was going to line up to give me a scholarship to play for them. I thought the stands & the backstops were going to be flooded with Major League scouts holding up radar guns for every pitch I threw. I thought I was going to go undefeated. I thought I was going to break every school record we had. I thought I was going to be the State Player of the Year. I thought we were going to win a State Championship. *I thought wrong.*

We did not win a State Championship. We did not even make it to the State Championship. We did not even win a Conference Championship. We went from having a record of 22-3 my sophomore season, to 15-7 my junior season, to 11-10 my senior season.

Personally, I went from having 6-1 win-loss record, & being named to the First-Team All-Conference Team & First-Team All-District Team my junior season, to having a 3-6 win-loss record, & being named to the Honorable Mention All-Conference Team my senior season. I went from hitting above .500 my junior season, to hitting below the *Mendoza Line* – which refers to the career .215 batting average Mario Mendoza hit in the Major Leagues – my senior season. I never had another game even close to the fourteen-strikeout game I had against Mt. Horeb. I lost to teams I should not have lost to. I gave up hits (*a lot* of them) to batters I should not have given up hits to. I gave up runs (*a lot* of them) I should not have given up. I struck out against pitchers I should not have struck out against.

Do you know how many Division I scholarships I was offered? *One.* Do you know how many Major League scouts showed up to my first game of the season? *One.* Do you know how many showed up after the first game? *None.*

Apparently, I was not as great as I thought I was.

The local newspaper did a featured article on me before the season began, & during the interview the journalist asked me, "how will you feel if you get drafted in the Major League Baseball Draft this year?" A lot of thoughts came to mind immediately, like ecstatic, overjoyed, & relieved, but I responded with "normal." The journalist seemed shocked by my answer. He probably assumed I was just another cocky kid with an entitled attitude. So, with a puzzled look on his face, he asked me a follow up question: "What do you mean by 'normal?'" My response quickly wiped that puzzled look off his face. I replied, "if you have worked as hard as I have, if you have put in as much time as I have, & if you love this sport as much as I do, you begin to *expect* these things to happen."

Despite all the failures & setbacks, having my name called in the MLB Draft is something I envisioned since I started playing baseball. More importantly, having my name called in the Draft is something I have worked so hard for since day one. *Why would I be surprised?*

I have always been a *big thinker.* When I make a decision to do something, I either want to do it to the best of my abilities, or I want to become the best at doing it.

When I was younger, I would go to Milwaukee Brewers games, or to Madison Mallards games, & I would envision myself on the field with the players. I loved the way they carried themselves; it was as if they were living legends. I loved going to games early to watch them prepare. I would study them as much as I could. I watched every pitch in batting practice. I was not interested in how many homeruns they would hit; I was interested in what they did before they got in the cage, & what they did in between pitches - every deep breath they took, what

54

they were focusing on, what their body language was, etc. I watched every throw they made while they were warming up. I watched every stretch they did, & every pre-game routine they had. I watched it *all*, & I wanted *every* part of it. I wanted to be on the field with them. I wanted to be the one signing autographs for the kids in the stands. I wanted to be the one everyone was watching.

I put in the work. I was the hardest worker on my team – I would bet a large amount of money that I was the hardest working baseball player in the state of Wisconsin - & I felt as though I deserved more. I thought all my accomplishments my junior season solidified myself as one of the greatest baseball players in the state, but it did not. I was overlooked by everyone, & it frustrated me. What I had in ambition, I lacked in patience. I wanted so badly to be a Major League Baseball player... *yesterday*. I learned the hard way that patience is not sitting around waiting for an opportunity. Patience is taking action, working hard, & not expecting immediate results.

Every great thing takes time to build, or create – *a lot* more time than we expect. When we are doing anything meaningful, or of any significant value, we have two options: stay patient, or quit. I was *not* about to quit.

Despite every outcome, & every missed opportunity telling me that I did not have a future as a Major League Baseball player, it was *my* belief that kept me going. There was something about proving everyone wrong that made it all worth it. Their disbelief only made me work harder.

Unfortunately, my efforts were misguided. I no longer had Coach Everson correcting me & telling me what adjustments I needed to make. I did not have *anyone* correcting me, or telling me what adjustments I needed to make. *I ran the show;* which, is a recipe for disaster for most seventeen-year-olds. Our new head coach inherited three highly-motivated, highly-experienced, & highly-talented athletes; me, our catcher, Zimm, & our centerfielder, Jerry Schleinz (also known as "Jam"). We were products of Coach Everson's program. The new coach trusted us to do what is right, & we always did. He empowered us to be the captains & leaders of the team; which, we already were. But he *never* coached us. We were on our own, & all three of us *struggled* our senior season because of it.

A coach makes all the difference. My junior year, Coach Everson knew how hard I was on myself, & he would remind me before *every* at-bat to not to do too much. He would tell me to hit the ball up the middle "like Tony Gwynn," & I did just that; which, ended with me having a batting average above .500.

My senior season, when I got into slumps (my whole season was a slump), my new coach would tell me that he did not think I had the bat speed to hit at the varsity level, even though he saw me hit the year before & knew what my batting average was. So, as many impressionable seventeen-year-olds do - I *believed* what my coach said, & my hitting suffered because of it.

Our batting averages were not the only things that suffered. The culture *completely* changed. There were times where I thought Jam, Zimm, & I were the only ones that wanted to be there. The only reason why we had standards was because Jam, Zimm, & I enforced & upheld them. But, we could only do so much. There were guys on the team that should not have been there. There were guys playing positions they should not have been playing. There was a posture of complacency among the rest of the team, & it frustrated all three of us.

In the middle of the season, I went to the coach before practice to convey my frustrations, & he responded with "what do you want me to do about?" It was at that moment, I realized we were on our own.

I had a conversation with Zimm in the locker room after that practice, to address my frustrations to him as well, & he let me know he felt the same way. Internally, I felt conflicted. I desperately wanted the team to succeed, & to win a State Championship, but I knew it was not going to happen because of the direction the team was going. We all knew what needed to change in order for the team to succeed, but it is almost impossible to change *anything* when the person who is in charge – the head coach who makes the final decision – does not support the leaders of the team.

That day, in the locker room, Zimm & I made the decision to focus on ourselves, & to start preparing for our college careers. We no longer allowed the decisions of the team to determine our destiny. We were ready for the season to be over, so we could move on.

You may be thinking, "how selfish of them!" You are right to think that; it was a selfish decision. I am not trying to justify our decision, but what were we supposed to do? We were seventeen- & eighteen-years-old, & we barely knew *anything* about leadership. The only thing we knew about leadership was to lead by example, & we did the best that we could.

Jam, Zimm, & I had the potential to play baseball at a *very* high level – Zimm & I both had Division I scholarships. If *any* high school baseball team has three athletes going on to play in college – more specifically, the catcher, pitcher, & centerfielder (three of the four most important positions on the field) – they should be able to win *a lot* of games. There was absolutely no reason as to why our team finished one game above .500, besides the coaching.

As John C. Maxwell, best-selling author & world-renowned leadership teacher, says, *"everything rises & falls on leadership."* The difference between my junior season, & my senior season, was a testament to that quote.

BATTERY MATE

When the season ended, Zimm & I got to work. There was not a day during the summer that him & I were not at the baseball field, working out in the weight room, or running at the track. We spent *a lot* of time together. Hilariously, some of the time we spent together included going to McDonald's after our workouts, because all we could afford was the food on the Dollar Menu, & we did not know anything about nutrition, & the detrimental effects of eating fast food.

I am so grateful for Zimm, because he helped me lay the foundation of my baseball career. There was a tenacity about him that inspired me. He *never* shied away from hard work, which caused me to work harder. He caught *every* bullpen I ever wanted to throw (there were *a lot*), & he *never* complained about any of them. If I ever wanted to go to the field, or workout, I would call Zimm, & he would *always* be there. There are not many people as loyal as Zimm.

We were *great* battery mates (referring to the bond between a pitcher & catcher), because our bond went *far* beyond baseball. We had very similar circumstances in the houses we grew up in, so without even knowing, we were drawn to each other for refuge. We understood each other, & how we were feeling, without even saying a word.

I have so many great memories with Zimm; too many to count. Not all of them include baseball, but most of them do. I am so honored to have called him my catcher, & more importantly, my friend.

THE CALL

It was the middle of July, the day of my high school graduation party, when I received a phone call that would change the trajectory of my baseball career. I was in the middle of helping my parents prepare for my party when my cell phone rang. I answered it, & it was the field manager for the Wisconsin Woodchucks – a team in the Northwoods League; one of the best collegiate summer leagues in the country. I had no idea why he was calling me, because it is a *collegiate* summer league. Needless to say, I was a little shocked when he asked me if I could come play for him. I asked him, "can high schoolers play in the Northwoods League?" to which he responded, "you would be the first one." I told him I would think about it, & I would get back to him as soon as I knew the answer. I did not have much time to think about it, because he needed to know my answer *that night*.

When I hung up the phone, I knew exactly who I needed to call, for guidance - Coach Everson. Much to my surprise, I found out he was the one who got me the opportunity. He was friends with the field manager of the Woodchucks, who called him to ask if he knew of any pitchers who were available to pitch, & Coach Everson gave him my name & phone number. So, *obviously*, Coach Everson wanted me to take the opportunity. As persuaded as I was to do it, I still did not know if I *really* wanted to, because it would cause a major change of plans.

This was a very hard decision for me to make. There was a month left of the season, & a month left of summer. If I left to go play for the Woodchucks, I would lose my summer (a hard thing for an eighteen-year-old to give up), because as soon I would get back from playing in the Northwoods League, I would have to immediately get ready to move to college. I was not ready to leave...at all.

The reason why I was not ready to leave was because I felt like my family was not ready for me to leave. I was the foundation of my family. I was the glue that held my family together. I was the highlight of my family's lives. I was the star athlete my family was so proud of. I was the encourager. I was the counselor; a hard job for a teenager. I was the one that gave them hope. I knew that if I left, the chances of my family falling apart significantly increased.

The truth is, I was ready to leave my family, but I was not ready to leave my friends, & I especially was not ready to leave my dog, King. Subconsciously, I wanted to get as far away from the house I grew up in as possible, but I did not understand why I wanted to escape, until recently.

I was so busy playing baseball, practicing, & working out that I did not see what was actually going on in the house I grew up in. I was a star athlete, & I received constant recognition & praise from the news & everyone else around me, which acted as a mask for my pain – pain I could not describe. On top of that, I had great friends, who had great parents, who gave me all the support & guidance I needed.

My parents grew up in a generation (the 70's) that partied *a lot*. The partying never really stopped for my parents, even after my brother & I were born. I did not think anything of it, at the time, because it was "normal" to me – it was not until I left the house & witnessed firsthand how "normal" families interact with each other that I realized how far from "normal" my family & my childhood was.

Ever since I can remember, *every* Friday night, like clockwork, my mom would pull into the garage from work, & the first thing she would unload from her car was two thirty-packs of Busch Light; a brand of beer I have grown to *hate*. Within forty-eight hours – by Sunday night – both thirty-packs would be gone. On occasion, depending on whether my dad had friends over, or not, they would have to get more beer. I thought this was normal. I thought this is what *every* family did. Worse yet, I thought they *deserved* it because they worked so hard during the week to support (financially) our family. They complained so much about their jobs & worried so much about money that I thought they needed the stress relief that they thought alcohol provided them.

As I said earlier, my dad worked nights, so I hardly saw him during the week. When he was home on the weekends, I hardly saw him either. He was *always* in the garage – that was where the beer was. Never once, do I remember going out to the garage & not seeing a beer in his hand. The only time he came into the house was to go to the bathroom. It was impossible to have a conversation with him, because if I started one with him, I would have to either go to the bathroom with him, or walk out to garage with him to keep the conversation going. I hated going out to the garage, because it was filled with cigarette smoke; which, caused my asthma to act up.

After my dad woke up on Saturday morning, & had his first cup of coffee, it was time for them to start drinking (they at least waited until noon to start). Once they started, they did not stop until late Sunday night. As I got older, dinner time became later & later on the weekends (sometimes after 9:00 PM), & I did not know why until I realized it was so they could drink more.

After dinner, my dad would go down into our basement to watch television, & within minutes of laying down on the couch, he would fall asleep. I did not put two & two together until recently. How could someone that works nights (6:00 PM – 6:00 AM) during the week, get a full night's sleep on Saturday morning, & fall asleep so quickly at 10:00 PM that night, & then again, the following night? It was because he passed out from being too drunk.

My mom, on the other hand, did not just drink on the weekends. She would not get drunk on the weekdays, but she would come home & "have a few."

She would constantly carry around this huge white & red plastic mug that was always filled with beer & ice; the mug got so much use that the logos on the outside of it were completely gone. To this day, the sound of ice sloshing around any liquid or clinking up against any cup, or any glass still makes me *cringe* every time I hear it. For the longest time, I did not put ice in *any* of my drinks for this reason.

Every weekend night, right before dinner, she would fall into this "trance-like" state where she would begin to walk pigeon-toed throughout the house, & her mouth would become fixated (almost as if she had a stroke), which caused her to slur her words. This *terrified* me. I thought there was something *severely* wrong with her, but she would always play it off like she did not notice what she was doing. She assured me that everything was fine but it was *far* from fine. Again, at the time, this was all *normal* for me.

I lost touch with my parents at a young age; probably around the time I could drive. As you can imagine, it was hard to even communicate with them. There were either working, or they were drunk. Besides that, I did not have much to talk about with them. None of what they did interested me, & they were not going to go to any of my baseball games, so why should I talk about that with them?

On most nights, as soon as dinner was over, I wanted to get the hell out of the house as quickly as possible. The problem was, our house was the house where all my friends hung out.

My parents were always generous & welcoming to them, & I am so grateful for that. My mom would always cook these huge meals – more like, *feasts* – for all my friends & I. There was *never* an empty stomach in the house I grew up in.

Having my friends over was another mask for me. We would always hang out in the basement, playing video games, playing euchre, or watching baseball games, & it would distract me from what was going on in the garage.

When I finally moved out of the house, I hated calling my parents after 4:00 PM, because I knew they were drunk, & they would not remember *anything* we talked about. If I did not call, my mom would make me feel *really bad* about it by calling me & leaving me hateful voicemails; I *still* have severe anxiety when people call & leave me a voicemail, because I always assume it is going to be an attack, or it going to be bad news.

Alcoholism destroys families. Alcohol causes way more problems than solves them. I never understood how anyone's life could be so bad, that they felt the need to escape reality, until I was depressed & became suicidal; which, I will talk about later. I loved my parents deeply (I *still* do), but I hated the choices they made. They did the best they knew how to raise my brother & I. It was devastating to watch them destroy themselves, & ultimately, destroy our family.

There were a few events that happened during my early childhood that completely changed the way my family – more specifically, my parents - interacted. The first event was my dad getting in a fight at work. The guy he beat up ended up suing us, & we had to file for bankruptcy. The second event was my dad allegedly cheating on my mom; I still do not know if it actually happened. I will *never* forget the car ride to one of my basketball games when my mom found the other woman's clothes in my dad's truck. I was the one that talked my mom & brother out of leaving my dad. I wanted our family to be together, but from that moment on, instead of seeking help, they sought alcohol, other means to fix their problems. Instead of talking to each other, they escaped reality as quickly, & as much as they possibly could.

THE DECISION

As the day of my graduation party progressed, & as some of my coaches, my friends, & my friend's parents showed up to the party, I began to ask them what they thought I should do. They all agreed that I should take the opportunity to play for the Woodchucks, but one piece of advice stood out more than others. One of my friends, who was an actor, had just recently moved to Albuquerque, New Mexico to film a popular television show, so he could not make it to my party, but his parents made it. His dad told me something that night that pushed me in the right direction:

"Riley, your dream is to play professional baseball, right? If you have a dream, you are going to have to makes sacrifices in order to make that dream to come true. No sacrifice, no dream. If you do not take this opportunity, you are going to spend the rest of your life thinking about what you should have done & what could have been. Do not allow that to happen."

That sealed the deal for me. The decision was made. After that conversation, I immediately called the field manager to let him know that I accepted his offer. The next day I packed up my truck, & headed to Wausau, Wisconsin to play for the Wisconsin Woodchucks.

BOY AMONG MEN

Opportunities are not always what they appear to be.

As soon as I got to Wausau, I quickly found out why no other high school baseball player had ever played in the Northwoods League. I was a boy among men. My team, & the entire league, was filled with some of the best college baseball players in the country - four of my teammates ended up playing Major League Baseball. Yet, there I was, a high schooler... & I was not even the best in my state.

I threw my first bullpen in front of the coaches, & afterwards, the field manager came up to me & said: "I hope you have more than *that* in you." I did not even ask what I hit on the radar gun, because I did not want to know, because of the fear of embarrassment. Besides, he let me know just exactly where me & my velocity (or, lack thereof) stood with him with what he said to me.

The fourth game I was there, was when I finally got my first opportunity to pitch. We were in Lacrosse, Wisconsin playing the Lacrosse Loggers. It was late in the game & we were getting beat *very* badly, so the field manager called my name to go down to the bullpen to start warming up to go into the game.

Those feelings I had right before my first varsity start my junior season – nervousness, anxiety, a big lump in my throat, elevated heart rate, & tense muscles - came back. I threw maybe ten pitches in the bullpen before the field manager went out to the mound to pull the pitcher out of the game, & call me in to come pitch.

This was my first time pitching in front of a large crowd. There was at least four thousand people there. The largest crowd I had ever pitched in front of before was *maybe* a couple of hundred people.

When I got out to the mound, I took a few seconds to look around at the crowd, & to let it all sink in – that was a *very* bad idea. In doing so, my nervousness got worse, especially, when I saw *all* the people watching *every* move I made. Home-plate looked like it was *at least* one hundred feet away from me (the actual distance from home plate to the pitcher's mound is 60'6"). I threw five warmup pitches; all of which were *way* out of the strike zone. One of the pitches, actually hit the back stop behind home plate, & the entire crowd erupted & started chanting "hit the bull!" – which, was a reference to a line in the movie, *Bull Durham*.

The first hitter stepped into the batter's box to face me, & just like my first varsity start, I walked him... & the next *four* hitters. The Pitching Coach came out to the mound to try to settle me down, & it worked... for a little while. I struck out the next hitter I faced. Then, my nervousness came back & I walked the next three hitters I faced before I was finally pulled out of the game. My confidence was completely deflated. I was yet again humiliated.

Not only did I fail in front of four thousand people, I failed my manager & my coaches - the ones who took a huge chance on signing a high schooler - & I failed my team – a group of men I inspired to be. When I got to the dugout, I was not greeted by any of my teammates, or any of my coaches. It felt like I was back in eighth grade, after I made the error in left field. I sat in the corner of the dugout, with a towel over my head, to hide my tears; just like after my first varsity start. I wanted to disappear, & that is what happened. I was like a ghost. No one acknowledged me in the dugout. No one said a word to me in the locker room after the game. No one said a word to me on the bus ride back to the hotel. No one said a word to me at lunch, the next day. I just sat by myself at the table & ate. *I felt alienated.*

As you may know by now, I do not quit things because they are hard, or because I failed. So, I did what I always did – *I kept showing up*. All I knew was working hard & being competitive. Days went by before anyone said a word to me, so instead of trying to talk to them, I *outworked* them. I watched what they did in preparation for every game, & I mimicked them the best that I could. If someone had sprints to run, I would run them with them, right next to them, & I would try to beat them *every* sprint. If someone had a medicine ball workout to do, I would do it with them, & I would try to do more repetitions than them *every* set. If someone had to throw long toss, I would do it with them, & I would try to throw the baseball harder & farther than them *every* throw. I *quickly* gained back the respect of my teammates – they knew I was not there just to be there & fill a roster spot.

A little longer than a week went by before I got another chance to pitch in a game. We were in Waterloo, Iowa, playing the Waterloo Bucks. They had a fan that would yell out between *every* pitch: "Hey! Hey! What do you say? Let's go Bucks!" It was funny at first, but then... it became annoying; especially, when I got out to the mound.

There was a song our left-fielder played for his walk-up song when he would go up to bat. He was from California, so it was fitting that the song was "Dani California" by the Red Hot Chili Peppers. I *loved* that song. It made me feel more confident, & more importantly, it calmed me down. So, I added it to my "pre-game playlist." If you can remember, I used to listen to heavy metal, which, would get me amped up for the games... *too amped up*. I was pitching with way too much tension, anxiety, & pressure, so I made the change to my playlist, & *it worked*. In my relief appearance that game against Bucks, I struck out the side. As I walked off the mound, I stared at my field manager with a *huge* grin on my face that let him know that he made the right choice signing me.

When I got to the bus after the game, I checked my phone to see I had a missed call. Do you know who the first person was to call me after the game? Coach Everson. I called him back, & he was so excited for me. He could not stop telling me how proud he was of me, & he kept saying, "that is the Riley Tincher I know!"

I pitched a few more times (some good, some bad) that season & he would call me after every single appearance. Thank you will never be enough for what he did for me, my baseball career, & my life. He gave me opportunities I did not deserve. He picked me up every time I fell. He did not give up on me when *everyone* else did.

TAKE IT

I may not have been ready to pitch in the Northwoods League, but I learned *a lot* of great lessons while I was there. One, in particular, stuck with me for the rest of my career:

It was the thirteenth inning of a tie ball game; the score was 5-5 against the Mankato Moondogs of the Northern Division of the Northwoods League. It was early August, so a lot of the players on our original roster had gone back home, to get ready for school; this included a lot of our pitchers. We were short on arms, & by short, I mean we had no arms left to pitch. The field manager was put into a tough situation, & he was forced to turn to some of our position players to pitch an inning, or two.

One of the best players I have *ever* played with was Daniel Descalso, our third basemen; who, is now playing in the Major Leagues for the Arizona Diamondbacks. It was not his sure-handed glove work, his discipline at the plate, or his outstanding athleticism that impressed me. It was the way that he always carried himself (on & off the field) that impressed me the most. There was something about him – the way he walked, the passion he played with, the way he talked to & treated people, & the amount of confidence he exuded – that told me he was going somewhere special, & *I was right.*

I will never forget the field manager asking Danny if he could pitch, & without hesitation, Danny said "yes, sir." Danny did not go down to the bullpen to warm up. Instead, he proceeded to warm up, on flat ground, with our shortstop, in front of our dugout. He threw five warmup pitchers, 4 of which were not even close to the strike zone, & told the field manager, "I am ready!" It was hysterical. Everyone in the dugout was laughing while he was warming up.

We all stopped laughing when Danny threw strike one & the radar gun flashed ninety-two miles-per-hour. We hardly ever saw ninety-two flash on the radar gun; not even from our best pitchers. Shortly after, Danny fell behind the hitter, & at a count of three balls & one strike, he threw a *change up* (where 99.9% of *pitchers* would throw a fastball) to get the batter to roll over a ground ball to the third basemen. If I did not know any better, I would have thought Danny had been pitching his whole life.

I learned an important principle that day – when your name is called, & you get your chance, *take it!* You may be nervous or scared, but take it anyways. You may feel like you are not ready, but take it anyways. You may have a lot of voices around you, telling you not to take it, but take it anyway. *Your* future depends on it, & it may be the only chance you get.

KNOWLEDGE APPLIED

I *firmly* believe that at the end of our lives we will only regret two things: the love we did not share, & the things we did not do.

There are so many things holding us back from sharing the love we need to share, & doing the things we need to do to pursue our dream – most of which, we create in our minds.

Every dream requires sacrifice – sacrifice of self, time, money, relationships, energy, etc. There is no dream without sacrifice. As my friend's dad told me: "no sacrifice, no dream." There is also no significant change without sacrifice.

Too often, we sacrifice the wrongs things. We sacrifice our dream for short-term gain. We sacrifice what we want most for what we want right now. We sacrifice the prize we have been given for pride. We sacrifice calling for comfort. We sacrifice our inheritance for safety.

Everything has a cost. *Everything!* There is a high price to pay for a higher calling. There are going to be things that we have to give up in order for our dreams to come to fruition – most of which, we will *not* want to give up.

We will never reach our full potential as a parent, or a spouse, if we are alcoholics. We will never reach our full potential as professional athletes, if we have a drug-addiction. We will never be the leader we were meant to be, if we are selfish. We will never become a champion – *at anything* – if we are not willing to put in the amount of time & work it requires; which is *a lot* more than we think. We will never experience the prosperity we have been promised, if we have a gambling-addiction, or we have a spending problem. We will never be the person we were called to be, if we are not willing to let go of the relationships we need to let go of, & get out of environments we need to get out of.

I am *begging* you - Do not live the rest of your life thinking about what you should have done, & what could have been. There is so much more to life than working for the weekends, & dreading Mondays. If you find yourself only thanking God for Fridays, then there are some *serious* changes & some *severe* sacrifices you need to make.

If you do not sacrifice for your dream, your dream will become the sacrifice.

"*Every dream requires sacrifice* – sacrifice of self, time, money, relationships, energy, etc. There is no dream without sacrifice."

"If you do not sacrifice for your dream, your dream will become the sacrifice."

@RileyTincher | #PitchingAgainstMyself

CHAPTER 4

ATTACK THE ZONE

M aking major life decisions can be *extremely hard* – especially, if you have to make them on your own. Have you ever made a major life decision you *instantly* regretted? The moment you stepped into it, & started doing the decision, you had a "what have I done?" feeling overtake you. Accepting the full scholarship, & going to Lincoln Trail College was that regretful major life decision for me.

It was the only Division I scholarship I received, because it was the first one I received. Due to my initial excitement, I accepted it right away. I had other *major* Division I universities call me, but I told them that I had already signed; I did not even give them a chance to talk to me & make me a better offer.

Coach Everson was the one that sent me to Lincoln Trail for a recruiting visit. Our centerfielder my junior year signed with them & was already there, so, Coach Everson wanted me to follow in his footsteps. Plus, he was dead set on me going to a junior college, as opposed to a four-year school.

He wanted me to go to a junior college for two reasons: one, I needed more playing time to develop my athletic ability & master my pitching skills, & two, for the Major League Baseball Draft.

In 2006, when I graduated high school, Major League Baseball had what was called a "draft & follow." If you were drafted, the team that drafted you had until the next year's Draft to sign you (now, they only have until the end of August to sign the players they draft). Because of this, a lot of baseball players, including myself, went to junior colleges, so we could still play (*a lot* of games) at the next level, & sign with the team that drafted us before the next year's Draft.

The letter of intent to a junior college was only for one year, as opposed to the letter of intent to a university being at least three years. If you were drafted, & decided to sign with a university, you would not be eligible to sign with a Major League team until after your junior year, or after you turned twenty-one-years-old.

All of the baseball players who went to junior colleges were there either because of the Major League Baseball Draft, or because they did not have the grades to play for a university in the National Collegiate Athletic Association (NCAA) – although, there were some exceptions (I played with a few).

The minimum requirement for a grade point average (GPA) to be eligible to play at a university in the NCAA is *terribly* low – It was a 2.0 grade point average (a *low* 'C' average) when I graduated high school, but in 2012, the NCAA raised the minimum requirement to a 2.3 grade point average.

On a side note, according to NCAA's research, 43.1% of men's basketball players, 35.2% of football players, & 15.3% of all student-athletes who enrolled as a freshman in 2009 to play Division I sports would not have met the 2016 standards. That is *so alarming* to me. I understand that school does not come easy for some individuals, but you can accomplish anything you want, if you care enough, & you are willing to put in the work that it requires to be accomplished.

These statistics tell me one thing: the focus is just on athletics, which is setting student-athletes up to *fail* after they are done playing their respective sport. They are student-athletes, *not* athlete-students.

To make matters worse, universities have created a degree for general studies. *Yes*, you read that correctly... general studies. *Who the hell does that serve?* It certainly does not serve the student-athlete. What are they going to do with that degree after they graduate college? It is just a one-hundred-thousand-dollar piece of paper.

Not every student-athlete has a full athletic scholarship, so the ones that do not have one are just giving away tens of thousands of dollars to the university, with little-to-no return of investment, & the universities are *ok* with that. I realize it is *their* choice to make, but why is it even an option in the first place?

Unfortunately, for the majority of the athletes I played with at junior college who did not meet the minimum grade point average requirement set by the NCAA, their grades were a direct reflection of their *character*.

There was *a lot* of partying. There were *a lot* of street drugs (all kinds) & there was *a lot* of alcohol abuse; even *during* the season. There was *a lot* of steroid usage. There was *a lot* of sex; this was my first time experiencing what the term "cleat-chaser" meant. There was *a lot* of cheating in school; the pitching coach I had at Lincoln Trail College would always say, "if you are not cheating, you are not trying." It was made very clear that we were there for one very specific reason: to play baseball – more specifically, to win a National Championship *for the coach*... by *any* means necessary.

It was also made very clear that we were pawns to his chess game, & we were *expendable*. The first day of practice at Lincoln Trail College, one of the first things the head coach told us was "we could be replaced, very quickly, at any time." Then, we proceeded to have a five-hour long practice. *Five hours!* It got dark during the middle of practice, & we did not have lights at the field, so I thought it was over. Instead, coach had us pull our cars around the fence of the field, turn our lights on, & shine them towards the infield, so we could continue practicing. The purpose of that practice was not to get better at baseball, it was to send a message: "I am your coach, your father, your master, & I own you & your life now."

The next nine months I spent at Lincoln Trail were absolute hell. It never got better, it got worse. It seemed like every day we were under some sort of punishment. We would do things no baseball players should have to do. We spent an enormous amount of time practicing. We ran more in that nine months than I have ever ran before... *in my life*. That was not even the worst part. During the offseason, we would have pool workouts every Sunday night, & we would swim, tread water, & swim some more until one of us cramped up, or puked. Then, we were done.

I lived every day in constant paranoia, because I had no idea what was going to happen next, & that was exactly what coach wanted. There were no rules, or restrictions in junior college, so we were at the mercy of him... at *all* times.

During the winter, near the end of the first semester, we were forced to volunteer as referees & scorekeepers for the local youth basketball program. I was always the scorekeeper, because of my attention to detail. During the last game of the basketball season (the first semester ended a few days before & I was going to head home right after the game) I accidently added points for the wrong team, & coach caught it. He walked over to me, & told me, "if you make that mistake again, you are not going home for Christmas." Thankfully, I did not make that mistake again, & after the game, I left the gymnasium as fast as I could.

I spent the entire Christmas break in torment about whether, or not I should go back. One day during break, the assistant coach called me to convince me to come back, & his silver tongue persuaded me.

When I returned, he came over to the house I lived in & the first thing he said when he saw me was "I am so surprised you are here. Thank you for coming back." I wish I did not go back.

In the first few weeks of the semester, one of our pitchers was arrested in a drug bust by the Federal Bureau of Investigation (FBI), because he was transporting & selling drugs across state lines. He was immediately kicked off the team (because he was in jail), but we had to endure his punishment.

There was a park next to the indoor facility we practiced in, & there was a trail that went around the entire park – the trail was a little over a mile in length. That day, we all had to run ten laps on this trail around this park – over ten miles, in total. I was one of the only ones that ran all ten laps. When I say that, I do not just mean there were others who walked some of laps (which, there were), I also mean that there were a few who did not run ten laps at all. I was so mad that we had to do this (to serve the punishment of a guy that was not even on the team anymore), that I ran the fastest I have ever run before.

My frustration got worse when I got back to the indoor facility & I saw some of my teammates, who I passed on the trail *several* times, were back at the facility before me. They cheated, & they would have gotten away with it if I did not do anything about it. I took my frustrations out on the first person I saw, our centerfielder. Three of my teammates had to pry me off him, & coach came running over to see what was going on. It was unusual for me to act that way - I am *not* a violent person – so coach asked me what happened. I told him that they did not run all ten laps, like we all were supposed to. He made them run again.

While they were running, he was sitting on the tailgate of his truck (while, the hitting coach drove) ahead of them ringing a cow bell after every lap they finished. I was not very liked by my team after that day.

This was the first time in my baseball career that I hoped our season ended as quickly as possible, & of course, it did not. I would actually sit in the corner of the dugout during the postseason & hope one of our batters would strike out to end an inning, or one of our pitchers would give up the go-ahead run, so we would lose, & I could *finally* get out of there.

We were a very talented team – there were several players on the team that were drafted the year before - & we won *a lot* of games. We won our Conference Championship. Then, we won Regionals to go to Super Regionals for the first time in school history. But I had *nothing* to do with the success of our team.

I was the *"oh shit pitcher"* (not my words, my head coach's words). During Spring Training in Florida, we were down by a lot, so coach called me & another pitcher (who also sat on the bench a lot) in to the bullpen to start warming up to go into the game. That is where he called us both the "oh shit pitchers" – Meaning, "oh shit, we are down by a lot, it is time to use our worst pitchers." Again, not my words, *his* words.

Since we won *a lot* of games, & we were hardly ever down by a lot, I hardly ever got a chance to pitch. I would always travel with the team (even when others did not travel), but I would *never* pitch.

I would not have minded the lack of playing time if I deserved it, but I did not deserve it. I may not have been the most talented, or one of the hardest throwing pitchers on the team, but I was not the worst. I was the hardest working player on the team. I was never late... *to anything*. I never partied. I never drank. I never did drugs. I stayed out of trouble. I got straight 'A's' in school. Every chance I did get to pitch, I did my job; I got hitters out & gave our team a chance to win. It did not make sense to me, at all.

I would sit on the bench & watch some of my teammates, who quite frankly did not deserve it, get opportunity, after opportunity, after opportunity to play. These were teammates who partied regularly; even, during the season. These were teammates who would not pass a drug test if coach made them take one. These were teammates who would not go to class; which, was a "requirement" to play. These were teammates who were failing school; I do not even know how they were eligible. These were teammates who would routinely skip workouts, & extra practices. These were teammates who cared only about themselves.

This sent a message to me, & the rest of my teammates who were overlooked, & underappreciated – Coach does not care about character, work ethic, or integrity; he only cares about winning... *at all costs.*

Towards the end of the season, I requested a meeting to talk to my pitching coach about my lack of playing time. During the meeting, the only legitimate reason he could give me as to why I was not pitching was because I did not have a "good enough pickoff move." As he told me this, I immediately responded with, "*Seriously?* Not having a good enough pickoff move was the only reason why I was not pitching?" He did not like me questioning him.

The funny thing about it was, I had one of the best pickoff moves on the team; it comes with the territory of being a left-handed pitcher. To add to the ridiculousness of his reason, during the offseason, I would go up to the indoor facility after *every* practice, to work on my pickoff move in the mirrors at the facility for hours at a time, & every coach knew about it, & many of them praised me for it.
This was not the only thing they lied to me about.

A few years later, a professional scout told me why I did not pitch at Lincoln Trail College. The coaches there were telling all the professional scouts that wanted to come see me pitch that I was hurt. The truth is, they did not want me to sign a professional contract.

Not only did they take a year of my life away from me, but they also ruined my chances of playing professional baseball.

When the season *finally* ended, we had our end of the season individual meetings with all the coaches. During my meeting, the head coach told me that they were going to give me the "privilege" of having another full-scholarship for next year – *what a joke*. He slid the letter of intent towards me, & before I could even read it to sign it, he told me "we want you to go home this summer & take time to really think about coming back next year. We also want you to look around for better options." It was a set up.

As soon as I got back to the house I grew up in, I started looking for "better options," & as soon as my pitching coach caught wind of it, he called me to let me know that "I betrayed the team" & that they took the full scholarship away from me, & I was not allowed back to Lincoln Trail College the next year.

I only have one thing to say about that: *Good riddance!*

FLY AROUND

It was the middle of June, when I *finally* was able to start taking recruiting visits to other schools. It was *very late* in the game. Most of the scholarship money was already used up by the early recruiting class back in the Spring.

My parents did not have enough money to support me going to college to play baseball, so I *desperately* needed a scholarship in order to continue my baseball career.

Coach Everson, *yet again,* came in to help me find another school. He passed my name around to everyone who knew (which, is *a lot* of coaches) to let them know I was available to pitch for them the next season. Most of them wanted to have me walk on at first & then give me a scholarship later, but we could not afford it.

Lucky for me, a small school in Mason City, Iowa – North Iowa Area Community College (NIACC) - called me & said they still had scholarship money left to give me.

Soon after I got the call, my Mom & I headed to Mason City to visit. When we got there, we were met by the pitching coach, Travis Hergert - the man who called me - & he showed us around the campus.

NIAAC's had a a big campus; *a lot* bigger than Lincoln Trail College's campus. The facilities were very nice; *a lot* nicer than Lincoln Trail College's facilities. The student population was *a lot* bigger than Lincoln Trail College's student population; they actually had regular students, not just student-athletes. He also showed us the baseball stadium, which, was *a lot* better than Lincoln Trail College's baseball stadium.

The scholarship helped *a lot*, but the thing that got me was Coach Hergert's genuine desire to have me come pitch at NIACC. He offered me a scholarship without ever seeing me pitch (which, is a huge gamble). It felt great to be wanted, for once. He trusted Coach Everson, & in turn, I trusted him. On that visit, I signed the letter of intent to pitch at NIACC.

I am still incredibly grateful for the second chance Coach Hergert gave to me. He took a huge risk on signing me – not knowing who I was, or what I was capable of. I wanted to make sure I gave him the greatest return of his investment.

That summer, I experienced depression for the first time in my life. As the summer progressed, I fell deeper & deeper into it. At the time, I thought this depression was because of all the terrible things that happened to me my freshman year at Lincoln Trail College… but, it was not. Then, I thought it was because of burnout from baseball… but, it was not. It really was because I moved back to the house I grew up in, & because I was thrown back into the environment I subconsciously wanted so desperately to escape from.

That summer, I slept more than I had ever slept before – it was rare for me to wake up before noon; the guilt I felt for "wasting the day" every time I woke up late, only added to the guilt & shame I already felt. All I wanted to do was lay around the house. I did not even want to hang out with my friends. I lost all motivation, & I quickly got out of shape because of it (I gained thirty pounds). I was invited as a date to a wedding, & I cancelled on the poor woman the day of the wedding – I *still* feel *terrible* about it. The only thing that got me moving was the baseball games I had every Sunday.

At the end of the summer, I loaded up my truck & trailer, & I moved to Mason City, Iowa. On the way there, Coach Hergert called me to see how the packing went, & to see if I was on the way. It was a pleasant surprise. It was something I was not used to - He *cared*.

As soon as I got there, I was welcomed by him, & he showed me to my dorm room. I had a dorm room to myself.

I am what most people consider a "clean freak," so I thought it was best for me to live by myself. I also had a t*errible* experience with roommates (one of them was a part of the drug bust) the year before – At one point, I moved into a different house with new roommates who were just as bad. I did not want to go through that again.

As I was moving in, I had several teammates, who lived on the same floor as me, come by my room to introduce themselves & offer a hand in helping me move in. They all seemed to know who I was before I even introduced myself. They referred to me as the "Division I transfer." It was ridiculous, & overwhelming, but I kind of liked it – again, it *always* feels great to be appreciated.

Up until this point, I had met everyone on the team, except the head coach, Todd Rima. Everyone on the team had an initial level of respect for me, because they knew where I was coming from & what I had "accomplished" … except Coach Rima. It seemed like he could care less about who I was, where I was coming from, or what I had accomplished. He did not recruit me, & honestly, at first, it felt like he did not even want me there, at all.

The first practice was *chaotic*, to say the least. I was shocked by *all* the players we had; there were at least fifty of them. We had enough players to have a junior varsity team; which, I did not know you could have in college.

Coaches had this term called "fly around" – which was their way of telling us to sprint. We flew around everywhere. When I say everywhere, I mean *everywhere*. If we were in practice, or playing in a game, we were not allowed to walk, or even jog, *anywhere*. If we were going out to our position on the field for defense, we sprinted. If we were walked or got a hit-by-pitch, we sprinted to first base. If we were going to the next station in practice, we sprinted. If Coach Rima, or Coach Hergert, called us over for them to talk to us, we sprinted to them – there were *several* times where we did not run fast enough to them, & they sent us "to the fence (outfield wall)" & back. *A lot* of my teammates hated it, but I thoroughly enjoyed it. I loved the rush & the competitiveness of it. When we played games against other teams who did not "fly around," we *looked* better.

In junior college, there is a fall baseball season (NCAA does not have a fall season) – another appeal for athletes to go to a junior college for more playing time & development. During our fall season, I started having *a lot* of success on the mound. I was throwing the ball the hardest I had ever thrown before. I was striking *a lot* of hitters out. I did not give up a single run until we played Des Moines Area Community College (DMACC); a team in our conference. To put it lightly, I got lit up; I think I gave up two homeruns that game.

The greatest threat to future success is current success. Success creates a sense of pride, & pride leads to complacency. That is *exactly* what happened to me.

At the beginning of the fall season, I was one of the hardest working players on the team (again, a common theme). I put in a ton of extra time at the field & in the weight room; I wanted to make the most out of the second chance I was given. When I started seeing success on the mound, I thought I did not need to put in extra work anymore. My performance on the mound suffered because of it, & Coach Rima was *quick* to let me know just how complacent I had become – A lecture that I *needed* to hear it.

I quickly changed gears, & for the rest of the fall season, I set my mind to being the hardest working player on the team again. I made sure I was the first one at practice, & the last one to leave, & fortunately, my performance improved because of it

Then, on a Friday night before one of the last games of the fall season – which was on a Sunday in Dubuque, Iowa against Clarke College – there was a party. At NIACC, we had a forty-eight-hour rule; which meant we were not allowed to drink any alcohol forty-eight hours before a game. Since we did not have a game on Saturday, most of my teammates felt the need to party on Friday night. When I say "most," I mean all but ten of us.

That night, I went over to one of our catcher's house, who lived with two other teammates. His house was right next door to the house where the party was; which, was on campus (not the smartest decision, considering two of our coaches lived on campus).

The party was *so loud*. There had to be well over seventy-five people there – all fitting into a *tiny* house. They thought they were clever by closing all the blinds & covering all the windows, so no one could see inside. The problem was, when it got later, & the alcohol started flowing more, it was harder to keep people inside. That was when campus security was called.

Can you guess who the campus security officer was that night? Our hitting coach.

On Sunday morning, we all boarded the bus to go to Dubuque. Before we took off, the captains got off the bus to talk to Coach Rima. When they came back, they told us that he knew about the party, & that if anyone was at the party, they had to get off the bus immediately to talk to him. All but ten of us got up & left the bus. We had no idea what was going to happen.

He sent all of them home, & told them to call their parents to tell them not to come to the game & explain to them why they were not playing that day.

On that bus ride to the Dubuque, I was filled with pride for two reasons: one, I was proud of my decision not to go to that party (even though I *really* wanted to), & two, I was proud of coach for sticking to the rules he created, & for sending a message to the team that no matter who you are, rules are rules, & *everyone* must adhere to them.

That game was one of the most fun games I have ever played in my baseball career. On top of that, my parents were *both* in attendance; which, was a rarity – they both came together to less than ten games in my entire baseball career.

If you do not know, it takes nine players to play baseball – we had ten. Of the ten we had, five of us were pitchers. I got a chance to do something that day that I had not had a chance to do in almost two years – play right field, play first base, & *hit*. I was 1-2 at the plate that day. I hit a double, & I scored a run. Plus, I pitched really well, & we won… *with ten players.*

82

REIGNITION

Fast forward to Christmas break; the best Christmas break of my life - the Christmas break that reignited my baseball career.

As a team, we put in *a lot* of work in the weight room & on the basketball court (running suicides) between the time fall season ended & Christmas break began. Before we left, Coach Rima told us that when we come back from Christmas break, we would have to run a timed-mile, & we would all have to run it in under seven minutes. If we were not able to run the sub-seven-minute mile, we would have to run it again, & again, & again, until we did run it under seven minutes.

I was nowhere close to being able to run a sub-seven-minute mile. I *needed* help. As I was driving home for Christmas break, I called the only person I knew who would push me more than anyone else would push me. I called Coach Diercks.

For the next four weeks, I would meet with Coach Diercks Monday through Friday at 9 AM, & he would take me through an hour long (sometimes, two hours) conditioning workout.

At the time, Coach Diercks was working full-time as a physical education teacher at Oregon High School (the high school I went to); he took Coach Everson's job when Coach Everson left to go work for the Florida Marlins.

Coach Diercks was also the head coach of the varsity boy's soccer team. Soccer was his passion, & coaching was his purpose. He had immediate success as the head soccer coach - winning multiple conference championships in a very talented conference, & taking the team to state for the first time in over ten years.

Coach Diercks is the perfect example of "great coaching & great leadership leads to success in *all* areas."

I know I used this quote before, but we all need the reminder – As John C. Maxwell says, *"everything* rises & falls on leadership," & in this case, Oregon High School boy's soccer (& the school, as a whole) rose because of Coach Diercks' leadership.

As you can imagine, he hardly had any time to give, but he *made* time for me - I could not even pay him for it. I still do not know why he was always so generous to me. He took care of me like I was one of his own. He saw something in me I did not see in myself. He was there for me *every* time I needed him.

When we first started working out, *it was hell*. The first thing he would always have me do when I got there was ten minutes of jumping rope... *straight*. At the time, I had hardly jumped rope before in my life. Needless to say, *I struggled*. I could barely jump rope for ten seconds at-a-time. Every time I stopped, he would yell at me to "get the rope moving."

After jump roping, we would do some sort of agility drill. Then, we would move into speed work. Then, we would do core work. Then, we would do medicine ball work. Then, we would finally finish with some sort of conditioning at the end (as if, what we did before was not enough) – usually, we ran suicides because we ran so many at NIACC. Then, it was time for lunch.

After lunch, I would come back to the weight room & lift. On Wednesdays & Saturdays, I would run a timed mile (timed by a kitchen timer) – which, on the first run, I ran an eight-minute mile.

At the end of Christmas break, I made some *incredible* progress - all thanks to Coach Diercks. I lost the thirty pounds I gained over the summer. I was able to jump rope for ten minutes straight. I beat Coach Diercks – who is a physical specimen that runs like a gazelle – running suicides. I was stronger than I had ever been before.
When I got back to NIACC, I ran a sub-seven-minute mile.

Not only that, but before Christmas break, I would always be one of the last ones to finish when we were running suicides, & after Christmas break, I was always one of the first ones to finish. One time, I beat our shortstop, who was a 5-time All-State football, basketball, baseball, & track athlete in the state of Iowa. Yes... *5-time* All-State athlete; he began competing in high school as an eighth grader.

The best part of that Christmas break, was when every once-in-a-while, my friends (who were also playing college baseball) would come & workout with us.

At first, I could not keep up with them, & they beat me in everything we did. At the end, they could not keep up with me. There was one workout where we did a medicine ball relay - where we would throw a medicine ball as far as we could & sprint after it to try to catch it before it bounces a second time. Then, we would throw it, & chase after it again. We did continuously, until we reached a certain distance. On one of the last days of Christmas break, we did this medicine ball relay, & two of the three friends that came with me that day, ended up puking, & could not finish. Not only that, but I beat the one who did not puke - my best friend, who is now a Navy SEAL.

What Coach Diercks did for me went far beyond the physical. He re-awakened my confidence. He helped me defeat depression (for the time being). He taught me how to compete again. He gave me a sense of pride. He showed me that I was capable of something I quite frankly *believed* I was not capable of. He not only completely changed the trajectory of my baseball career, he also completely changed the trajectory of my life.

I went into the next semester ready to compete & ready to prove to the coaches I was the guy they needed to carry the team to the National Junior College Athletic Association (NJCAA) World Series.

FIVE-GAME LIMIT

Right before the season started, we had individual meetings with Coach Rima to discuss our roles in our upcoming Spring Training trip to Florida - I *loved* the transparency of the entire coaching staff.

At the time, I was uncertain of where I fit in the rotation. There was another lefty who transferred in from another Division I school. Coach Rima *loved* him, despite, the reputation that preceded him, & quite frankly, *proceeded* him. Even with all that went on behind the scenes, Coach Rima thought this lefty could do no wrong. He was a shoe in for being the opening day starter.

As for the rest of the pitchers, there were six of us competing for the final three starting roles in the weekend rotation (every weekend we played a four-game Conference series).

When I sat down to talk with Coach Rima, I was thrilled to hear that I would be the third starting pitcher in the rotation; even though, he made it sounded like he was reluctant to tell me that. He told me I would have two starts in spring training, & then we would reassess where I was at in the rotation. He made sure that I knew that my spot was not solidified & that there were other guys on the team that he would love to give my spot away to.

Coach Rima treated me this way for a reason – He was one of the first coaches to *truly* know how to motivate me. He recognized that I carried a huge chip on my shoulder in everything I did, & he knew how to add to it.

Spring training came & went, & I left with a record of two wins & *zero* losses. I solidified my spot in the rotation.

Then, our conference schedule started, & my win-loss record improved to 4-0. The other lefty (Coach Rima's favorite) & I were the only undefeated pitchers on the team.

Then, the weekend came where we played DMACC. At the time when we played them, DMACC was in the top ten in the NJCAA, & we were in the top twenty. There was *a lot* of hype going into the weekend, because the winner of the series would most likely go on to be the winner of the Conference.

On day one, DMACC set the tone. They did not just beat us, they *destroyed* us – they "ten-runned" us (referring to the game being ended early due to one team beating the other team by ten runs) *both* games. Truth be told, they beat us before we even got off the bus.

The DMACC hitters *crushed* Coach Rima's beloved Ace (referring to the number one pitcher on the team), & they crushed our number two pitcher (who had been solid all year). Coach Rima was not happy about it... at all.

When we got back to campus that night, we did not get to go home right away. Instead, Coach Rima had us all meet him in the gym (where we would practice if the weather did not permit us to go outside). We then ran bunt coverages & first & third situations (referring to the defensive plays we ran when runners were on first base & third base) for over *an hour*.

Remember, we *flew around*, so, we were not jogging for over an hour, we were *sprinting*.

I was *pissed,* because I was supposed to pitch the next day, & my legs felt like *jello.*

When he *finally* decided that we were done, he told us to stop & he had us all gather around him. He then gave us a great speech about second chances; one, that I refer to a lot when I am experiencing setbacks, or feeling down. He told us that "no matter how bad the circumstance, no matter how bad the outcome, no matter how dark it may seem, the sun *always* rises in the morning." It is *true*!
As Coach Rima predicted, the sun rose again.

The next day, we went back to Des Moines, & we were the ones that set the tone. We beat them both games, & I pitched one of the best games of my baseball career. I experienced a "zone" I had never experienced before. It was like I was in a *trance.* I had tunnel vision; all I saw was the catcher's glove. I also could not hear *anything.*

Coach Hergert was *very intense* whenever it came time for the practices & games. He would *constantly* be yelling "you have got to compete!" I cannot tell you how many times I heard him yell that phrase; it was a countless amount. He *hated* free bases (walks & hit batters), & would slam his clipboard *every* time they happened. There were several broken clip boards that season.

He had a special saying he would yell only to me. It was: "attack the zone!" It seemed like he yelled it in between every pitch I threw.

Unfortunately (more like, fortunately) I could not hear him the day I pitched against DMACC. There were a few times I was sitting in the dugout between innings & he would try to get my attention, to no avail. So, he had whoever was sitting next to me hit me to get my attention; I *hated* it. I was pitching one of the best games of my life, against one of the best hitting teams in the country. I was in *the zone* - which, is what *every* coach wants their players to be in during games - & he kept on breaking my trance. Fortunately, it did not hinder my performance. I ended up allowing just three runs to score that day to a team that scored twenty-eights runs on us the day before.

The reason why he would yell "attack the zone!" at me was because when I pitched at NIACC, I was a perfectionist. I wanted every pitch I threw to be perfect. My drive for perfection made me a very tentative pitcher. I would try to "nibble" at the corners. I would throw with finesse, rather than with conviction. I would pitch scared, & it took away my velocity. It drove Coach Hergert *crazy*. He would yell "attack the zone!" to encourage me to let it go, & trust my stuff.

My fear of failure outweighed my will to win. Ultimately, it hurt me. I won the first five games I started, & began the season with a win-loss record of 5-0. Then, in the last five games I started, my win-loss record was 0-2. I was very aware of this. I called it the "five-game limit." I obsessed over it. It became all I thought about, & all I talked about. It drove me crazy.

Coach Rima & Coach Hergert tried almost everything to break me out of this "funk." They would come out to the mound, get right up in my face, & *yell* things at me that most people should not hear. Sometime, when they came out to me, they would question me if I wanted to be there. They would also try to add to that enormous chip on my shoulder by saying things like, "I do not think you have what it takes," & "you came all this way for nothing." Coach Rima even tried complimenting me. It was during our post game meeting after we lost to our Conference rival, Iowa Central, by one run - I pitched that game,

& I threw a complete game. He said, "there is no other pitcher I would have on the mound for that game than Riley Tincher. He competed his ass off. He gave us a chance to win, & we let him down."

His compliment caught me off guard, because it was something he *rarely* did – especially, towards me. It was a pleasant surprise.

Unfortunately, everything they tried did not work. No matter how great I pitched, I could not win my sixth game. I would come out of the game tied, or with the lead, then, whoever relieved me would give up the lead. This is exactly what happened the last game of the season.

It was game three of the Regional tournament, & I came out of the game with a *ten-run lead*, & the reliever who came in after me proceeded to walk hitter, after hitter until the ten-run lead was gone. We lost the game, & our season was over.

I finished the season with the most innings pitched on the team, the lowest earned runs average (ERA) among the starting pitchers on our team, & the third most wins in the Conference. Yet, I had zero scholarships offers from *any* schools.

I was back on my own again. I needed to figure out what I was going to do the next year, & I needed to figure it out *fast*.

KNOWLEDGE APPLIED

Let me say something that we all know, but we have a very hard time *fully* comprehending - *Life is not fair*. It is incredibly hard. This world does not owe us anything. It will not give us exactly what we want. It will confuse us. It will make us frustrated. It will tear us down, & destroy us… if we allow it to.

I know we live in an era of instant gratification, but that is not how the world works. *Any & everything* meaningful takes time… A lot more time than we think.

There will be setbacks. There will be storms. There will be people with less talent than us, or who we feel are less deserving than us, who are given opportunities that we are not given. There will be people who make worse decisions than we do, yet it seems like they catch all the breaks. There will be people who are going to take advantage of us. There will be people who are going to lie to us & hurt us... *intentionally*. There will be people who are going to use us for their personal agenda; oftentimes, it is people we least suspect. There will be times where everything we know & believe will be questioned. This world is set up for us to fail, but that does mean we will fail.

The *real* problem is we think that there should not be any problems.

When things do not go our way (which, they will not), it is all about how we respond. If we truly want something to happen, no matter what occurs in our journey to get there, nothing should be able to stop us from pursuing our dreams & taking constant action towards actualizing them. *Nothing!*

I know how hard it is to keep going when you cannot see your progress, when you have lost your perspective, & when the pain of failure has pushed you past your breaking point. But, now is not the time to quit. It is not the time to back down. It is not the time to give up & turn around. We must keep going.

In everything we do, there are dues we must pay; there is no way around it. There are going to be things we have to do that we do not want to do. Everybody has talent, but ability takes hard work. There is no substitute for it. There are no shortcuts. We must be determined to finish. We must be determined to keep going.

Consistency separates champions from losers. *Diligence* is the difference between all-time greats, & first-round draft pick *busts*. The race is not won by the strongest, the fastest, the smartest, or the best-looking. The race is won by the one who perseveres until they reach the finish line. What we start, we must have the determination to finish. We will *win,* if we do not quit.

When it does not make sense, we must keep going. When all odds are against us, we must keep going. When it feels like we are fighting this battle by ourselves, we must keep going. When everything seems to go wrong, we must keep going. When it appears that everyone else around us is succeeding, & we are not, we must keep going. When it feels like we are not gaining any ground, no matter how hard we try, we must keep going. When it feels like all hope is lost, we must keep going. We are closer than we think we are. We are closer than we have ever been before. Get back up, & keep going.

We cannot go into another year of our lives, "hoping it is going to get better." Hope is not a strategy! If we want something for the rest of our lives, we have to stop quitting. We have to stop quitting when we feel scared. We have to stop quitting when we feel discouraged. We have to stop quitting when we get tired. We have to stop quitting when things do not happen as quickly as we would like them to happen. We have to stop quitting when people tell us to (especially, people closest to us). We have to stop quitting when it gets hard; it is *supposed* to be hard, or else everyone would do it.

How bad do you want it? I know this question gets tossed around *a lot*, & it sounds so cliché, but there is truth behind it.

Too many of us quit right before our breakthrough. What if we quit today, & tomorrow our breakthrough was supposed to happen? What if we quit our jobs today, & tomorrow we were supposed to get the promotion, or the raise we have hoping for? What if we close our business today, & tomorrow a client was supposed to walk in who would completely change the trajectory of our business? What if we stopped calling, & the next day someone was supposed to answer who would give us the opportunity we had been looking for? We will never know when our breakthrough is, if we quit. Keep attacking the zone! *It is not about getting there as fast as you can. It is about getting there... period.*

"What we start, we must have the determination to finish. We will *win*, if we do not quit."

"It is not about getting there as fast as you can. It is about getting there... *period*."

CHAPTER 5

I'M COMING HOME

One of my least favorite things to do is move. I am not talking about physically moving my body, I am talking about packing up all of my stuff into boxes, & moving them to a new location. Moving is *never* easy. It becomes even more challenging when you know where you are moving to is only temporary, because that means you are going to have to move *again*.

Moving back to the house I grew up in after my season at NIACC was over was the *last* thing I wanted to do. I did not even bother unpacking that summer, knowing, I would just pack it up again a few months later to move on to the next college – wherever that may be.

The first month I was back in Wisconsin was a busy one. I had to update my baseball resume, & send it out to a bunch of coaches, hoping, their rosters were not already full, & a couple of them would actually give me a chance to come visit them. I had to find a job, because my mom insisted on me working during the summer. I also had to find a place to pitch that summer.

I made the decision to try to stay close to the house I grew up in, so, I sent my resume to all the universities within a 3-hour radius – there was no discrepancy with Divisions (I, II, or III). At the time, I thought I wanted to be closer to the house I grew up in, because I wanted to be closer to my friends, & closer to my parents. But, subconsciously, I wanted to be closer, in case anything happened to my parents, & because I wanted to give them a chance to see me pitch as much as they possible could. I thought being closer to them would eliminate all the excuses they had not to come & watch me pitch, before. *I was wrong.*

The first college (Lincoln Trail College) I moved to was six hours away, & they *never* came down to watch me pitch that year; due, in large part to the fact that I never pitched. The second college (NIACC) I moved to was four hours away, & they only came to see me pitch twice (once, in the fall, & once, in the spring). The third college (to be named later) I moved to was less than forty-five minutes away (I made it in less than thirty minutes, one time), & they both came down together to watch me pitch, maybe, five times… *in three years.*

The families of my future teammate came out to *every* game; even, the away games. It seemed like every player on the roster had parents at every game… except for me. I was envious of that. After every game, I would always be asked by at least one of the parents where my parents were (more specifically, where my dad was), & I never knew what to tell them. My mom came to a lot of games - as much as she thought she could – but my dad did not. It was incredibly hard to answer the question of, "is your father around?" It was incredibly disappointing to see the look on their face when I told them "yes," because they had assumed he was "not in the picture" anymore.

I made excuses for them not being at the games. I thought that they were not there because of how much they worked, even though I pitched primarily on the weekends, when they did *not* work.

Then, I thought that they were not there because they were exhausted from the week of work that they had. To be honest, it frustrated me that they could not sacrifice rest to see their son pitch.

Then, I thought it was because of my dog. Yes… my *dog.* He was getting older, & he needed extra care, & I did not know anyone who would have been able to take care of him while they were gone to see me pitch (there were plenty of people who would have helped).

Then, I thought that it was because it was their only chance to be together, since, they worked separate schedules, & never saw each other during the week. But, if they came to the games, they would have been together watching their son pitch.

Years later, I stopped agreeing with the excuses I made for them, & I finally recognized that it was not the sleep, nor the time together, nor taking care of my dog, that they were not willing to sacrifice to come see me pitch... it was the beer.

A GREAT SALESMAN

To my surprise, almost every college I reached out to, reached back out to me. Nearly every college in Wisconsin called me; none of which, had scholarships to offer me. They all acted like they were surprised I did not have a team to play for yet. Nevertheless, it was great to feel *wanted* again.

Through all the phone calls, one, in particular, stood out the most to me. That phone call came from Coach David Perchinsky – Coach Perch, for short. He was the assistant baseball coach for the University of Wisconsin – Whitewater Warhawks. The Warhawks have traditionally been a powerhouse in the Wisconsin Intercollegiate Athletic Conference (WIAC), especially, in the last five years (since 2004). They had been to the Division III World Series three times, including the past season (2008). They won the National Championship in 2005. They also had several players get drafted to play professional baseball (more than every Division I school in Iowa, Minnesota, Illinois, & Wisconsin). To be honest, I never paid attention to them, because they were Division III, & my mind was so focused on playing Division I, because that is what every coach I had talked about. To be honest, I was very reluctant to play Division III, because I thought it was going to be a huge step backwards for my career, but the phone call I had with Coach Perch completely changed that.

We spoke on the phone for over an hour, & we maybe talked about baseball for a total of five minutes. Coach Perch was more focused on what I wanted to study, & what I wanted to do after college. He told me something in that phone conversation that I will never forget. He said, "Riley, you have potential to be a great baseball player, but if you do not leave the University of Wisconsin – Whitewater a better man, than we did not do our jobs as your coaches."

Never once did he tell me about how much playing time I would have, or what spot I would be in the rotation. He never bragged about their facilities (which, I would find out later are *incredible*). He talked to me about education, my future, & being a better man.

After that phone call, I was pretty convinced I wanted to go to Whitewater, but I wanted to visit there first, & I wanted to hear out the rest of the coaches who had contacted me. Plus, I knew better than to take the first opportunity I was handed, because of my experience going after the first scholarship I received from Lincoln Trail College, & immediately regretting that decision as soon as I got there.

The other coaches who contacted me were... interesting. They all had very nice things to say, but there was a level of bullshit that came with everything they told me. They promised me *a lot*. It was nice to feel wanted again, but the things they promised me were, quite frankly, outrageous. They promised me that I was going to see significant amount of time on the mound; some even told me that I would be the Ace of the pitching staff. They promised me that I could pick whatever number I wanted; some even told me I could design the new jerseys they were getting. One coach even promised me that I would never have to pay for rent, gas, or food if I went to his school; which, is *illegal* throughout every Division in the NCAA.

One thing they all had in common was they all told me how great their programs were & how much they had accomplished as coaches; which, was *nothing* in comparison to the success Whitewater had.

Despite all the phone calls, *& promises*, I ended up visiting only two schools; both of which, had incredible traditions of winning, & developing players into the professional ranks.

The first school I visited had newly renovated facilities, which were entirely paid for by alumni who made it to the Major Leagues (or so the head coach told us). My mom & I were instantly impressed; it was beautiful. Having played at junior colleges for two years, I was not used to seeing a baseball stadium that nice.

My mom was already very partial to me going there, since we were very familiar with the area because we had family members who lived in the area. I also had friends who attended the university; & they spoke highly about the education they received there.

To our surprise, one of my former teammates greeted us as we arrived on campus – I had no idea he was playing there. It was great seeing him again, & catching up. He took us out to lunch, & gave us a brief tour of the campus. On the tour, we met up with the head coach. He was a legend in the entire baseball community… & he knew it. He had *a lot* of success early in his coaching career – going to the Division III World Series nine times in his first fifteen seasons, & winning one National Championship; it took, maybe, three sentences into the conversation for him to tell us all of this. He also had two pitchers go on to play Major League Baseball; which, he told us on the fourth sentence of the conversation. As a matter of fact, the *entire* conversation we had was about how great *he* was. He was a great salesman. He convinced my mom that I needed to go there (which, I heard about for the entirety of the car ride home). I, however, was not convinced. I wanted to go somewhere where we could win, & I wanted to go somewhere where I could get noticed & have a greater chance of getting drafted. He & his school gave me the opportunity to do both, but there was something off about him.

POWERED BY TRADITION

The second school I visited was the University of Wisconsin – Whitewater. Like I told you before, I never paid attention to Whitewater, so I had no idea what I was in for that day.

This visit was a little different from my first one. Instead of going with my mom, I went with Zimm. He also came back to our hometown that summer, & he needed to find a place to play the next year, as well.

Our paths through college were very similar. He heeded the advice of Coach Everson & went to a junior college in Iowa his freshman year (which, was in the same conference as NIACC). To say his team was terrible would be an understatement.

To give himself a better chance of getting recognized by professional scouts, he transferred to a junior college in Illinois (which, was in the same conference as Lincoln Trail College) for his sophomore year; we literally switched conferences.

We also had very similar experiences with coaches. He was also on his own trying to find a school for next year. Coach Perch had also recruited him, so we visited Whitewater together.

Whitewater, Wisconsin is a relatively small town (the population is a little over 14,000), but in the middle of this small town is one of the biggest Division III campuses in the country (a little over 12,000 students). The population of Whitewater doubles from August to May.

As soon as Zimm & I got on campus, we both were blown away. There were a ton of buildings, & they all were *huge* (compared to the building(s) at our tiny, little junior colleges). The landscaping was immaculate. There was purple (the school color) *everywhere* - Now, I know what you may be thinking, *"Purple? Really?"* But let me tell you something, it was beautiful. There was a *perfect* amount of purple, & there is such thing as a perfect amount of purple.

After Zimm & I drove through the campus, we arrived at Prucha Field (Whitewater's baseball field). There, we were met by Coach Perch. He was *very* excited to see us - he hugged us both, which had never happened to me by *any* coach on *any* visit. His passion & excitement reminded me a lot of Coach Diercks. He *loved* Whitewater Warhawk baseball, & you could tell that just by the way he carried himself around that campus; he was so proud to be there.

He showed Zimm & I around the baseball field, & the clubhouse that was attached to it. I had never been in a clubhouse like that before – beautiful, hand-crafted lockers with everyone's numbers & names above the locker. Upstairs, above the clubhouse, was the Head Coach's office, but we did not go up there yet.

After we got the tour of Prucha Field, he drove us over to the Williams Center – A building on campus where the Kachel Fieldhouse was located, as well as the Wrestling Gymnasium, Basketball Gymnasium, Gymnastics Gymnasium, Volleyball Arena, Indoor Swimming Pool & Dive Well, Indoor Track, Locker Rooms, Athletic Offices, Athletic Training Room, Weight Room, Racquet Ball Courts, Dance Studios, & Classrooms.

The Williams Center was *huge*. I have never been in a building as big as it. Everything seemed brand new, even though it was almost ten years old. I about lost my mind when we walked in the Kachel Fieldhouse. It was *enormous*. There was a six-lane, two-hundred-meter track inside; which, was colored purple. There were four basketball courts; which, were also colored purple – again, the *perfect* amount of purple. There were four batting cages hanging from the ceiling (this is where they practiced in the winter). There was even a putting green. What amazed me the most were the pictures of all the All-Americans Whitewater has ever had. There were too many to count - the pictures filled the walls of this enormous fieldhouse.

Just when I thought the facilities could not get any better, Coach Perch walked us into the Weight Room. All I had to say was – *"Wow!"* Up until this point in my life, I had never seen a weight room like this - there were twelve Olympic lifting platforms, eighteen squat racks, & loads of boxes, free weights, & machines. The weight rooms at Lincoln Trail College & NIACC seemed tiny & outdated compared to this weight room.

I almost told Coach Perch right then & there that I was going to come to Whitewater in the Fall. But... I waited.

After we walked through the weight room, we toured the rest of the Williams Center; which, was just like the Kachel Fieldhouse, & the weight room – nothing short of *spectacular*.

When we finished the tour, Coach Perch drove us back over to Prucha Field, so Zimm & I could finally meet the head coach of the Whitewater Warhawks, John Vodenlich – Coach Vo, for short.

When we got to Prucha Field, Coach Vo was waiting for us at the gate of the field. He greeted Zimm & I with a *firm* handshake & told us how excited he was to meet us. He called us the "package deal."

Coach Vo is not a big man (average size – around six feet tall, maybe one-hundred-seventy pounds), but he carries himself like he is a giant. He walks with a *swagger*, & is a *smooth* talker. Confidence & charisma pours out of him, just like it pours out of Coach Everson. He also had these bright blue eyes that would pierce through you when he looked at you.

He took us back into the clubhouse, & walked us upstairs to his office. His office was filled with awards & trophies. The walls of his office were covered with pictures of former teams, former players, & captured moments of some of his former teams dog-piling on the field after they won Regional & World Series Championships.

One picture caught my eye the most. It was a picture of a left-handed pitcher (I did not know who it was at the time) in the middle of his windup, & in the background of that picture was probably twenty, or more, professional scouts holding up their radar guns waiting, in anticipation, for this pitcher to throw his fastball. Coach Vo caught me staring at the picture, & told me, "one day, that could be you." He was right.

Zimm & I sat in his office for maybe twenty minutes, & we talked about how Whitewater could benefit us. He never promised us anything. He told us the *truth*. He told us that we would have to fight for a spot on the roster because there were *a lot* of talented players already on the roster - many of which played in the World Series the year before. He also told us that there were going to be *a lot* of other players trying out in the Fall alongside us. I asked him what he looks for in his players, & instead of telling us about what a player should look like, or how talented the player should be, he told us what he *expected* from his players – a willingness to work harder than everyone in the country, a character that is second to none, & a passion to win at a very high level.

Zimm & I matched his expectations *perfectly*.

We finished our meeting, & walked out of the clubhouse, & he asked us if we had any questions, or comments. I thanked him for having us, & I said to him "Zimm & I have been through a lot the last two years, & we just want to be somewhere that we are wanted & appreciated." To which he replied, "I cannot guarantee you that this is the right place for you, but I can guarantee that if this is not the right place for you, we will help you find the right place." That is not what you would expect to hear from a coach trying to win over two Division I transfers to his school. Again, no bullshit, just truth.

I was sold. I knew right that day that I wanted to go to the University of Wisconsin – Whitewater in the fall. On the car ride home, I asked Zimm what he thought, & he felt the exact same way I did. We then talked about living together, & how much fun we were going to have. We also talked about how we were going to come in & dominate because we were coming from very high-level programs. We both were extremely excited.

When we got back to the house I grew up in, before Zimm got out of the car, he turned to me, & said, "Whitewater has *no idea* what is coming their way."

When I walked into the house, I told my mom that I was going to go to Whitewater in the fall, & instead of congratulating me, she asked, "are you sure you do not want to go to the other school?" She was still sold on the idea of me going to the other school. An argument ensued, which finished with her walking away from the argument & out into the garage (as she always did when we got in an argument, & it did not go her way) yelling "I think you should just quit playing baseball & focus on school," as she slammed the door behind her.

Those words cut through my heart like a hot knife through butter. It was bad enough to hear it from my coach in eighth grade (which, always echoed in my mind), but it was even worse to hear it from my own mom. The sad thing is, I have heard it from her before (*several* times), & just like the last time she said it to me, I tried my best to ignore it.

I know she did not mean many of the *nasty* words she said to me, but it still does not make it ok that she said them; especially, to her own child. I never understood why my mom never believed in my dream of becoming a professional baseball player... & I still do not understand. You would think all the awards, the scholarships, & the notoriety would have given her confirmation that I was a great baseball player, but it did not convince her.

It seemed like every summer, or every time I was back in the house I grew up in for an extended period of time, I was fighting to convince her that I am going to keep playing baseball. She always resorted towards me "needing a job & baseball getting in the way of that," but there was *a lot* more to it than that.

THE FINAL DECISION

Towards the end of June, I received a phone call that would eliminate my chances of getting a job that summer. The call came from the pitching coach of the Green Bay Bullfrogs; another team in the Northwoods League. Our shortstop from NIACC was playing for the Bullfrogs at the time, & when he heard that they needed a starting pitcher, he mentioned my name.

During the phone call, the coach told me they had an open spot in the pitching rotation, & he asked me if I wanted to take it. Without hesitation, & without asking my mom, I enthusiastically said *"yes!"*

That night, when my mom got home from work, I told her about the opportunity. She, of course, tried to talk me out of it. She was worried (& rightfully so) that I would have the same experience I had when I played in the Northwoods League before. She was looking out for me, but casting her fears on me was not the best way to do that.

When that argument did not work for her, she resorted back to what she *always* worried about the most – getting a job & money. In which I responded, "I have the rest of my life to work."

It did not take her very long to realized there was no way of talking me out of this opportunity, & she reluctantly let me go. Shortly after, I loaded up my truck, & took off.

On the three-hour drive to Green Bay, all I could think about was the decision I had to make about where I was going to go to school in a couple of months. I was about ninety-nine percent sure that I was going to go to Whitewater, but I needed more clarification, & I knew exactly who I needed to call to get the clarification I needed. So, I called Coach Everson.

As always, he picked up & was excited to hear from me. It had been a long time since we talked last, & we had *a lot* of catching up to do. It took almost an hour to even get to the whole reason for calling him. I told him about my two options, & to my surprise, he eliminated one immediately – the school other than Whitewater. He emphatically told me he would *never* allow any of his players to play for that coach, & he proceeded to tell me a few horror stories of how this coach abuses his players – mentally & physically.

One of the stories Coach Everson told me was about how one of this coach's pitchers said something to him under his breath after this coach pulled him from the game. After the next pitcher came in, the coach charged after the pitcher he just took out, tackled him to the ground in the dugout, & choked him out. It took the whole team to tear this coach off of this pitcher. This pitcher's career was over, but somehow, this coach kept coaching. The worst part is, I have an even more horrific story about this coach to share with you later, because, over the next three years, I would pitch against this coach & his team, & I would witness his abuse in person.

Thank God, Coach Everson did not allow me to go to that school.

The next portion of our conversation shifted towards what I should expect when I go to Whitewater, & play for Coach Vo. Coach Everson told me that Coach Vo is very hard on his players, & demands a lot from them. He also told me that *a lot* of players try out for the baseball team every year – over one-hundred players tried out the year after they won the National Championship. Coach Everson ended the conversation by telling me (actually, warning me):

"I think you are making a great decision, Riley, but be careful. I admire & respect Coach Vo, but he puts winning above everything, & he is willing to do whatever it takes to win, & if you cannot help him do that, he will get rid of you without even thinking twice about it."

The next day, I signed the contract to play for the Bullfrogs, but there was a problem – players cannot play for two different teams in the Northwoods League without a release from the first team, & the Woodchucks had not released me yet, so I had to sit out until they did. It was a (*long*) couple of days before I was finally able to suit up to play. Until that day, I was only allowed to do batting practices, & throw bullpens with the team, but I was not allowed to sit in the dugout with them during the games. The funny thing is, the first game I was allowed to suit up was when we played the Woodchucks in Wausau, & I was scheduled to start.

On the bus ride to Wausau for the game, I called Coach Perch to tell him my decision. When I told him I was going to be a Warhawk, he was very excited (to say the least) – I have never heard a grown man yell the way he did. After he calmed down, he got straight to business telling me what I needed to do next to ensure a smooth transfer (applying for school, sending transcripts, signing up for student loans, finding an apartment, etc.). When the business talk was over, he told me "I am so glad you are a Warhawk. This will be one of the best decisions you will ever make in your life." He was right.

The next phone call I made was to Coach Vo. When he answered, he was thrilled to hear it was me. He knew about me going to play for the Bullfrogs, & somehow, he knew I was starting that night against the Woodchucks, so he wished me luck. After all the small talk was over, I finally told him that I was going to go to Whitewater in the fall. There was a slight pause, then all he said was *"Welcome Home."*

KNOWLEDGE APPLIED

We are where we are today because of the choices we have made, & we will get to where we want to go (or do *not* want to go) because the choices we *will* make. Fortunately, we have the power & freedom to make whatever choice we want to make, at any given time. Unfortunately, we are not free from the consequences of the choices we make.

The choices we make today determine the lives we live tomorrow – choose *wisely.*

The greatest impact on the choices we make is the environment we live in. There is absolutely no way around it - the environment we live in *will* either make us, or it will break us. It will either pull us up, or keep us down. It will either help us succeed, or force us to fail. It will either keep us going, or make us quit. There is no gray area, it is either *this*, or *that*.

Why do you think there is a cycle of fatherless homes in African-American communities? Why do you think there is a cycle of domestic violence with people who grow up in battered homes? Why do you think children of alcoholics are four-times more likely to become alcoholics themselves? Why do you think drug addicts who go to rehab fall back into the same drug addictions? Why do you think people who go to jail are more likely to return once they are released? Why do you think destructive relationship patterns get passed down from one generation to the next? Why do you think dysfunction begets dysfunction? I will tell you the answer - *It is the environment.*

There is a reason why I do not call the house I grew up in "home." In this house, there was always strife. There was always hardship. There was always tension. There was always oppression. There was always guilt. There was always shame. There was no peace. There was grace. There was no faith. As soon as I graduated high school, I could not get far enough away from it.

It is nearly impossible to thrive in an environment that suppresses us. It is nearly impossible to break the cycle of alcoholism &/or drug abuse when the best examples we have (our parents) are alcoholics &/or drug addicts. It is nearly impossible to break the cycle of domestic abuse when that is the only modeled behavior we know, & it has been taught to us that violence is how we resolve conflict. It is nearly impossible to stay out of trouble, when all our friends & family are constantly going in & out of prison. It is nearly impossible to stay clean in a dirty environment.

How do we change our environment? We have to first become aware of it & recognize that the environment that we are currently in is destructive to us, our wellbeing, & our future. Then, we have to *believe* that we are better (& deserve better) than the environment we are living in, & we are better than the choices we are making.

I had no idea how dysfunctional my family was until a family welcomed me into their home & into their family as a young adult, & I got to witness firsthand how a functional family loves & interacts with each other. I thought drinking was the only way to relieve stress, or the only way to celebrate, until I was introduced to better, non-destructive ways to relieve stress, & to celebrate.

The second thing we must do is *take ownership*. We can place the blame on our environment, our parents, & our upbringing only for so long. There comes a point in all our lives where we have to grow up, & stop placing the blame on everyone else. What we allow is what will continue. We have the power to choose the environment we want to live in. We have the power to break the cycle.

If we do not want to play with lions, then we *need* to stop going into the lion's den. If we want sobriety, then we must stop going to bars, or stop spending time with people who drink. If we want purity, then we must stop going to the clubs, or inviting the opposite sex over to our homes. If we want to break a cycle, we must remove ourselves from the environment in which the cycle occurs, otherwise, the cycle *will* continue. It is not a matter of *if*, it is a matter of *when*. We may be strong enough to tame the lion, but why should we even put ourselves in that situation in the first place?

Who & what we surround ourselves with is who & what we become. If we want to succeed (at *anything*), then we must put ourselves in an environment that not only allows us to succeed, but *demands* that we succeed.

If we want to learn more, then we must read more. If we want to become smarter, then we must ask better questions. If we want to raise our standards, then we must surround ourselves with people who expect more from us than we do from ourselves. If we want to stop complaining, then we must put ourselves in an environment that does not allow us to complain. If we want to become more confident, then we must surround ourselves with confident people. If we want to become more positive, then we must surround ourselves with positive people. If we want to increase our work ethic, then we must surround ourselves with people who work harder than us. If we want to grow, then we must surround ourselves with others who *want* to grow, & will challenge us to grow. If we want to change some of our behaviors, then we must surround ourselves with people who model the behaviors we wish we had. If we want to make more money, then we must surround ourselves with wealthy people. If we want to have a healthy, thriving marriage (even if we are not married yet), then we must surround ourselves with people who are in healthy, thriving marriages. If we want to have a highly-functional, loving family (even if we do not have children yet), then we must surround ourselves with highly-functional, loving families. If we want more wisdom, then we must surround ourselves with wise people. If we want to become better leaders, then we must surround ourselves with people who have more influence than us.

Are you paying close attention?

Are you reading this clearly?

Are you understanding the point I am trying to get across?

I hope you are, because the trajectory of your life depends on this.

We do not have to be victims of our environment, we can be victors. Our environment (past & present) does not have to be our destiny. We may not be able to change the past, & we may not be able to change the environment we grew up in, but we can change the environment we live in now, to ensure that we have a better future.

Our life does not get better by chance. It gets better by change.

"If we do not want to play with lions, then we need to stop going into the lion's den."

"We do not have to be victims of our environment, we can be victors. Our environment (past & present) does not have to be our destiny."

@RileyTincher | #PitchingAgainstMyself

CHAPTER 6

SCRUBBING BUBBLES

Remember how hard & how often Zimm & I worked the summer after our senior year? Well, things did *not* change – Not even two years apart from one another could break the bond we had with each other, & the one thing that brought us closer together... our work ethic.

As soon as we moved to Whitewater, we got to work. We moved in a week before school started, & we spent hours *every* day at Prucha Field & in the weight room at the Williams Center - throwing bullpens, hitting in the batting cages, running, & working out.

Fortunately, the apartment we lived in was only a couple hundred feet away from Prucha Field, so all we had to do when we woke up was get dressed, grab our equipment, & walk to the field. We were also within walking distance (less than a half mile away) from the Williams Center. It could not have been *any* more convenient for us.

We were not the only ones who were spending a significant amount of time at Prucha Field before school started. The three-time All-Conference centerfielder (who I had met playing in the Northwoods League that summer) was there with us *every* day. He was accompanied by the All-Conference third basemen, who hit a school-record nineteen homeruns the year before, & the All-Conference second basemen.

There was a reason why they were the best on the team... they worked harder than *everybody* else on the team.

It was a great feeling to work alongside other players who were awarded for their work ethic.

It was also a glimpse into the *standards* of the Warhawk Baseball Program & who they were led & upheld by.

Throughout the week, a few other players would join us, including the highly-touted, All-Conference left-handed pitcher who had been named to the All-Star team in the Northwoods League during the summer, & was a certainty to be drafted in the MLB Draft the next year. He was tall, like goliath; *much* taller than I was. It was intimidating to throw a bullpen beside him – I often stopped pitching, just so I could watch him pitch. He threw *fast;* a lot faster than I threw. He had an *amazing* curveball, that looked like it literally dropped off a table. He was also *very* arrogant – he knew how great he was, & he did not hold back telling everyone about it. However, he was the type to tear you down to let you know how much better he was than you; which, only showed his insecurities.

There were also two other goliaths who came to throw a couple of bullpens throughout the week; both were right-handed pitchers, & both were *massive* in size. When I saw them, I was reminded of how I felt when I went to Milwaukee Brewers & Madison Mallards games when I was younger, & how blown away I was by the size of the baseball players on the field. These two goliaths looked like they could have been tight ends in the National Football League.

One of the goliath's name was Jason. He was a Division I transfer who threw incredibly fast. I would go to camps with him when I was in high school, & all the professional scouts that were at the camp flocked to him whenever he started throwing.

As fast as he threw, he was equally as wild. In high school, I read an article in the paper about how he struck out eighteen hitters, & walked fifteen hitters… in *one* game. Things did not change.

In his bullpens, he would throw a dart to an exact location one pitch, then on the very next pitch, he would sail one ten feet over the catcher's head. He reminded me of the character "Nuke Laloosh" in the movie, *Bull Durham* - both on & off the field.

The other goliath's name was Ben. I did not know him prior to coming to Whitewater. However, I soon would *never* forget his name after hearing the *pop* of the catcher's glove whenever he threw a fastball. It was a sound I had *never* heard before. It was also a fastball I had *never* seen before – it was like the baseball would gain speed as it got closer to the plate. He was easily the *hardest* & fastest throwing pitcher on the team.

There is a huge difference between a fastball, & a *hard* fastball. A hard fastball usually has a lot of movement & it seems likes it gets to the plate a lot faster than a regular fastball gets there; even if they are the same velocity. Here is an example: Let's say there are two pitchers - one throws ninety miles-per-hour, the other throws eighty-eight miles-per-hour. However, the one who throws eighty-eight miles-per-hour throws a *harder* fastball than the one who throws ninety miles-per-hour. To a hitter who is standing in the batter's box against both pitchers, the *hard* fastball that comes in at eighty-eight miles-per-hour will look faster than the regular fastball that comes in at ninety miles-per-hour. Plus, trying to hit the *hard* eighty-eight miles-per-hour fastball is like trying to hit a bowling ball. This is something radar guns, & statistics cannot measure.

I had a hard fastball, but I did not throw as fast as these two did.

On the first day of school, all the returning players & those who were transferring in were asked to meet in the stands of Prucha field with Coach Vo, that afternoon.

Since Zimm & I lived so close to the field, we showed up earlier than everyone else. As it got closer to the meeting time, one-by-one, & two-by-two the rest of the players started to trickle in. There were *so many* familiar faces - Guys I played against in the Northwoods League, guys I went to baseball camps with in high school, guys I have read about in the papers during high school, & guys I played against in high school; all of which were All-State award winners (some were players/pitchers of the year in the state of Wisconsin).

There was one guy I recognized from playing in the State Tournament my sophomore year of high school. He pitched against us game one of the tournament. Prior to that game, we were given the wrong scouting report on him. It said he was "a left-handed pitcher with a *soft* fastball (velocity high seventies - low eighties) & a "Frisbee-slider" (no sharp break). When he got on the mound, he proceeded to throw fastball, after fastball eighty-seven miles per hour & above; some, touching ninety miles-per-hour. On top of that, he had a *filthy* slider that made the best hitters on our team look *terrible*. He only allowed one hit that game, & struck out ten of our batters; we did not have double-digit strikeouts in a game all season. It was amazing to watch him pitch. I had instant admiration for him.

I did not keep up with him after that game, so I had no idea where he went to college… until now. Needless to say, I was happy he was now my teammate, instead of having to face him again.

There were also a lot of unfamiliar faces at this meeting. The more of them I met, I realized they *all* were also transferring in from other schools – many of them being Division I schools.

The team was *loaded* with talent, & quite frankly, it *scared* me. Coach Vo was telling Zimm & I the truth, when he told us that we were going to have to fight for a spot on the team. To be honest, I thought I was going to walk into Whitewater & immediately become the Ace of the staff. I thought I was going to dominate every hitter I faced. I thought I was going to win every award I could possibly win (technically, I was not wrong). I thought all of this, because I played at a Division I level, & Whitewater is only a *Division III* school, & my perception was that Division III was the least talented out of all the Divisions. I was *dead wrong*.

It is a shame that Division III has the reputation it has. It is the most laughed at & underappreciated out of all the Divisions.

Throughout my career, I played with & against players in all Divisions (some of them went on to play Major League Baseball), & *none* of them were as talented as some of the players I had the fortune of playing with at Whitewater.

The worst part is, some of these teammates I had at Whitewater did not even get a chance to play professional baseball, for the sole reason that they played Division III baseball.

There are *zero* Division I baseball programs in the state of Wisconsin, besides UW-Milwaukee (but they do not count, because winning seasons are a rarity for them & they have been beaten several times by Division III schools in Wisconsin). With that being said, the most talented baseball players in the state of Wisconsin have to travel far away from home in order to receive a scholarship to play Division I baseball. Most of them go to their school of choice, & either get homesick very quickly, or they do not play as often as they would like. So, after their first year, they transfer back to a Wisconsin state school (like UW-Whitewater) & play baseball there. This happened at all the state schools, so the Wisconsin Intercollegiate Athletic Conference (WIAC) - the conference for all the Wisconsin state schools - was *stacked* with talent; which is why the majority of Division III National Championships for *all* sports are won by a school in the WIAC.

On top of that, there are not any *full* scholarships for Division I baseball (11.7 scholarships divided up between a roster of thirty-five). With out-of-state tuition costs, it is going to cost a player more to go to play *with* a scholarship at an out-of-state Division I school than it would cost for that same player to play with no scholarship at an in-state Division III school in Wisconsin.

FALL BALL

Fall practices at Whitewater were completely different from Lincoln Trail & NIACC. We hardly ever did drills, or threw bullpens. Instead, we scrimmaged pretty much every practice.

At the time, I did not understand why, but now I see that it is a great way to evaluate players, because what you see in games is what you are going to get. There are *a lot* of practice All-Americans, but there are very few *true* All-Americans.

After class every day, we had to stop by Coach Perch's office to see what lineups were posted on the board outside of his office, & to see who was throwing that day. If our names were not on the roster to throw that day, we still had to show up to the field, because we always did some form of conditioning (running) instead.

Conditioning at Whitewater was also completely different from Lincoln Trail & NIACC. We did a lot of sprints... *a lot* of them. Even if we ran long distance, we mixed in some form of sprinting. I ran more sprints that fall than I had ever ran before in my life (& I ran *a lot* before Whitewater). It seemed like every day we were running sprints; some long, some short. Just when I thought we could not run anymore, we did.

If we were scheduled to pitch that day, we would often pitch anywhere between one & four innings, depending on if we started, or if we came on in relief. It also depended on our performance as well; if we sucked, we probably were not going to pitch multiple innings.

Since we practiced every day besides Sundays (sometimes), we would throw two or three times per week. This went on for the entire months of September & October, until we started the "Steak Series."

The tone of each scrimmage was *very* competitive. There was *constant* heckling, & trash-talking among the team. I heard things yelled out of the dugouts during the games that I had never heard yelled out before. It was *a lot* of fun.

I had quite a bit of success early on, but as we scrimmaged more & more, I quickly realized that there were a few things I needed to change in order for me to continue my success & solidify a spot on this team. For one, I had to get rid of some of my pitches. I was under the impression that because I did not have an overpowering fastball, I had to have four or five off-speed pitches to make me a better pitcher. Up until that point, it did. Or at least I *thought* it did. But truly, I had a good fastball (a lot better than I thought), & four mediocre off-speed pitches that moved in every direction (not very sharply). I got rid of my splitter & my cutter, so I could focus more on mastering the command & the movement of my fastballs (4-seam & 2-seam), curveball, & changeup.

For two, Coach Perch recommended that I start bringing my glove over my head in my delivery, like my favorite pitcher, Andy Pettitte. I lacked rhythm in my delivery (sound familiar?), & bringing my glove over my head helped create the rhythm I needed.

I did not have to make these adjustments, but I did. I did not have to listen to my coaches, but I did, & I am *so* glad that I did. It was *exactly* what I needed to break through to the next level.

Did I see improvement right away? *Absolutely not.*

For a while, I had a hard time understanding that having three pitches was more than enough to be a great pitcher. I also had a hard time getting comfortable with bringing my glove over my head in my delivery. But over time, & after many bullpens, after many towel drills, after many dowel drills, & after many times practicing my delivery in the mirror (all too many to count), these two adjustments would pay dividends to the success of my career.

THE STEAK SERIES

In the last week of October, we began a Warhawk tradition called the "Steak Series."

The Steak Series was the intersquad World Series, where we split the entire roster up into two teams, & we would play a seven-game series. The losing team of the seven-game series would buy & cook steaks for the winning team; hence, why it is called the "Steak Series." *Everybody* looked forward to the Steak Series.

The Steak Series meant the end of Fall Ball. The Steak Series also meant the start of another Warhawk tradition – *initiation*. During initiation (which, the coaches knew *nothing* about), all of the newcomers were separated into groups, & each group had to report to a veteran on the team.

The week of the Steak Series was also the week of initiation. Throughout the week, we had to accomplish tasks as a group; most of which required a photo to be taken. At the end of the week, when the Steak Series was over, we had a party to go over all the tasks completed. During this part, we would tally up all the points each group collected, & declare the winner of initiation, because at Whitewater, there was a winner & loser in *everything* we did.

Since I am in the fraternity of current & former Warhawk baseball players, I cannot discuss the things we did during the initiation process, or at the initiation party. However, I can tell you that it was one of the most fun times I ever had at Whitewater. I cannot say they were the most memorable, because the memories I have of them are very *hazy*, if you know what I mean. I am so fortunate to have been a part of three of them; one, as a participator, & two, as a leader.

Besides the season, the Steak Series week was the greatest time of the year. It was really our first chance to get together as team, get to know each other on a personal level, & *celebrate*. This was also a chance to get to learn some of the Warhawk traditions, & hear some of the legendary Warhawk stories.

On top of that, we were also competing against each other for steaks... & for pride in saying we won the Steak Series. But most importantly, *steaks*. There was *a lot* on the line. We treated these games like we were playing for a National Championship.

Throughout the week, we would not talk to the opposing team, even if they were in the same classes as us (unless, we were in the same initiation group). We would show up early to the games, just so we could get some extra work in.

The tone was *very* different from the rest of Fall Ball. There was still trash-talking, but there was a level of seriousness to the trash-talking now. There was no joking around anymore.

We played to win, & we did anything to win, even if that meant losing a few friends during that week.

I was very fortunate enough to play on, or be a part of the winning team of the Steak Series all three years I was at Whitewater, & every year, the steaks seemed to get more tender & juicy. I think that also may just be the sweet taste of victory.

As a matter of fact, I never lost any intersquad World Series I played in during college at Lincoln Trail, NIACC, & Whitewater. I also played a major role in all of them (except the last).

At Lincoln Trail, I came in & closed out game 7 of the World Series to get the save, & the entire time I was pitching, the head coach was standing behind me trying to get inside my head by telling me how big of a game it was, how important the win would be for me & my team, & how nervous I should be.

At NIACC, I started & won two games of the seven-game series; one, being the final game to win the series.

During my first two years at Whitewater, I started & won two games of the seven-game series. My third year was different; which, I will talk about later in the book.

A *REAL* OFFSEASON

After Fall Ball ended, after the steaks were eaten, & after the newcomers were initiated, the real work began. The offseason meant two things. The first thing was winter workouts. The weight room I marveled about in the previous chapter finally got put to use; I finally had a *real* weight room & a *real, structured* training program to follow. This was also when I met another coach who would have a significant impact on me, Coach Lee Munger.

At this point, the coaches had narrowed our team down to about fifty players. There were still cuts to be made, but they did not need to be made until the first game of the season.

Since there were fifty of us (which, was too big for Coach Munger to handle alone), the team had to be split up into two groups: position players & pitchers. We met at different times, & had *slightly* different workouts. However, we had the same conditioning every day, & Every day the conditioning & the agility drills were different. They were not announced until the first group (the position player) showed up to workout. So, going into each day, we had no idea what to expect.

I always showed up early to foam roll & stretch out, but I *really* showed up early to ask Zimm what we were going to do for conditioning that day, so I could "mentally prepare" myself. Thinking back, it is so funny to me now, because knowing what the conditioning was did not make it any easier. All it did was add more anxiety & worry, which did not help (*never* does), or change *anything*.

This was the first time in my life I got to actually measure how athletic I was. It was also the first time I got to measure how strong I was. It felt great to get under a bar with *a lot* of weight on it. It felt great to throw a heavy medicine ball as far as I could. It felt great to run as fast as I could. It felt great to change directions as quickly as I could. It felt great to jump over high hurdles & high boxes. It felt great to see & feel *real* progress; due, in large part, to the coaching & program design of Coach Munger.

Because of the progress, I fell in love with winter workouts. The weight room was where I separated myself from the rest of the team.

While so many others on the team tried their best to avoid the challenge, I *never* backed down from it. I embraced it. As a matter of fact, I *loved* it. I constantly sought out new ways to challenge myself, because if there is no challenge, there is no change. I did not want to remain the same, because I knew that where I was, was not going to get me to where I wanted to go – Major League Baseball.

The weight room gave me the challenge I was looking for every time I stepped foot inside of it.

That offseason, I saw *significant* improvement in everything we measured, & that improvement translated onto the mound, which only fueled my obsession even more. I got *a lot* stronger (specifically, in my lower body), & I got a lot more agile; I was jumping higher than I have ever jumped before. I also put on quite a bit of size (both good & bad weight), which caused my velocity on my fastball to increase.

In baseball, there is a quote for pitchers that refers to the correlation of body size & velocity, & it says, "mass equals gas."

I remember the first time getting back on the mound after my first offseason of winter workouts at Whitewater, & the first pitch I threw, it felt like the baseball exploded out of my hands.

The second thing the offseason meant was baseball camps... *a lot* of them. We held camps three times throughout the year. The first camp - the fall camp - was held on the Friday & Saturday after Thanksgiving. The second camp – the winter camp - was held two days after Christmas, & went all the way through New Year's Eve. The third camp – the spring camp - was held in the spring, usually between our first games, & our spring training trip. We were required to work... I mean *volunteer* at all of them.

Within each day of camp, there were three separate camps – pitching, hitting, & fielding.

I was not prepared for these camps at all. Quite frankly, nothing could have prepared me for these camps. All the veterans warned us about these camps, but it did not matter. They were like death & taxes; they were *guaranteed* to happen, even though none of us wanted them to happen. They were impending doom that we could not avoid. No matter how much we complained, all of us had to "suck it up" & go through them.

The worst part about the camps may not be what you think. It was not having to drive back to Whitewater on Thanksgiving Day. It was not having to cut days out of my Christmas Break to be there. It was not the consecutive days of being on my feet from 8:00 AM until 6:00 PM. It was not having to deal with the bratty little kids who would never listen. It was not standing in the front of the camp when it started hoping coach would not call my name to demonstrate something. It was not having to coach the same drill an unbelievable amount of times. It was not getting drilled by baseballs, whiffle balls, & tennis balls by all the hitters in the camp. It was not having to throw hundreds of pitches in the batting cages. It was… the Rocky Rococo's pizza.

Do not get me wrong, it was good pizza, but after three straight years of having it every single camp, it became unbearable to eat.

I have not had *any* Rocky Rococo's pizza since my last camp at Whitewater, over 6 years ago, & I do not see myself eating ever again.

To be honest, the camps were not as bad as I may be portraying them to be. They served a *great* purpose & they were actually quite valuable to the entire Warhawk program. They brought in a significant amount of money for the program. They brought us together as a team, & forced us to work together. They were great recruiting platforms for the coaches to use. They were a way of keeping us players out of trouble. They were also a way for us to learn more about the game.

I believe the best way to *truly* learn anything is to teach it. Research says we retain ninety percent of what we learn when we teach it to someone else. We taught *a lot* during these camps.

Camps also served as a great reminder that the season was right around the corner. Although most of us did not like being there, we all knew it meant that we were one day, one camp, closer to the start of practice, & the start of the season.

HOPE LOST

Every year at Whitewater, there was a period of time between the end of Christmas Break, & the first official day of baseball practice. This period of time was usually around two weeks long, & during this time, we started the second semester, got settled in to our classes, & began our "Captain's Practice." Since coaches were not allowed to run practices until the first official day, the captains of the team ran them.

Also, during this time, we got re-acclimated to the weight room, & we did some physical tests to see who was working out during Christmas Break, & who did not. One test, in particular, was the "beep test" – where we had to run a certain length & back in the time given between "beeps." As time went on, the time between beeps got shorter, & as soon as we could not keep up with the beeps, we were out. The whole point of the beep test was to run as long as you could.

As you can imagine, this test was not fun… by *any* means.

I had another amazing Christmas Break with Coach Diercks, so I was ready to attack any physical test they threw my way, including, the beep test. I actually ran the beep test every day during Christmas Break. I remember running it the first day & only being able to do a few rounds before my lungs & legs gave out on me. As the days progressed, I got better & lasted longer than the day before.

On one of the last days of Christmas Break, we had to stop the best test, because I was running for so long that we ran out of time.

When I got back to Whitewater, & I ran the beep test against my teammates, I finished in the top five, & I beat guys I should not have beat; which, is *another* common theme of my life.

I was *so* excited for the season to start. As a matter of fact, we all were. There was *a lot* of hype around our team. We had a few guys who were supposed to be drafted at the end of the year. We had a few All-Conference players – including, one I had not yet met, because he was busy winning his second National Championship as the starting Quarterback for the football team. We were returning *a lot* of veterans who played in the World Series the year before. We had *a lot* of talented players who transferred in from other prestigious schools. We were predicted to win conference by a large margin, & everyone thought we were going to head back to the World Series, & win it all this year. The amount of talent we had on the roster at the beginning of the second semester validated all of the hype.

Everything was going as planned, until the first Captain's Practice.

We started the first Captain's Practice at 5:30 AM, because that is when we were going to practice when we could officially practice with the coaches. I showed up at 5:00 AM, because I like being early, &

not having to rush. To my surprise, I was not the first one there. Matt Millar, a senior catcher, & one of our captains, was there before me. He praised me for being there early, & advised me about the rule that "if you are on time, you are late. & if you are five minutes early, you are ten minutes late." He also told me about some of the consequences of being late, & that sometimes, the coaches like to start early, just to see who was actually there on time.

Fortunately, of the three years I was there, I was *never* late.

It was a *strange* morning. The entire time we were warming up & stretching, we were silent; over fifty players in one giant fieldhouse, & you could have heard a pin-drop. Maybe, it was because we all were not used to waking up that early, yet. Or maybe, it was because we were all nervous. Whatever the reason, it was very unusual.

After we got done warming up, we picked our throwing partners, & we began our "throwing progression." During our throwing progression, we all threw in a cadence – meaning, we got set together, we went through the motion together, & we all threw together at the same time. At certain distances, we had different set positions to throw from, & different motions to go through. We all would start our throwing motion together after one of us yelled, "Ready... Throw!"

On the 8th throw of the first day of Captain's Practice, the fate of my season was decided. My throwing partner threw the baseball too high, so I had to jump up to catch it. When I was coming down from jumping, another baseball rolled underneath me, & my left-foot landed & my ankle rolled on top of the baseball, & I *busted* my ankle.

Since we were throwing in a cadence, you could hear the simultaneous pop of the gloves when the baseball hit them, then, you could hear the *pop* of my ankle shortly after. I fell to the ground, & everyone looked over at me, then went back to throwing. I was in denial. I had never been injured before, so I tried getting up to start throwing again, & I could not stand on my left foot. Shock set in shortly after, & I passed out on the floor of the field house.

I woke up still on the ground, with my foot elevated on a chair. The size of my ankle was enormous; nearly three times the size of my other ankle. My ankle swelled so much that it hurt to keep it in my shoe, so I tried to untie my shoe to take it off, & one of my teammates stopped me, & told me to keep it on, so I do not make anything worse.

Since it was only Captain's Practice, we did not have any athletic trainers on site, nor did we have access to the trainer's room to get ice, so I had to lay there, *in pain*, with my foot elevated until one of the trainers showed up; which was an hour & a half later.

When the trainer got there, he wrapped my ankle up with ice, gave me some crutches (temporarily), & told me to go to the hospital to get X-Rays. Thankfully, Zimm did not have class that morning, & was gracious enough to drive me to the nearby hospital. It was there that I got the news that my injury was a lot worse than I wanted it to be, & it was going to take me eight to twelve weeks to completely recover, & four weeks before I could even take the walking boot off.

The season was *six* weeks away.

I had a hard choice to make. I could either sit back, watch the team practice, get the necessary rest, dedicate myself to physical therapy, & hope I make the roster (remember, I have not made the roster, yet), *or,* I could still go to practice & do as much as I can on one leg, double down on physical therapy, be available to pitch at the start of the season, & take a huge risk of coming back too early, & never recovering correctly.

What do you think I chose to do?

The next day I showed up to day two of Captain's Practice - thanks in large part to a great pep talk & Ben & Jerry's Ice Cream delivered by my good friend, Suzanne, the night before. I was still in an incredible amount of pain (they gave me pain killers, but I did not want to take them), so there was not much I could do, but *I was there.*

Unfortunately, my injury was not the only bad news the team received that week. Our All-Conference first-baseman & starting quarterback for the National Champion football team, who hit twelve homeruns the year before was deemed "ineligible," & the coaches made him sit out the entire season. This became a *huge* fiasco that caused his brother, one of our captains, who was also supposed to be one of our starting pitchers, to quit the team.

On top of that, one of our starting outfielders also was deemed "ineligible," & had to sit out the entire season (this was not as big of a shock as our first-basemen being ineligible).

We also found out that the shoulder injury our three-time All-Conference centerfielder suffered during Fall Ball was worse than we thought. He had orthoscopic surgery done, & they found that he tore his rotator cuff, so they repaired it, which forced him to be out for the remainder of the year.

Looking at it from an outside perspective, most people would think, missing three hitters & one pitcher would not affect such a talented team, but two of the hitters (the first baseman & the centerfielder) were the two of the best hitters in Whitewater history; I would bet a lot of money that the first basemen was *the* best hitter in Whitewater history. When they were in the lineup, they completely changed the batting order & how other team's pitchers would pitch to us. It is like taking Babe Ruth & Lou Gehrig out of *Murderers' Row* (referring to the New York Yankees batting order in the late 1920's – in particular, 1927). *They were irreplaceable.*

TEARS REQUIRED

When the day came for the first official practice, I had to forget about the pain. I was still in my walking boot, & I still had crutches, so I had to do *everything* on one leg. When we were warming up, I would throw to my partner on one leg, & he would throw it back. Then, I had to grab my crutches to step back for the next series of throws. I had to do this several times throughout the warmup.

It was *miserable,* for me & my throwing partner.

126

Since my injured ankle was on my back leg – my power leg – I had no lower body power when I threw the baseball. It was hard to throw the ball farther than 50 feet.

Imagine trying to throw a baseball in a seated position as far as you could. You are probably not going to get it very far. Now repeat that for seventy-five to one-hundred times a day. How do you think your upper body – more importantly, your shoulder & elbow of your pitching arm – would feel? This is what throwing was like for me, the first couple of weeks of practice.

When we moved on from warmups to throw off the indoor pitching mounds, I would throw every pitch with my lower body in a stationary position (square to the catcher), on one leg (my front leg), while I would twist my upper body to try to throw it to the catcher. I had to torque my body so hard just to even get the baseball to the catcher, that I started to have lower back issues.
It was *incredibly* hard.

It was not only physically demanding, but it was mentally taxing, especially, when I failed the majority of the drills I tried to perform.

To make matters worse, occasionally, I would lose my balance, & I would have to plant my walking boot on the floor, & put weight on my busted ankle. The pain was so bad that tears would run down my face while I was trying to throw.

After practice, I was so exhausted, & my entire body was so sore that I would sit in an ice tub for at least twenty minutes. Sometimes, I would fall asleep in the ice tub, & the athletic trainer, Chad, had to wake me up. Then, I would go right into the hot tub for ten minutes to warmup for physical therapy.

For the first couple of weeks, I had to hard time deciding which one was worse: practicing on one leg, or the physical therapy afterwards. Both required *a lot* of my tears.

Since pitchers & position players practiced at two different times every day (pitchers in the early morning, & position players in the afternoon) for the first couple of weeks, I would come in when the position players practiced, so I could go through a second round of physical therapy. Chad & I got to know each other *very* well. I am incredibly grateful the patience he had with me, & the time he dedicated to getting me back as quickly as possible to practicing (on both feet); even though, it took *a lot* longer than expected.

I approached every single practice & every single physical therapy session as if I was going to lose my spot on the roster; that *never* changed throughout my career. I always felt like I had to prove to my coaches & to all my teammates that I deserved a spot on that team, & I tried to prove it every day. If coach asked me to do something, I *always* did at least one more than he asked for, or expected. The same thing applied if Chad asked me to do something, or if Coach Munger asked me to do something.

I cannot tell you the number of ice & hot baths I sat in. I cannot tell you the amount of times I went through spelling the alphabet with my foot, nor the number of jacks I picked up with my toes (if you have been through any ankle rehab, you know what I am talking about). Anything I had to do to make the opening day roster, I did it, & then some. & I mean *anything!*

CALLY

When I arrived at Whitewater, one of the very first things that was taught to me by current & former Whitewater baseball players was to not take anything the coaches said *personally*. I had to learn to apply that advice given to me very quickly, within the first couple of practices in the spring.

The coaches were notorious for getting onto players, for even the littlest things; they understood the importance of doing the little things right & paying attention to detail.

The coaches set very high standards for us, & they demanded that we performed up to those standards *every* day. When we did not perform up to that very high standard, they *freaked* out, & for good reason; excellence is a byproduct of consistency.

These "freak outs" were a daily occurrence.

Sometimes, they even kicked someone out of practice for not performing up to the standards that were required of us. I will never forget the day we had two or three professional scouts show up to watch the All-Conference left-handed pitcher (the one I told you about earlier) throw a bullpen, & Coach Vo kicked him out of practice right in front of the scouts. This sent a message to everyone on the team that it did not matter who you were, if you did not meet the standards required of us, you were gone.

Unfortunately, they also viewed injuries as not performing up to the standards required of us. When Coach Perch saw me right after my injury happened, when I was in a walking boot, walking with crutches, the very first thing he said to me was "you need to figure your life out." I did not know how to interpret what he meant by it, & it drove me crazy. On one hand, I knew it was not my fault & there was nothing I could have done to avoid it, but on the other hand, I did not want to disappoint him. I cared a lot about what he, & the rest of my coaches thought of me. Every time I saw him, I thought of those words he said to me, & it only made me want to try even harder to prove to him that I deserved to be on that team.

Not every coach communicated this way. There was a saving grace among them, & his name was Coach Ryan Callahan, our pitching coach. I, & the other newcomers, did not get a chance to meet Coach Callahan (Coach Cally, for short), until the first official day of practice. He had a heavy workload in the fall, as an academic advisor for the University, so he was unable to dedicate time to coach us during Fall Ball.

Coach Cally was a former Whitewater great - leading the Warhawks to a third-place finish in the World Series his senior year in 2004. After his Whitewater career, he went on to play a few seasons of Minor League baseball in the Minnesota Twins & San Francisco Giants organizations.

He had a very easy-going, calm presence about him. He carried himself with a "quiet-confidence."
Plus, he was left-handed, so he had *immediate* influence over me.

Since it was Coach Cally's second year as our pitching coach, Coach Vo did not give him full control over the pitchers, yet. He led all of our practices, & he taught & demonstrated all of our drills, but Coach Vo *always* had the final say. Quite often, Coach Vo would coach over him, & I could tell it bothered him.

He was our voice of reason. He knew what it was like to play for Coach Vo, so whenever Coach Vo said, or did something that bothered us, Coach Cally was quick to encourage us, & to let us know that everything was going to be ok.

He had an infinite supply of Rickey Henderson (MLB's all-time stolen base recorder holder who always spoke in the third person) stories that would *always* lighten the mood.

He also fought for us. Whether Coach Vo would like to admit it, or not, for quite some time, he had a thing against all of us pitchers. He would constantly call us "mental midgets" & tell us that we babied our arms too much. He would have us throw, even if we were too sore, & he would constantly remind us that "if we are going to get injured, we are going to get injured, so throw anyway." Coach Cally was the gray area to Coach Vo's black & white mentality. He forced Coach Vo to give us rest when we needed it.

The more I got to know Coach Cally & his story – more importantly, his upbringing with his mom – the more I admired & respected him. We were *very* much alike. He understood me more than *any* other coach has ever understood me, because he made the time to understand me. He taught me how to *actually* pitch, not just throw the baseball as hard as I could. He taught me about peaks & valleys. He also taught me a lot of life lessons.

I owe *a lot* of my success in baseball & in life after baseball to Coach Cally. Of *all the great* memories I have of playing baseball at Whitewater, some of the greatest were the times I spent with him before & after the games I started, talking about life.

FINAL CUTS

Despite the doctor telling me I would be walking with crutches for three weeks, I ditched them after the first week. Despite him telling me that I would not be able to take off my walking boot for four weeks, I was out of it in a little over two weeks. Despite him telling me I would not be able to run in eight to twelve weeks, I was running in the sixth week of physical therapy. Was it too soon? *No doubt about it.* But I had a roster spot to make, & a season to prepare for. Plus, in the fourth week, the pitchers were starting to throw live batting practice to the hitters, & there was *absolutely no way* I was going to miss that.

For the next couple of weeks before the season started, I would show up twenty minutes before I usually showed up to practice, to get my ankle taped. My ankle was so heavily taped that I could not move my foot at all. Chad would use double the amount of tape he would usually use for an ankle tape job, & it was so thick, that I could hardly put my shoe on over it. Regardless, I was able to practice again, & pitch off of the mound with both legs, & that is all that matters.

I could still hardly use my back leg – my power leg – in my delivery. When we would throw live batting practice to the hitters, we would get videotaped, & Coach Cally would go over our videos with us, individually, the next day.

Every time we met to watch my video of me pitching, Coach Cally would always ask me if my ankle still hurt (which, it did). He would ask, because every pitch I threw, it was almost like I had a prosthetic leg on. I was incredibly flat-footed on my left foot (my back foot - the foot of the busted ankle), & I would hardly push off the mound with my left foot. Then, in between pitches, I would limp back up the mound. The velocity on my fastball suffered because of it. The movement on all my pitches suffered because of it. My performance suffered because of it.

He would constantly tell me that I was rushing the recovery process too much, & he was right. I *should have* listened to him, but I was too worried about making a spot on the team.

A few days before the season started, the final roster was posted... or, so we thought. At the time, both Zimm & I both made the roster. We were both *very* excited. In our minds, we both believed we had a chance of being starters. The spot for starting catcher was up for grabs, & Zimm had a *legitimate* shot of being the starting catcher. He was *by far* the most talented of all the catchers we had. He was the most-technically sound catcher we had, he had the most experience behind the plate, he knew how to handle pitchers, & he could swing the bat better than most of the players on the team. I was excited, not only for him, but for the fact that I got *my* catcher back.

He caught *every* game I pitched in high school. He caught *every* bullpen I threw during our offseasons.

We had been separated for the last two years, & now we were *finally* back together... or, so we thought.

On the day we were supposed to travel up to the Metrodome in Minneapolis, Minnesota, Coach Vo called Zimm into his office a few hours before we left, & told him he had been cut, & replaced by a freshman outfielder. This was after Zimm's name was put on the roster on the Whitewater Athletics' website. I did not find out about this until I was on the bus to Minneapolis, & was wondering where he was. I was devastated for him. At the same time, I was *pissed* at Coach Vo.

How could he do that to someone a few hours before he was supposed to played his first game as a Whitewater Warhawk? How could he do that to Zimm, after he told him that he made the team? How could he do that to *my* catcher? How could he do that to my roommate, & my best friend?

I saw the demise of Zimm coming.

Before we moved to Whitewater, he had his heart broken by a girl he was dating at his former junior college. He thought this girl was going to be the one he married.

To suppress his broken heart, he turned to drinking. There was a period in the fall where he drank *heavily* for over forty days in a row. The worst part was he would brag about it. There was not a time when I came back to the apartment we lived him, & he did not have a Natural Light beer can in his hand.

The Whitewater environment only made his drinking problem worse. *Everybody* drank at Whitewater - there was so much drinking going on that Harvard did a study on binge drinking at Whitewater.

As soon as he turned twenty-one, shortly into the fall, he spent *every* night out at the bars, & every night, he would call me at bar time for a ride home.

He was falling apart right in front of my eyes. He stopped taking care of himself. He quickly got out of shape. Although, he was still very talented, he became inconsistent. One day, he would be the best player on the team, & the next day, he would be the worst. It was very hard to watch this happen. I felt bad for him that his heart was broken, but I hated that he resorted to drinking to cope with his pain.

I did not have the heart, or the courage to tell him that what he was doing was wrong, & that he was risking his baseball career every time he put the beer can to his lips. Plus, I had no right to tell him what to do & what not to do, because I would drink with him, sometimes. Unfortunately, the drinking did end his baseball career.

MISERY LOVES COMPANY

My first appearance as a Whitewater Warhawk did not go as I planned. I came on in relief against one of the best teams in the country, the University of St. Thomas Tommies - they went on to win the World Series that year. To say I got hit around, would be an understatement. I walked the first batter I faced, & then I proceeded to give up four hits in a row, allowing two runs to score. Coach Vo came out for a mound visit, & he had some *very unpleasant* words to say to me. Coach Vo has piercing blue eyes (almost crystal clear), & when he was yelling at me, it was like he was staring into my soul - I have never felt more afraid after a mound visit in my life. I wish he would have taken me out, but he did not.

Fortunately, I got out of the inning with no more harm done. I got back to the dugout & received another tongue-lashing from Coach Vo, & also from Coach Perch. Then, I was pulled from the game.

Coach Cally did not travel with us to the Metrodome, so I had no one to turn to for advice. As I sat in the dugout in my own pity, I was reminded of my first game of baseball I ever played, & the first error I made playing left field. I was then reminded of my first varsity start in high school, & how I never got an out. All of the doubt that followed both of those events began to consume me again, & I started questioning everything:

"Am I really good enough to play professional baseball?"

"Will I *ever* get a chance to pitch again?"

"Do I even deserve a spot on this team?"

"What if my eighth-grade coach was right?"

I blew what I thought was going to be my only opportunity to pitch that season. I honestly believed I was *done*. I was *convinced* that I would never see the field again. I was wrong.

A few weeks later, when we were on our Spring Training trip in Orlando, Florida, I was given another chance.

I was *shocked* when Coach Vo called my name to go warmup to pitch. It was the seventh inning, & it was a close game; we were down two to one. We were playing another great team, the Otterbein University Cardinals – they were a perennial powerhouse on the east coast. There were a lot of pitchers he would normally call upon in this situation, but to my surprise, he called my name instead. I quickly hustled down to the bullpen to get warmed up to pitch. Thank God, Coach Cally was there to go down to the bullpen with me.

The pressure I felt while I was warming up was *enormous*. The same nervous feeling I had before my first varsity start in high school came back. I was rushing. I was shaking. I had shortness of breath. I kept thinking, "do not blow this opportunity, Riley," & "if you fail, you are *never* going to pitch again." I was all over the place - *every* pitch I threw missed its spot.

Shortly after, one of my teammates ran down from the dugout to the bullpen to let me know I was going in to pitch the next inning. Instantly, my nervousness got worse. I threw a couple more pitches in the bullpen, the inning ended, & it was time for me to make my entrance. I tried to take a deep breath, but I could not. As I was running out of the bullpen onto the field, Coach Cally stopped me & said, "Riley, you would not be going in to pitch, if we did not believe in you." Thanks to those words, my nervousness went away.

I threw two scoreless innings to close out the game. We ended up scoring the tying run in the eighth inning, & the winning run in the ninth inning & I got my first win as a Whitewater Warhawk. The entire time I was pitching, Coach Vo would yell from the dugout "show me your nuts, Riley!" It was comical.

After the game, I felt like I was on "cloud nine." That was a big win for our team, who had been struggling to score runs, & win games, & I was so proud that I got a chance to help the team win. I *finally* believed I proved my worth to the coaches – more specifically, to Coach Vo. I thought I finally showed them that I deserved a spot on the team; maybe, I finally showed myself. I was so sure of myself in that moment, that I started thinking "I might get a chance to start, now." In all reality, my thinking was just hoping & wishing.

I did not get a chance to pitch the rest of the time we were down in Florida for our Spring Training trip. As a matter of fact, I did not get a chance to pitch until two weeks later.

Coach Vo hardly ever talked to me, so I had no idea why I was not pitching. The only time he would talk to me was when I was throwing a bullpen in practice, & at the end of each bullpen I threw, he would always ask me "why don't you throw like this in a game?"

I *desperately* wanted him to like me & to trust me, & I felt like he did not like me, or trust me.

I quickly fell back into the trap of thinking "I will never get a chance to pitch again." I believed it so much that I stopped preparing to pitch before every game. I would just go through the motions, to show the coaches that I was doing "something."

Once each game started, I would resort to the end of the dugout, with the rest of my teammates who were not playing, because *misery loves company.*

During the game, we would sit there & complain... about *everything.* We would complain about our playing time, & how we were not getting a fair chance to play. We would complain about the other players who had more playing time than us. We would complain about our roles on the team, & how we believed we should be starting instead of coming off the bench. We would complain about Coach Vo, & how we thought he was the reason why we were struggling. We loved complaining, but not as much we loved *not* doing anything about what we were complaining about.

Here is the thing about complaining: it is the easy thing to do, but it is *never* the right thing to do. Complaining *never* makes anything better. If we have time to complain, then we have time to do something about it, & if we are not going to do anything about it, then we have no right to complain.

Here is the thing about playing time: Players think "play me & I will show you!" Coaches think "show me, & I will play you."

When situations came where Coach Vo would call on pitchers to go warm up, I always hoped that he *would not* call my name. Guess what happened? One day, when we were playing one of our conference rivals, the University of Wisconsin – Oshkosh Titans, *he called my name*, & I was not ready. I came into the game in the sixth inning, & we were tied five to five. I faced four hitters, & gave up four extra base hits, including a monster three-run home run before I got pulled from the game.

I got one out… *One!*

Coach Vo did not say a word to me when he came out to the mound to pull me. As a matter of fact, no one said a word to me when I got back to the dugout. Since Coach Cally did not travel with us to Oshkosh, I was left alone again to sit in my own pity.

We ended up getting ten-runned both games of the double-header that day. Up until point, Whitewater had *never* been ten-runned in a doubleheader before.

The next day at practice, Coach Vo had us meet him at the football field. All of us were *terrified*. We all started worrying about & assuming what our punishment was going to be. That is when we manifested what we called the "Wrath of Vo." Luckily, it was not as bad as we assumed. Actually, it was *nothing* like what we assumed. Coach Vo gave us what I like to call a "real talk" (also known as a pep talk). He told us that he believed that "we are better than we are performing," & he was right. He also referred to the same analogy that Coach Rima used while I was at NIACC the prior year about the sun coming up tomorrow, & how tomorrow always presents a new opportunity to reverse the outcome of the day before.

Then… we ran… *a lot.*

There was no way we were going to go unpunished.

We ran stadium stairs for about twenty minutes. Then, we had a competition. From the bottom of the stairs to the top of stairs was about two-hundred feet in length (well over one-hundred steps) & the stairs went all the way down to the field. At the bottom of the stairs, there were four entrances to the stairs, so we broke up into four teams. We then went across the football field to start our relays. A player on each team would sprint across the width of the football field to the entrance of the stairs, then sprint all the way up the stairs. When the player running reached the top of the stairs, the next player would go. This would go on until all the players were done running. The team who finished the fastest, won.

We ran these relays *several* times that day.

While most of the team hated running the relays, I *loved* it. This was the first time since my ankle injury that I could sprint at one-hundred-percent. There was no more walking boot, there were no more crutches, there was no more heavily-taped ankle, & there was no more pain. I felt *free*.

It was like that scene from my favorite movie, *Forest Gump*, where the main character, Forest, was running so fast that he broke out of his leg braces, when he was getting chased by the bullies in the truck, & Jenny was yelling, *"Run, Forest! Run!"*

STAY READY

The next weekend, we played our biggest conference rival, the University of Wisconsin – Stevens Point Pointers, at Stevens Point.

On the way there, I received a phone call that would change the course of my baseball career. Can you guess who the phone call came from? Coach Darin Everson.

He was calling to catch up with me, since we had not talked in a while; at least, since the beginning of the second semester. He asked me how the season was going, even though he *knew* how it was going. I aired out my frustrations, & told him the same complaints I was hearing at the end of the dugout. Instead of getting sympathy (like I was hoping) from Coach Everson, I got a lecture. He actually stopped me in the middle of one of my complaints, & said: "Riley, you get what you put in. It sounds to me like you are not putting in the work. Instead of complaining, start contributing. Complaining is the easy way out. You are better than that."

Then, I made the mistake of trying to justify my complaints, by telling him that Coach Vo was not giving me a fair chance to play, & Coach Everson cut me off again, & proceeded to tell me:

"You have *no* control over what Coach Vo decides to do. You have no control over what your teammates decide to do. The only things you can control are your attitude & your actions. Right now, your attitude *sucks,* which is causing you to not take action."

I asked him how I could take action, since I was not getting any chances to pitch, & he responded:

"It is all about your *approach.* You need to prepare for each game as if you are going to start, even if you are not going to. You need to do the same pre-game routine you did in high school & warm up before every game like you are going to start. You must *stay ready!* So, when the times comes, & your name is called, you do not have to get ready."

He would not hang up the phone until I told him what I was going to do that night to prepare for the games the next day. I told him that I was going to buy scrubbing bubbles. He was very confused by my answered, & he asked me if I was going to clean the bathrooms at the hotel. I told him no, & explained to him:

"When I was playing with the Wisconsin Woodchucks, I always roomed with our second basemen, who was from UCLA, when we traveled. Every night before our games, he would clean his cleats & his turf shoes with scrubbing bubbles. His cleats & his shoes always looked brand new. One night, I finally asked him why he cleans his shoes every night, & he told me it was symbolic for him to clean the 'old' away, so he could start over new the next day. Plus, he liked the look of clean shoes."

As soon as we got checked in to the hotel in Stevens Point, I walked across the street to the convenient store to buy scrubbing bubbles, so I could clean my cleats & my turf shoes that night.

The next day, I changed my approach.

I went through the same routine I went through in high school (it was like muscle memory, because I did it *so many* times before), & I prepared for both games as if I was going to be the starting pitcher.

Although my name was never called to pitch the first day, I cleaned my cleats & turf shoes again that night (even though, they were not dirty), & prepared the same way the next day.

Although my name was never called to pitch the second day, I cleaned my cleats & turf shoes again the night before the next game, & I prepared for it as if I was going to start.

I went into to every game for the remainder of the season, thinking I was going to start, & I prepared accordingly.

We did something as a team that weekend we had never done before; we swept the Stevens Point Pointers. We had great pitching performances, & there were two *clutch* grand slams (from two unlikely homerun hitters) that helped us win two of the four games.

Sweeping Stevens Points was a huge turning point for our team, that propelled us to win the Conference Championship for the fifth time in six years under the tenure of Coach Vo.

We were all riding a high on the bus ride back from Stevens Point; which, could have been from everything we ate at the Golden Corral. The bus was the loudest it has ever been, & there was not even a movie playing. We could not stop talking about the two grand slams that were hit, & how we swept Stevens Point for the first time ever.

When we got back to Whitewater, as we were getting off the bus, Coach Vo had me stay behind. As always, I automatically assumed the worst.

When everyone else got off the bus, he did something he had never done that season. He told me that I was going to start game two of the doubleheader the next day against the Carroll University Pioneers.

Telling me that I was going to start (which, he had never told me before) was not what I meant when I said he did something he had never done before. Coach Vo was notorious for not letting *any* of us know who the starting pitcher was going to be for the next game until about thirty minutes before the game. It drove all of us pitchers crazy. We absolutely hated it.

Just like all the other things he did that I did not understand when I was playing for him, I *now* see why he did it. He wanted us *all* to prepare for *every* game as if we were going to start.

I was beyond excited to finally be given the opportunity to start a game. I could not wait to get home to call my parents to let them know, so I called them on the drive home. They were happy for me, but not as happy as I was, & not happy enough to come see me pitch.

A large part of me was hoping that they would come to see me pitch, since the game was late in the afternoon, after my mom got done working, & before my dad started working, but of course they "could not come" to the game... for whatever reason. I felt selfish for even asking them to come, but it was going to be a big day for me. I did not understand why they could not drop everything they were doing to come & see their son pitch.

Too bad for them, because they missed one hell of a performance.

The next day, I pitched one of the best games I had ever pitched in college (up until that point). I threw five innings, gave up two hits, allowed only one run to score, & had a career high eight strikeouts. Plus, I threw the hardest on the radar gun I had ever thrown all season, & for the first time, I started throwing my *new* slider (which, led to all the strikeouts). Most importantly, *we* won.

It felt *great* to start a game again.

Although, this was the last game I would start that season, it did not stop my approach. I never wavered in my preparation, & I prepared for *every* game as if I was going to start. Whenever my name was called, I was *ready*. Because of this, my performance significantly increased; I only gave up two runs the remainder of the season.

I became a name that Coach Vo would call on *regularly*, especially when the playoffs started.

KNOWLEDGE APPLIED

One of my favorite quotes of all-time is from Abraham Lincoln, & he said this: "If you give me six hours to cut down a tree, I am going to spend the first five hours sharpening the axe."

This quote speaks volumes about the importance of preparation.

Are you prepared for where you want to go? Are you doing every necessary thing to get you there? Every little thing? On a daily basis? Or, on a "whenever I feel like it" basis?

If you are not doing the necessary things to get you to where you want to go, especially when you do *not* feel like it, what makes you think you deserve to get to where you want to go?

Is the work you are willing to do equivalent to the win you say that you want? For too many of us, what we say we are going to do is not in alignment with what we *actually* do.

We are what we do, not what we say we will do.

Everybody says they want to be a National Champion. Everybody says they want to be an All-American. Everybody says they want to be a leader of their organization, or a captain of their team. Everybody says they want to be a millionaire. But, when it comes times to do the necessary things to become a National Champion, an All-American, a leader, or a millionaire, *a lot* of people do not follow through.

A lot of people love the concept of winning until it comes time for the commitment. A lot of people want to be successful without the sacrifice. A lot of people want to be rich without the risk. A lot of people want the glory without the grind. A lot of people want the blessing without the burden.

We should never hope for something more than we are willing to work for it. Hope is not a strategy. Someday is not a goal.

There are three questions we should all ask ourselves: 1) "Where do I want to go?" 2) "What it is that I *really* want?" & 3) "What am I willing to *struggle* for?" The answer to the third question tends to be a greater determinant of how our lives end up.

Preparation is the foundation of all success. Often times, preparation is not what it appears to be. The best athletes are not always the most-talented; they are the most-prepared. Unfortunately, all we see is their talent. We do not see the amount of time they have spent in the gym, in the weight room, & in the classroom, doing repetition after repetition, & drill after drill, mastering their craft.

The best athletes understand that repetition is not punishment, it is the mother of all learning; it is how we improve any skills; it is how we create consistency. They never waste an opportunity to get better.

The best athletes make it look *so easy*, because they prepare not until they get the job right, they prepare until they have the utmost confidence that they cannot do the job *wrong*. The same thing applies to us – no matter what we are doing.

The more we prepare, the harder it becomes to give up.

I *firmly* believe that we do not rise to the occasion, we fall to the level of our preparation. No pep talk (no matter how great it is), or amount of motivation or incentives, will help a person who has cheated on their preparation. We are either ready, or we are not.

It is simple: if we are not ready, it is because we have not worked hard enough, or we have not prepared enough.

I believe Coach John Wooden, the greatest coach of all-time, said it best: "I will prepare & someday my chance will come, but when that chance comes, it is too late to prepare."

No matter what situation we are in, if we stay ready, & an opportunity presents itself (which, it *will*), we will not have to rush to get ready. That is why we practice.

The whole purpose of practice is to help us prepare for the most important moments of our life. Whatever those moments might be, our practices need to simulate the conditions of those important moments as closely as possible.

The people that hate to practice hardly ever succeed when the most important moment of their life comes to fruition.

Our talent will open many doors for us, but our preparation, & our ability to maximize the talent we have will keep us there.

The difference in how our lives end up, & the difference between whether we are successful, or not, has nothing to do with our talents. It has everything to do with our ability to maximize the talents we have. We all have potential, but potential alone, will get us fired.

We all know someone who had an unbelievable amount of talent, but they were surpassed by someone who maximized their talents. We all have played with athletes, or have witnessed athletes, who are *far more* athletically gifted than everyone else, but they were lazy, or they were in the wrong environment, & they did not maximize their gifts. Because of this, they had a short-lived career, & will forever be known as a *"bust."* The quote "hard work beats talent, when talent does not work hard" is *true.*

If talent were enough, then every number-one pick in the Draft (no matter the sport) would be a Hall-of-Famer.

No dream was ever accomplished without hard work. However, hard work is not the *only* variable of preparation. Another, much larger variable of preparation is being coachable.
Everyone needs to be coachable. *Everyone!*

In order to grow & achieve, we need to be coachable. In order to be coachable, we need to listen to & *accept* feedback. In order to listen to & accept feedback, we need to be prepared to be wrong, & be willing to be corrected.

Believe it or not, we do not have it all figured out. The minute we think we do, *we lose.* There are *always* going to be things we need to learn. There are *always* going to be adjustments we need to make.

Having a coach, a leader, or a mentor is absolutely pointless, if we do not listen to them, or make the adjustments they suggest we make.

If we do not have a coach, or we are not coachable, we can practice something for hours every day, but if our technique is wrong, then all we accomplished was being good at doing something the *wrong* way.

Being coachable is one of biggest determinants of long-term success.

More opportunities come to those who are willing to be taught, who are willing to change, & who are willing to surrender control.

People change for only two reasons - when they want to, & when they have to.

The unwillingness to surrender control is the biggest reason that most *authentic* changes only happen because of a crisis. This is why it always takes a death of someone close to us, or a terrible diagnosis, for us to realize that life is short, precious, & fragile.

People who are not coachable almost always reach a plateau in their development. They stop getting better, despite numerous repetitions, or they keep making the same mistakes, repeatedly.

We all have seen a movie where the main character keeps making the same mistakes, & to us, it is so obvious what they are doing wrong. Yet, they keep doing it, & getting the same results. As viewers, we get so frustrated. But the truth is, we are that character in our own lives, sometimes. We live out our day-to-day, & go through the same routines, & we become blinded to what we are doing, & what we may be doing wrong.

Fortunately, being coachable is a choice we all can make. Working hard is a choice we all can make. Being prepared is a choice we all can make. Having a great attitude is a choice we all can make. However, these are not easy choices to make, & they are not a one-time choice to make. These choices need to be made every single day, especially, when we do not feel like making them. These choices require an unshakeable character, a willingness to struggle, a promptitude of patience, & an eagerness to sharpen the axe – no matter how dull the axe blade might be right now.

It is not what we start with, or what we will have; it is what we are willing to do with what we have *right now* that leads us to our success. *Do not let the years pass (which, they will, regardless) without making any progress towards the life you were called to live.*

"We should never hope for something more than we are willing to work for it. Hope is not a strategy. Someday is not a goal."

"It is not what we start with, or what we will have; it is what we are willing to do with what we have *right now* that leads us to our success."

@RileyTincher | #PitchingAgainstMyself

CHAPTER 7

WHO ARE YOU TRYING TO IMPRESS?

E verything about my first year at Whitewater was *different*. There was *a lot* of inconsistencies. There were incredible highs, followed by devastating lows. Everything that could have gone wrong, did go wrong... in *dramatic* fashion. Hardly anything went as I expected – or should I say, *hoped* for.

I fell in love with a girl the first month I lived there, & then, shortly after, she cheated on me... & blamed *me* for it.

I moved in to an apartment with my best friend, Zimm, & then I watched him fall deep into alcohol abuse, which ultimately ended his baseball career, & put a huge damper in our relationship.

During the offseason, I worked my ass off, to be the strongest I had ever been, & to get in the best physical shape I had ever been in, only to bust my ankle on the first day of practice.

I went to a Division III university thinking I was going to be the king right away, & then I only pitched thirteen innings.

The inconsistencies, & disappointments did not just happen to me, they happened to the entire team.

There was a dark cloud over the team the entire year... *literally*. It seemed like every game day, the weather was cold & rainy, with no sign of the sun at all. I remember having to wear my jacket during the playoffs in the middle of May.

Yes, I know that is "typical Wisconsin weather" in the spring, but it was very symbolic to how our season went.

We lost a lot of *very* talented players, due to ineligibilities, injuries, & them choosing to quit. We lost games we should not have lost, & we won games we should not have won. We did things the program has never done before, like getting ten-runned in a double-header, then sweeping an entire series against our biggest conference rival... at *their* place.

We never had a consistent batting order, or a consistent pitching rotation. Due to a couple of mid-season injuries, we had to move players around, & some of them had to play positions that they had not played in many years, or *ever* before in their lives. Our starting third basemen was playing in right field, our starting catcher was playing first base, & one of our pitchers was playing in center field. Our starting left fielder, was a freshman, who replaced Zimm when he got cut on the day of our first game (so, he was not even supposed to be on the roster in the first place) led our team in homeruns. We also had players who consistently sat on the bench, that became heroes with one swing of the bat.

We ended the regular season in a three-way tie for first place in the conference; which, had *never* happened before in WIAC history. When we were ten-runned in the Conference Tournament Championship by the conference rivals we swept earlier in the season, we all believed with the *utmost certainty* that our season was over, & we were done for the year. Even the coaches thought so. In fact, Coach Vo gave an end of the year speech after the game.

That night, many players on the team went out to the bars one last time together, only to find out right around bar time, that we got a bid into the NCAA tournament. Then, we - a team that was barely over .500 - went to the Central Region Tournament in Moline, Illinois, & lost in the Regional Championship game - the deciding game to go to the World Series.

Can you see how strange the year was yet?

This may come as a shock, but I was ok with our season ending. Actually, I was more than ok with it ending - I was ready for it to be done. Of course, I wanted to go to the World Series, but now as much as I wanted to wipe the slate clean & start over.

DRUNK WITH DISAPPOINTMENT

The day we traveled back to Whitewater from the Central Regional Tournament, was the eve of my twenty-first birthday.

As we were riding the bus home, a piece of paper on a clipboard was getting passed around from the front of the bus to back of the bus. On the paper, there were time slots for us to fill out to indicate when we were going to have our end of the year individual meeting with Coach Vo the next day.

I sat towards the back of the bus, so I was one of the last ones to pick a time slot. As you can guess, the last time slots available were the ones that were early in the morning. I chose the 8:00 AM time slot. Which meant that I was going to meet with Coach Vo at 8:00 AM on my twenty-first birthday.

Let me say that again, so it sinks in… I signed up to meet with Coach Vo at 8:00 AM *on my twenty-first birthday.*

It was also our starting third basemen's 21st birthday. His name was Nick, & him & I decided to have a party together that night to celebrate. This party also served as an end of the year party for the rest of the team. The party was at one of our other teammate's house; I cannot remember whose house it was (I wonder why). We hung out & drank beers at the house until the clock struck midnight, & Nick & I finally turned twenty-one. We did a celebratory shot of whiskey, then we headed down to the bars.

Graduation was the weekend before, so there were hardly any students left in Whitewater, & the bars were *empty.*

When we got to the bar, we proceeded to take shot, after shot until we reached a total of twenty-one shots, each. Because… twenty-one shots on your twenty-first birthday is the *logical* thing to do.
It was a fun night, but as you can imagine, it got very blurry, very fast.

I woke up the next morning on one of my teammate's couches, having no idea how I got there & having no recollection of what happened after my twenty-first shot. Luckily, I had the wherewithal to set an alarm the night before for the next morning, so I would not be late to my 8:00 AM meeting with Coach Vo.

To my surprise, I actually felt sober; like I did not even drink the night before. That was until I realized I was still drunk. I got up & walked out to my car. Then, I drove (*drunk*) to Prucha Field, & got there just in time for my meeting.

The meeting was upstairs in Coach Vo's office, where Zimm & I sat during our first visit to Whitewater.

When I go there, he was finishing up his meeting with our catcher & captain, Matt Millar. When they finished, Matt came down to get me, to let me know that it was my turn for my meeting. He also asked me if I could meet with him as well the next day, to which I said "yes, of course." Because Matt was one of our captains, I held him to a high regard. I was thrilled that he wanted to meet with me.

When I got up to Coach Vo's office, he greeted me with a handshake, & closed the door behind me. I am surprised he did not smell the alcohol on me (although, he probably did). He told me to have a seat, & he wasted no time with small talk, & got straight to the point. He asked me what I thought of my performance throughout the season. After thinking about the question for a couple of seconds, the only word that I could come up with was "disappointed." I told him I was disappointed with the outcome of the season, I was disappointed with my performance, I was disappointed with the fact that I did not get to pitch as much as I would have liked to, & I was ultimately disappointed with myself. He agreed with me.

He responded to my answer with a few reasons as to why he was disappointed with me, but to be honest, I did not hear a word he said, because I was too busy telling myself "stay focused" & "look sober" over & over again in my mind.

When he finished with his response, he asked me what I wanted to accomplish next year. He actually had to repeat himself, because I did not hear him ask the question the first time. I then told him I wanted to be a starter, to be a captain, & to win a National Championship. I only said that because that is what I thought he wanted to hear, but it was not what he wanted to hear *at all.*

He quickly countered my response with "you are not going to be a captain." Then, he explained, that "no one on the team would listen to someone who performed as poorly as you did this year."

Even though it hurt to hear those words, it was the truth. Why would anyone take advice, or guidance from someone else who performed more poorly than they did?

He then followed his response up with:

"You will lead the team through your actions. You have a great work ethic; one of the best I have *ever* seen. Your teammates admire it. But, they will not listen to you until your work ethic translates onto the field."

I nodded my head in agreement. Then, he asked me if I was playing anywhere that summer, which I was, & he told me to come back in the fall with a better breaking ball. To which I responded, "that is not the only thing that is going to be better in the fall."

Once the meeting was over, I left, & I drove (*still drunk*) to the house I grew up in (forty-five minutes away), to meet my friends who all were already home from school for the summer.

When I got home, the birthday celebration began. My friends & I went to a local restaurant that is known for being the place to go on your birthday, because if it was your birthday, you would get free beer *all night.*

We hung out there for a couple of hours, then we drove back to Whitewater (I did *not* drive), to go to a bar that had a special every Wednesday night for "all-you-can-drink" for five dollars - *Yes*, you read that correctly. They did not just give us glasses, or mugs to drink from, they gave us buckets, that could fit about thirty-six ounces of our alcoholic beverage of choice in them.

And people wonder why there is a drinking problem in Whitewater?

That night got out of hand *very* quickly. I drank *way* too much, &
I got sick. I was in the middle of dancing on the dance floor, when the
sudden urge to puke came. I ran to the back bar that was close to the
dance floor, & I threw up in a plastic bin; which, was *not* a trash can.
No one was back there, & I did not think anyone saw me, so I left my
puke there, & went right back to dancing. I blacked out shortly after.

The next morning, I woke up in my bed at my apartment in
Whitewater. I had no idea how I got there. I got up & went out to the
living room to see my friends were scattered throughout my living
room on the couches & on the floor. I was *extremely* hungover (the
most hungover I had ever been before) & I was hungry, so we all got
dressed & went to breakfast at a local diner.

After breakfast, they all headed back home, but I stayed, because
I had a meeting with Matt Millar early that afternoon.

A ROCK IN THE POND

I met Matt in the Williams Center parking lot. He greeted me with
the biggest smile & the warmest hug (he *always* did); He has the
biggest & whitest teeth I have ever seen. We walked into the building
together, & he guided me upstairs where there were tables & chairs
for us to sit at & talk.

Every one of us athletes has played with another athlete who made
a significant impact on our life. Typically, that athlete that had an
impact on us had a lot of talent that we wished we had, or they always
made difficult plays look easy, & they inspired us. We often talk about
them like they are legends, & tell mythical stories about things that
they did. Matt was that athlete for me. However, he was not very
talented, or very athletically gifted, but there was something about him
that I wanted to have.

Matt always had a way of making me feel *really* good. Half of the
time, it was without even saying a word; it was that smile of his. He
was *always* positive, & he always had encouraging words to say to

me. Plus, he carried himself with dignity & distinction – I never once saw Matt down, disappointed, or frustrated, even in situations where he had *every* right to be.

If he struck out at the plate, he walked back to the dugout with his head held high, & before he would run out onto the field the next inning, that smile was back on his face. If Coach Vo was yelling at him – which, he did quite often (Coach Vo was the hardest on all the catchers, because that was the position he played, & he knew how critical the position & leadership of the catcher was to the success of the team) – he rolled with the punches, & never let them defeat him, nor change his demeanor.

He strained his hamstring *badly* in the fall & he spent countless amount of hours rehabbing it, only to injure it again on his first day back, & then again in the middle of his senior season. But that was not enough to steal his joy.
Matt's constancy & steadfastness inspired me.

On top of all of that, Matt had an incredible story of redemption. Matt was a red-shirt freshman on the 2005 National Championship team. During his freshman & sophomore years (academically) at Whitewater, he *loved* to party. He shared his explicit drinking stories with us, quite often. Because of his partying, his grades suffered, & he was barely eligible to play. After they won the National Championship, they had a parade on Main Street in Whitewater. During the parade, the baseball players rode on top of a Fire Truck. Matt thought it was a good idea to drink while on the fire truck, & he got so drunk, that he got caught, & was immediately kicked off the team. He was not allowed back on the team until two years later, after he got sober, conquered his alcoholism, & cleaned up his act.

The year after he returned, he was named captain of the team - which, is a *big deal*.

Judging by who he was when I first met him, I would have *never* guessed that he had a severe problem with alcoholism, & was kicked off the team because of it. It was a complete shock to me when I found out about it. I had no idea *how* he redeemed himself, & became the man he was his senior year, until that day I met with him in the Williams Center.

Up until this day, Matt & I had not really had a chance to sit down & have an uninterrupted conversation. We had different groups of friends, so we never spent much time together outside of baseball.

He would always invite me to the Fellowship of Christians Athletes (FCA) meetings he led, & I would come occasionally, but only because of the free food, & the pretty girls that were there.

He also invited me to go to church with him, which I *always* turned down, & felt bad about it. So, it was very nice to *finally* have the opportunity to meet with him & talk to him.

When we sat down to talk, he asked me how my birthday was, & I responded with "well, I do not remember much of it & I am extremely hungover, so it must have been good." He laughed, then shared a story with me about how he once had a three-day hangover during his sophomore year. I then asked him how he went from that his sophomore year to not drinking at all his senior year. He responded with "I had to, or else could not play baseball anymore." I had hard time accepting that answer, so I told him "there has to be more to it than that," to which he responded with "do you *really* want to know how?" I emphatically said *"yes, I do!"*

Then he shifted the conversation, with a big smile on his face, & he asked me what I thought of my first year at Whitewater. I told him the same thing I told Coach Vo: "It was disappointing." He then asked me why I thought it was disappointing, & I again told him the same thing I told Coach Vo. Matt had a different response, though. He asked me, "who are you trying to impress?" I quickly answered in a prideful manner with *"no one!"* He knew right away I was lying, so he asked me again, & told me to be honest, so I answered, "Coach Vo." He responded with "And?" Then, I answered, "My Parents." He responded with "And?" again. We kept going back & forth until I could not come up with an answer for him.

The tone of the conversation suddenly changed when he said, "there is only one person you should be trying to impress, & you have yet to mention Him." After a long period of silence, I sat up in my chair & eagerly asked him, "Who is it?" To which he responded with, "God." Before, I could even say a word, he continued: "And guess what? He is *already* impressed with you."
I sank in my chair, & tears started rolling down my eyes.

Up until that point in my life, I was looking for the right things – love, attention, appreciation, & significance – in all the wrong places. I tried so hard to impress my coaches (especially, my eighth-grade coach), my parents, my friends, my teammates, my family, professional scouts, girls, & even complete strangers (fans). I tried to do everything I thought they would like me to do, & it made me miserable. I had no idea who I *really* was, or what I *truly* believed in. I always knew there was a higher power, but I never knew Who it was.

In the house I grew up in, we never went to church (except, sometimes on Christmas Eve), or read the Bible, so I never got to hear the Gospel. We had this plaque of the Ten Commandments that hung on the wall of our kitchen & collected dust, but I never knew what they meant. The only time I heard about God & Jesus Christ was when we went over to my grandparents' house on Christmas & Easter, & my Grandpa led the prayer before we ate.

My perception of God was that He was this ruler, & judger of all people, who sat on this mighty throne in the clouds & punished people for disobeying Him, because that is how everyone in my family perceived Him to be.

I thought I had to earn my way to Heaven by following a bunch of rules (commandments), & going through confirmation in the church, like my brother did. I thought I had to do a whole bunch of stuff (works) in order for God to love me, & accept me.

When I was young, I used to play a lot of video games – more specifically, a lot of Madden Football games. Whenever it was close to the end of a game I was playing, & the score was tied, & I needed to score in order to win, I would pray "God, if you are real, you will help me score here!" When I did not score, I would cry, & I would blame God, or denounce Him completely.

That was the gist of the relationship I had with God. I only called on Him when I needed Him, & I thought He never showed up, so I started to believe I was not good enough for Him.

Matt Millar completely changed that perception. *Thank God.*

For the first time in my life, I heard "God" & "love" in the same sentence, when Matt told me "God loves you, Riley. More than you could ever imagine." He proceeded with:

"He loves you so much, that He sent His only son, Jesus Christ, to die on a cross our sins, so that we could have eternal life in Heaven *with* Him (John 3:16)."

Matt then then asked me, "do you want eternal life, Riley?" With my head hanging down, & tears rolling down my face, I quietly said "yes." He responded with:

"The Bible says that if we believe in our hearts, & confess with our mouths that "Jesus Christ is Lord of all," then we will have eternal life (Romans 10:10)."

He then asked me the question that led to my salvation: "Do you believe that Jesus Christ died for your sins, was raised from the dead, & is alive today?" As I lifted my chin, & wiped my tears away, I said, "yes." With a huge smile on his face, he asked me, "Do you want to make Jesus Christ the Lord of your life?" To which I said, "yes" as I nodded my head. He responded with, "Then close your eyes, & repeat this prayer after me." I bowed my head, closed my eyes, & brought my hands together (just like I did when my Grandpa would pray for us before we ate). I confessed with my mouth that "Jesus Christ is the Lord of my life," & in that moment, I was *saved!*

As soon as we got done praying, Matt stood up & gave me hug. He told me he was proud of me, & I cried again in his arms.

That day, a Rock dropped in my pond, that would create ripples that would eventually change my life *completely.*

Did my behavior change right away? *No.* My twenty-first birthday was only the start of my alcohol abuse. But, my *heart* changed, & that is what God cares about the most.

KNOWLEDGE APPLIED

For the first time in the history of mankind, we have an entire generation of children who have had access to the internet for the entirety of their lives. More so, these children are growing up with their identities tied into everything that is on the internet – more specifically, social media. On the internet, we have been blinded with the illusion of perfection, & we have been bombarded with the thief of all joy that is comparison. *Nothing* kills contentment & feeds insecurity more than comparison.

Because of the ability to use "filters," we only see everyone else's highlight reels, so we only want to show our highlight reels. It has become a perpetual cycle, but it is not the real issue. The real issue is, we like to compare our "behind the scenes," with everyone else's highlight reels. Because our friends, coworkers, &/or peers only post statuses & share pictures that make them appear happy, we assume they are *always* happy. Because our friends, coworkers, &/or peers only post statuses & share pictures to show people how successful they are, we assumed that they did not have any struggles getting there. Because our friends, coworkers, &/or peers only post statuses & share pictures to show people how great their marriage is, or how *perfect* their kids are, we assume they never have problems.
It is a lie, & a trap we have all fallen into.

The worst part is, we have become addicted to it. We spend countless number of hours taking pictures – selfies, in particular –

trying to find the right angle, & the right lighting. Then we spend more time trying to come up with a clever caption that we think people would like to read. We only share pictures that we think will get the most likes & comments. We only share stories on Snapchat & Instagram if we are doing something that we think is *important*, or we are somewhere that we think other people wish they could be. We even come up with schedules to post things at certain times, because that is when we think it will get the most attention. When we finally find the "perfect picture," & create the most-clever caption, we post it, & when it does not get the amount of likes we want, we delete it.

Why? For credibility? For likes & followers? To make us feel good about ourselves?

Worse yet, our entire self-esteem is wrapped up in this. We actually have apps on our phones that track our followers on Social Media, & when someone does not follow us back, or *heaven forbid*, unfollows us, it devastates us.

"Insta-famous" & being an influencer on Social media has become a thing that most kids inspire to be. We have girls who have *millions* of followers for the sole reason that they take half-naked pictures of themselves. This sends a message to every other little girl who wants to become "Insta-famous," that if you want more followers, you are going to have to show some skin. Because of this, Instagram has become soft-core pornography.

This is causing *detrimental* side effects to our younger generations. Depression has increased *significantly* in the last ten years. Colleges have had more leaves of absence due to depression than ever before. Suicide is the highest it has ever been in thirty years; it is the second leading cause of death among those who are thirty years old & younger. The most startling of all these statistics is: The age group that has had the highest increase in suicide over the last five years, has been girls, ages ten to fourteen – the number of suicides nearly *tripled* from five years ago.

Our phones are not to blame. The internet is not to blame. Social media is not to blame. They are tools of destruction (just like televisions, video games, & rock & roll music), but they are not the source of the problem.

Have you ever asked yourself: Am I good enough? Do I measure up? Do I fit in? Do they approve of me? If you answered "yes" to any of those questions, you are not alone.

Over the last ten years, I have had the fortune of playing with, working with, & mentoring *a lot* of great athletes. The more of them I meet, the more I realize that despite what the media portrays, we all have issues. I am not talking about small issues, I am talking about *major* issues. I have met Heisman Trophy winners, who are glorified in the media, & are portrayed as an esteemed individual, but they cheat on their wife every chance they can get. I have met All-Pro athletes who have more money that you could ever imagine, yet they are miserable. I have met All-Americans, who are on top of their respective sport, yet they feel like they are not good enough. I have met Olympic medalists who have every material thing they have ever wanted, but they feel empty. I have met future Hall of Famers, who are considered "a-list celebrities," & they have an entourage of five to ten people around them at all times, yet they feel lonely.

Why are they struggling? Why do we struggle? Why is depression, suicide, & drug abuse (specifically, prescription drugs), increasing at such a young age at an *alarming* rate?

Like the Samaritan woman in the Bible (John 4), we are drinking from the wrong well, & we are continually *thirsty.*

The Bible says "seek *first* the Kingdom of God, & *all* these things will be added to you. (Matthew 6:33). " Notice it says, seek *first* the Kingdom of God. Yet, we are seeking "all these things" in the world (likes, follows, popularity, approval, riches, fame, glory) first, & hoping the Kingdom of God is there. When it is not there, we keep looking, & keep looking, & keep looking, & never find it.

We are *constantly* auditioning. We are auditioning for our teams. We are auditioning for our coaches. We are auditioning for colleges. We are auditioning for jobs & internships. We are auditioning for friendships & relationships. We are auditioning for our parents.

We all are guilty of it. This is the reason why we dress the way we do. This is the reason why we buy the shoes we wear. This is the reason why we style our hair the way we do. This is the reason why we drive the cars we drive. This is the reason why we say the things we say. This is the reason why we post the pictures & statuses we post.

Unfortunately, this is also the reason why we party. This is also the reason why we drink. This is also the reason why we do drugs. This is also the reason why we crumble under peer pressure.

We are looking for all the *right* things – love, attention, appreciation, & significance – but we are looking for them in all the wrong areas. *We all thirst*, but what matters most is where we go to quench our thirst.

I am going to ask you the same question that Matt asked me. This question changed my life, & *always* corrects my heart, & fixes my focus: *Who are you trying to impress?*

I want you to think about that for a moment – Who are you *really* trying to impress?

Let me tell you something that may be hard for you to fully comprehend: It is *impossible* to impress everybody. We can say & do *everything* right, & there is *always* going to be someone who has a problem with us. Jesus Christ showed us this – The Pharisees (the self-righteous) killed him, & He was an innocent man who *never* sinned, nor committed *any* crimes.

The only one we should be trying to impress is God. Guess what? He is already impressed with us, no matter what we have done, how we feel, or how bad we think we are.

He created us. He knew us long before we were even born (Jeremiah 1:5). He knew our entire story, even the deepest, darkest parts of our story. He knew the choices we would make, even the terrible, unthinkable ones we are afraid to tell everyone else about. Yet, He continually chooses us, & He does think because He loves us.

He wants the same things we want – something more; He *desperately* wants a relationship with us. He is so desperate for a *real* relationship with us, & for us to join Him in His Kingdom, that He gave His only son as a sacrifice, to hang & die on the cross, to forgive us for the sins we should not be forgiven of.

The only way to find out how much He loves us, & how impressed He is with us is to read His Word... *every day*; especially, when we do not feel like it. Faith comes by hearing (luckily, the verse does not stop there), & hearing the Word of God (Romans 10:17). So, instead of seeking what everybody else says about us, we should be seeking what He says about us in the Bible.

The Bible is the *greatest* love story ever written, & in it, we will find that there is value in being liked by people, but there is *greater* value in being loved by God. There is value in having fun with friends, but there is *greater* value in faithfulness to God. There is value in being popular, but there is *greater* value in serving God's purpose. There is value in impressing others, but there is *greater* value in impressing God.

You may be feeling a pull on your heart, right now, which is the same pull I felt the day I sat down with Matt in the Williams Center. There is reason why we feel this way. We all have a *constant* innate feeling (thirst) of wanting something more. It is hard-wired in all of us. The only way to quench that thirst is to surrender your life to Him & confess that *"Jesus Christ is my Lord."*

Only Jesus Christ can change our lives. *Only* He can fix the messes we have created. *Only* He can give us peace (beyond understanding). *Only* He can give us freedom. *Only* He can give us grace for what we have done. *Only* He can redeem & restore us. *Only* He can heal us. *Only* He can transform us, & make us new.

In order for all these wonderful things to happen, we must give up control; which is simple, *but not easy*. I promise you, the kingdom we think we have created, & do not want to give up (because it is *ours*), is *worthless* in comparison to the Kingdom of God, & all the riches He has *promised* us (Philippians 4:19).

God's approval is not based on performance, or behavior. He does not want our behavior. He does not want us to keep a ton of rules. He wants us to follow him. *He wants our heart!* The Bible says, "where your treasure is, that is where your heart is. (Matthew 6:21)" If we give Him our heart, our behavior *will* change. There is no doubt about it. It is not a matter of *"if,"* it is a matter of *"when."*

Will our behavior change right away? Maybe… but more than likely, it will not. It is a process. We will mess up & that is *alright*, because it is never about what we have done, what we do, or what we will do, it is about what He has done!

God is not interested in who we were, He is interested in who we are becoming. I am a *completely* different person from who I was before I made the *best* decision of my life. As a matter of fact, I am a *completely* different person from who I was last year. It is not because of something that I did, it is *all* because of Jesus Christ.

The Bible says, "all things are possible for those who believe (Mark 9:23)." Believe in what? Believe in Him & believe in the power He has given us. One of my mentors, & the greatest father figure in my life, Dr. John Saurino always reminds me: "If you do not change what you believe, *nothing* will change tomorrow."

God wants to bless us beyond measure (Ephesians 3:20), but He cannot bless who we pretend to be. He cannot bless who we portray to be in order to impress everyone around us. We cannot simultaneously impress people & impress God. Our intention should always be to impress Him first!

The world teaches us that in order to have value, we need to achieve, but God says we are valuable right now… just as we are.

That is *great* news, because Greater is He who is *in* us, than he who is in the world (1 John 4:4). He is our Rock (Matthew 7:24-27), & with Him, *nothing* is impossible (Luke 1:37). He is the same yesterday, today & *forever* (Hebrews 13:8). He has never failed. He has never faltered. He has never wavered. He has never stopped short. He has never surrendered. He has never lost, & He is not about to start with you, or me.

He *promised* that He will never leave us, nor forsake us (Deuteronomy 31:6), & if we *believe* that, then we should have the utmost confidence that He is *always* going to take care of us.

He also promised that in *all* things He works together for the good of those who *love* him, & have been called according to His purpose (Romans 8:28). If you love Him, then you have been called according to His purpose.

As long as we have Jesus, we *always* have hope. His promises are *true*, & His word is *everlasting* (1 Peter 1:25). So, when He says that we can do *all* things through Him who gives us strength (Philippians 4:13), then He means it!

Too many of us are trying to fight a war that has already been won, by the resurrection of Jesus Christ. If He is for us, then who can be against us (Romans 8:31)? In the end, He *always* wins. That means, in His name, we are *unstoppable.*

When I look back at my life, & see all that I have been through, & all that I have been rescued from, I cannot help but see miracle, after miracle that God has performed. I should be dead right now, but by the grace of God, I am still alive. I am His miracle.

If you made the decision to make Jesus Christ the Lord of your life, I must warn you: Once you invite Him in, He will take over, & your life will *never* be the same; that is a *good* thing.

Nothing can stop the power of God in your life… except your unbelief.

"*Nothing* kills contentment, & feeds insecurity more than comparison."

"It is *impossible* to impress everybody. We can say & do *everything* right, & there is *always* going to be someone who has a problem with us."

@RileyTincher | #PitchingAgainstMyself

CHAPTER 8

THIS IS MY GAME!

The summer after my first year at Whitewater was the beginning of something *very* special. It was the beginning of a new journey. It was the beginning of something I could never have dreamed of, nor imagined. It was the beginning of my comeback. It was the beginning of my reinvention.

I used to *hate* hearing the phrase "your time is coming." It was so cliché to me, because it seemed like it was the auto-response *everyone* gave to me after I told them about my problems, or after I vented my frustrations to them. To annoy me even further, it was usually followed up with the quote: "a setback is only a setup for a comeback."

I cannot tell you how many times those quotes were told to me. I was sick of hearing it, because I never believed it to be true... until I experienced it.

After my meeting with Matt Millar, & after he dropped the Rock in my pond, *a lot* of things changed. I began to see things differently. I also began to question *everything*.

That summer, I went on a mission to figure out what I was going to do the next year, & to figure out what it was I was called to do. Some call this "soul searching," others call it "reflection." I like to call it "introspection," because it sounds more *productive* to me.

At the end of my first year at Whitewater, I knew three things: 1) I was not happy with where I was... *at all.* 2) I did not want to be there anymore. 3) I was willing to do *whatever* it took to change it.

I considered quitting baseball all together, & just focusing on school; which, my mom strongly encouraged. But even the thought of quitting made me cringe. I was tired of the constant frustration &

disappointment baseball gave me, but I was not tired of it enough to live the rest of my life thinking, *"what if?"*

I also considered transferring schools, but I had no idea where I was going to go. Plus, the whole transferring process is grueling, & I did not want to go through it again. I already went to three different schools in three years, & I did not want to add a forth.

The *only* option I had was to find a way to maximize the gifts I had been given, & become the best pitcher I could possibly be. There was no way I was going to end my baseball career on the note I ended my first year at Whitewater on. I knew I was better than I performed, but I had *no idea* how great I was going to become.

The first day I got back to the house I grew up in, I went down to my high school baseball field to workout with Jam (our centerfielder in high school) & Zimm. I was happy to hear Zimm was still going to play baseball that summer for the local team that him, Jam, & I had played for, for the previous three summers. I was also happy to hear he still wanted to work out that summer, even though his baseball career was over; a strong work ethic is hard-wired in Zimm - he *never* shied away from working hard (at *anything*), & he never backed down from anything physically challenging.

The first thing we did as soon as we got to the field was long toss – which, is where you start on the foul line, close to the foul pole, & play catch with a partner, & you both try to gradually increase the distance between the two of you after each throw, until you both cannot throw any farther without the ball hitting the ground.

As soon as we began to throw, my anger & frustrations immediately came to the surface.

Every throw I made was at one-hundred-percent; meaning, I threw as hard as I could every single throw. With each throw, we gradually got further & further away from each other. We got so far away from each other that we were literally throwing from foul pole to foul pole – a little over four-hundred feet. I was not making huge, arching throws, I was throwing the ball on a line, every single time. I had *never* been able to throw that far on a line before. It was one of those moments we all have experienced where we surprise ourselves, & realize we are capable of *a lot* more than we think are.

I had a teammate when I played for the Wisconsin Woodchucks who I would long toss with the day after one of his starts. At the time, I could only throw about three-quarters (if that) of the distance he could… *one day after his start*, when I am sure his arm was sore. It was *very* embarrassing.

For the rest of the summer, Jam, Zimm, & I would long toss every other day (if we did not have a game). Every time we long tossed, we would throw from foul pole to foul pole, & every time, it gave me a sense of pride, letting me know that I was *significantly* better than I was when I would long toss just two years before.

MY NEW SLIDER

I mentioned my *new* slider in the last chapter, but I did not mention where it came from. If you remember, when I started at Whitewater, one of the first major adjustments I made was getting rid of some of the pitches I had in my arsenal (the cutter, & the splitter), in order to focus on mastering my fastballs (4-seam & 2-seam), my curveball, & my change-up.

My fastball has always been my best pitch, because of the movement it had, & how hard it was. The second-best pitch I had was my change-up, because of the movement it had, & how it looked like a fastball coming out of my hands, until it "hit the brakes" when it got to the plate. My curveball was a different story. To put it plainly, it *sucked*. It was more of a gravity ball – meaning, the only reason why it moved was because gravity was pushing it down.

Every pitcher has a different arm-slot where they release the baseball. Some pitchers are "submarine" pitchers (for example, Chad Bradford & Byung-Hyun Kim), where it looks like they threw

167

underhand. Some of them would literally scrape their hands on the ground as they were throwing.

Some pitchers are "sidearm" pitchers (for example, Satchel Paige & Don Drysdale), where they release the baseball, & their arm is perpendicular to their body, & their hand is shoulder level.

Most pitchers throw over-the-top (for example, Andy Pettitte & Roger Clemens), which, is self-explanatory.

Then, there are pitchers like me, who throw from a three-quarter arm slot (for example, Randy Johnson & Pedro Martinez), which is any arm angle between a side-arm pitcher, & an over-the-top pitcher.

Because I threw from a three-quarter arm slot, it was nearly impossible for me to get on top of the baseball to throw a "12-6 curveball" (12-6 is referring to the numbers on a clock); where the ball breaks in a straight vertical line.

One day in practice, during my first year at Whitewater, I was throwing a bullpen with Coach Cally by my side. During the bullpen, I voiced my frustration to him about my curveball, & that no matter how often, or how hard I tried, I could not figure out how to make it break sharper & harder.

Every time I threw my curveball, I had to change my natural arm slot in order to get on top of the ball to make it have a 12-6 break. It was obvious to every hitter I faced that I was throwing a curveball, because of the different arm slot I had to throw it from, in comparison to the arm slot I threw my fastball & changeup in.

Coach Cally suggested that because of my arm slot, I should try throwing a slider (slider's break from 3-9 on a clock) instead; which, turned out to be another one of the greatest adjustments I was suggested to make while I was at Whitewater.

The year before, I threw a cutter, which is *very* similar to a slider (just thrown a little bit harder, so it does not have as much of a break), so the transition in my mind from cutter to slider was easy. However, the transition on the mound took a little bit more time.

Since Coach Vo told me to come back to Whitewater in the fall with a better breaking ball, I made sure I dedicated the *entire* summer to mastering my slider. I threw it playing catch. I threw it in my bullpens. I threw it in games. I threw it as often as I could. I also did this thing, where I would practice my windup anywhere I was standing ((the kitchen, the basement, the garage, standing in line for food at a restaurant, etc.), at any given time, & I would throw all three of my pitches. When I would phantom throw my slider, I would snap my fingers, & it drove my mom crazy; I did it *a lot*, so I can see why.

So much of pitching is *feel* – being able to feel certain pitches coming out of your hand. So, the more you throw something, the better you have a feel for how to throw it. It is *a lot* of trial & error.

As the summer progressed, my slider got better. It went from being a pitch I threw to hitters to catch them off balance, to being a strike out pitch. The more games I started, the better my slider got, & the more strikeouts I had.

It was not until my last start of the season, when I struck out twenty-one hitters, that I realized I finally had something *special*; something I could take back to Whitewater, & Coach Vo would be proud of.

JAMES B. MILLER STADIUM

The success I had on the mound in the summer, carried over to fall ball. A better breaking ball was not the only thing I brought back to Whitewater. I was a *completely* different pitcher. I was throwing the hardest & fastest I had ever thrown before. My new slider was not only striking out local recreation league hitters, it was striking out Whitewater hitters as well. I had a better pickoff move. I was getting hitters out at an alarming rate. In fact, I did not allow an earned run the *entire* fall.

I was not the only thing that was completely different at Whitewater. Prucha Field was different, as well.

The veterans did not start Fall Ball until the middle of October. The reason for the delay was because Prucha Field was under a remodel... actually, a *complete transformation.*

When I moved back to Whitewater a few weeks before school started, I was shocked to see a brand-new scoreboard in the outfield, & the construction of a new infield. No one told me that we were getting artificial turf. I think no one told me because no one knew... except, the coaches.

The day I moved back, the entire infield, the warning track, & the bullpens were all torn up & gutted. Instead, there was a thick layer of gravel that was laid & packed where it all used to be. There was also cement laid where home-plate & the batters boxes used to be, & where the pitcher's mound used to be on the field. All of this had to be done so we could lay down the artificial turf; which, happened over the next couple of weeks.

Having lived so close to Prucha Field, it was incredible to watch the process of the new field being made.

An artificial turf infield was something I had *never* seen before. The closer it got to being done, the more excited I was about getting the opportunity to play on it.

During the month of September, the coaches were holding tryouts for the incoming freshmen & transfers at Whitewater High School. While the newcomers were in tryouts, us veterans were in the weight room, working out.

We usually did not start working out with Coach Munger until the end of Fall Ball, but circumstances dictated otherwise. I had no problem with it, because I loved being in the weight room. The other veterans did not love it as much as I did, probably because we had to go in early in the morning.

There were not as many veterans as I expected. Of the twenty-five players who were on the roster the previous year, that *should* have returned, ten of them either quit, or were asked not to come back, &

one of them (the All-Conference left-handed pitcher) got drafted & signed to a professional team.

It was a *strange* sight to see. We used to have to split the team up into two groups to work out, & now there were less than fifteen of us.

For the first couple of weeks, while the turf was being laid, the morning workouts were our only responsibility throughout the day. The freedom we had was unusual.

Several of us pitchers would go to the practice fields behind Prucha Field to throw & keep our arms "in shape." I continued to long-toss whenever I got the chance. Unfortunately, not many of the pitchers wanted to long toss with me. So, when I had no one to throw with, I would recruit Zimm to throw with me. Fortunately, he was *always* willing to throw with me if I asked.

There was something different about Zimm that fall. He drank very little in comparison to how much he drank the year before. My guess is he saw Graduation coming, & he knew he need to get serious about straightening out his life. Thank God that he did, because he now has a *great* story to share about overcoming *extreme* odds, & becoming the leader he always wished he had.

Once the turf was finally laid, the freedom we had in the afternoons went away, & the real work began.

We had responsibilities to do to get the field ready so we could have Fall Ball, & play our Steak Series. We had to build a new pitching mound… from scratch. We had to build new pitching mounds for each bullpen. We had to build new batting cages just outside the third-base dugout. We had to cut & place new rubber mats inside each of the dugouts. We had to place new wind screen slots in the outfield fence (this took *forever,* because there were at least a thousand of them). We had to hang new banners up. We had to lay new sod in the outfield. We had to carry in *a lot* of bricks & help build a three-foot wall that went from the bullpen on the first-base side, around the backstop behind home-plate, to the bullpen on the third-base side.

This is just a *short* list of the things we had to get done in less than a month, so we could finally play on the brand-new field.

Much like everything else we were *"forced"* to do, I hated doing it, at the time. I used to think it was Coach Vo taking advantage of us for *free* labor; which, in all reality, it partially was. Looking back at it, I see why he did it. He wanted to give us a sense of ownership of the field. Now, when I go back & watch games, I cannot help but proudly think to myself "I helped build *all* of this."

When we finished getting the field ready for Fall Ball, the transformation was *incredible*. There were still things that needed to get done (putting up stadium lights, & building the gate for the entrance to the stadium), but nevertheless, it was *incredible*.

There were several nights after practice where I would sit at the top of the stands & just look at the field in awe.

To make this new field even more special, on the first practice we had *on* the field, Coach Vo told us that we would be naming the stadium after legendary Warhawk Baseball Coach, & Coach Vo's predecessor, Coach James B. Miller, also known as *"Mills."*

Coach Vo played for Coach Mills, then became his assistant coach, until Coach Mills passed over the baton to Coach Vo to take over as head coach.

Coach Mills *bled* purple. He was our biggest fan. He was *always* around. Whenever I got a chance to talk to him, he hardly ever talked to me about baseball. Instead, he always asked me how I was doing, how school was going, & how my family was doing.

That Fall, in order to make some money, I was given the chance to work alongside our All-Conference centerfielder (who was completely recovered from his shoulder surgery) & one of our infielders around Coach Mills' house & yard.

This job entailed us doing anything Coach Mills asked us to do. We worked every weekday afternoon until his wife, Carol, got home from work. It was beautiful to see how excited he would get when she got home. I loved watching him greet her *every* time like it had been a *long* time since seeing her last. I am so honored that I got to witness, firsthand, the love he had for Carol.

I want a love like that someday.

FALL BALL

On the first day of Fall Ball, we did only two things. The first thing we did was take groundballs on the brand-new artificial turf infield. It was amazing how every bounce the baseball took on the turf was a *true* hop; there were no short hops, or hops off any divots or rocks. The only bad thing (& it was not that bad) was the groundballs were *a lot* faster, which forced the infielders to play back a couple of steps.

The second thing we did that day was learn how to slide into second & third base.

Now, I know what you might be thinking – "college baseball players *should* know how to slide into every base." There is truth to that statement. However, there is a *huge* difference between sliding on dirt, & sliding on turf. Sliding on turf is *a lot* faster. Everybody who slid on the turf for the first time, slid *past* the base. It was hysterical – the coaches had a great time watching us.

Since it was already the middle of October, & we were supposed to be done with Fall Ball at the end of October, we did a couple of scrimmages, then jumped right into the Steak Series.

I was excited for the Steak Series, because... it is the *Steak Series!* It was one of the best times of the year. I was also excited to showcase my new slider, & to find out just how good of a pitcher I had become. I was also very nervous, because I thought my spot on the team was in jeopardy, & I thought my performance in the Steak Series dictated whether I would make the team, or not.

I approached *every* start I had in the Steak Series, as if I was going to lose my spot on the team if I lost that game. I approached every inning of my starts, as if it was going to be the last inning I ever pitched. I approached every hitter I faced as if I was pitching against the best hitter on the team.

Because of this approach, I won both of the games I started; including my last start which decided who won the Steak Series. I have *never* tasted a steak so good.

My performance in that Steak Series let everyone know, including myself, that I was there to stay.

At the end of every Fall Ball season, every player on the roster had an individual meeting with Coach Vo to go over Fall Ball evaluations.

When I met with Coach Vo, one of the first things he told me was how pleasantly surprised he was of my performance. Then, he immediately followed it up with a warning, telling me not to get complacent, & what would happen if I did.

As our meeting was concluding, Coach Vo & I started talking about the upcoming season, & he asked me what goals I had for myself & for the team. I told him that I, personally, wanted to be a starting pitching, & win ten games. Then, I told him that I wanted to lead the team to a National Championship. He neither agreed with me, nor disagreed with me. Instead, he began to tell me a story about a former Warhawk legend, who was also a left-handed pitcher. This legend won *fifteen* games in 2005, & one of games he won was the National Championship game.

Since I had *never* won more than 5 games in a season before, I began to write off his story in my mind as *unattainable* - a story of legend, like Babe Ruth calling his shot. Then, he told me something that changed my perspective, & my unbelief:

"Here is the thing about goals, Riley: If you keep telling yourself that you are going to win ten games, that is all you are going to win. Winning ten games is great, but what if you are capable of winning more? I told you that story about the pitcher who won fifteen games, to let you know that since it has been done before, it can be done again. *You* are going to be the one to do it."

The next season, I won more than ten games.

GET TO THE FRONT OF THE LINE

Let's go back to the summer before I came back to Whitewater for my second year. Like I told you, I was willing to do *whatever* it took to change the circumstance I was in. So, throughout the summer, I read several books - three, to be exact (which, is several for me & my dyslexia). One book, in particular, changed the trajectory of my baseball career, & ultimately, inspired me to get my Master's Degree in Sports Psychology. That book was *Mind Gym: An Athlete's Guide to Inner Excellence* by Gary Mack & David Casstevens.

Gary Mack is a renowned sports psychology consultant, who is best known for his work with Alex Rodriguez, & helping him overcome the pressure of performing in the postseason. If you recall, Alex Rodriguez's first couple of years with the New York Yankees (2005-2008), he struggled in the postseason (hitting below .200), which many blamed him for the team's postseason struggles. 2009 was a different story. After seeing Gary Mack, his performance in the postseason significantly increased, & the Yankees won their twenty-seventh World Series champions.

Prior to reading *Mind Gym*, I never really thought of my mind as a "muscle" that I can strengthen, & I definitely did not think about how it affected my performance on the field; which, it did... in a *detrimental* way.

There were two chapters (two lessons) in the book that stood out to me the most. They helped reveal some of the "mental issues" I was having. More importantly, they showed me how to overcome them.

The first lesson was how to overcome the fear of failure – more specifically, the pressure that comes from the fear of failure. In this lesson, Gary Mack gave the illustration of having someone stand on a chair. He defined the simple, specific objectives of how to stand on the chair properly. Then, he gave the illustration of having someone stand on a chair on top of a one-hundred-story building. The objectives stayed the same, but now the chair was one-thousand feet in the air. He talked about how the height was the pressure that we create for ourselves, even though the objectives stayed the same.

I translated this into my fear of pitching in front of a large crowd. If there were less than five-hundred people in the stands, I was perfectly fine, but if there were any more than five-hundred people in the stands, I became nervous. The nervousness was so bad that it would cause me to tense up, & not allow me to use my arm as a whip (loose, free-flowing) when I pitched, which, decreased my velocity, & ultimately, hurt my performance.

I was still playing the same game I had played since I was in eighth grade. The distances did not change. The rules did not change. The objectives did not change. But, my mind distorted my perspective, because of my fear of failing; more specifically, my fear of failing in front of *a lot* of people. The funny thing is, my fear of failing in front of a lot of people is what caused me to fail.

My fear was not just in failing in front of large crowds, it was also in failing in front of my coaches, & the people I cared about most, because I valued their opinion of me, & I *desperately* wanted their approval & recognition.

In *Mind Gym*, Gary Mack talks about fear being an illusion, & that it is just a feeling that comes & goes, & ebbs & flows. Since it is a feeling, it does not define who we are. We may feel afraid, but that does not mean we *are* afraid. Since we are not afraid, we can still take action, & complete the objectives needed to succeed at any given task.

The feeling I had of fear of failing never went away, but it did not control me, or my actions anymore.

One of the things I started doing my second year at Whitewater to help me overcome this feeling was getting to the front of the line.

Before, whenever we did pitcher's fielding practice (PFP's), bunt coverages, first & thirds, or any other drills, I would constantly go to the back of the line. I did this hoping that I would only have to do the drill one time, before we moved on to the next drill. I thought I was protecting myself from the embarrassment of failing in front of my coaches & teammates, but really, it was only taking away from me getting better at the things I *needed* to get better at – like, fielding my position (which, I will talk about later on in the book).

Making a simple change like going to the front of line in *everything* we did, not only gave me more repetitions, it also taught me a great lesson in leadership – leaders always have the courage to go first, which puts themselves at personal risk, but show others the way to follow.

3-1 DAY

The second chapter (lesson) in *Mind Gym* that stood out to me was about our inner-dialogue & the words we say to ourselves – especially, in high pressure situations. In this lesson, Gary Mack illustrated a hitter at the plate with two-strikes against him. Most hitters (especially, young hitters) in a two-strike count are repeatedly saying to themselves, "do not strike out."

Gary Mack goes on to point out the last two words in the sentence – "strike out" – & how they cause the hitter to focus on a negative outcome, instead of a positive one. He also points out that the words "do not strike out" are very reactive, instead of being proactive. As athletes (& as human beings, as well), we always want to be on the offense with the words we say, *not* the defense.

After reading that chapter, I audited & became very aware of the words I would say to myself while I was pitching.

To say that these words were awful & *very* self-destructive, would be an understatement. If I ever walked a hitter, or gave up a hit, my immediate responses would be: "You have got to be kidding me!" or "I am a loser," *or* "I *suck* at pitching," *or worse yet,* "I should just give up." Of course, I am leaving out *a lot* of expletives I would say.

Those are just a few of the harmful, destructive words I would say to myself. The problem was, I said them *so much*, that I believed them to be true.

One time, after I gave up a homerun, I caught myself saying, "I should just kill myself, I will never be good at anything." That was the moment when I decided I had enough, & that I needed to totally change the words I was saying to myself.

I wrote down several phrases & words I wanted to say to myself instead. Then, I started practicing saying them in the mirror, during bullpens, & when I would pitch in scrimmages during Fall Ball. Some of these phrases included:

"I am the *greatest* pitcher in the country."

"I *will* win this game."

"I *will* strike this guy out."

"I *will* put up a zero this inning."

"I *will* get out of this jam."

On top of that, right before certain pitches, I would repeat (several time) specific words, or short phrases like: "first pitch strike," or "strike three," or "outside corner (or any other location in the strike zone I was trying to throw to)."

There was another phrase I would use, & this one topped them all.

After I got done throwing the seven warmup pitches before every inning, & the catcher threw down to second base, & I received the ball back from the third-baseman, I would go behind the mound, face away from home-plate, tuck my chin under my undershirt, & pray. I *always* said the same prayer (which, I will tell you later). When the prayer was done, I would turn back toward home-plate & walk up the mound to face the first hitter. Then, I would cover my mouth with my glove, & I would yell *"this is my game!"* right before the first pitch.

To be honest, I actually would yell: *"This is my f@#%ing game!"*

There were two things I did in high school that led to my success. The first thing I did was pitching at a very fast tempo, & not wasting any time in between pitches (to keep me from overthinking & help me get into a rhythm). The second thing I did was coining the phrase *"this is my game!"*

After every big inning, & after I got out of any tough situations, I would yell it as loud as I could, as I was running back to the dugout, pounding my chest like a gorilla.

Over time, I continued to pitch at a fast pace, but the phrase *"this is my game!"* slowly went away – due, in large part to me worrying about what my new coaches & teammates would think of me if I said it. That was until one day in spring practice, my second year at Whitewater, when we were doing live matchups in the cage.

Live matchups were already *highly* competitive, with a *ton* of trash talking, but there was always one day every year, where the competitiveness increased *dramatically* - the 3-1 day.

During the 3-1 day, hitters would enter the cage with a 3-1 count (3 balls, 1 strike). They had a *huge* advantage, from the beginning. If we (the pitchers) threw a ball the first pitch, they walked, & the at-bat was over. We not only had to throw one strike, we had to throw two strikes. In most (probably, ninety-nine-percent) 3-1 counts, pitchers throw fastballs, so every hitter that entered the cage that day knew what pitch was coming.

It became a matchup of who's best is better. As a pitcher, my mentality was: "here's my best fastball, go ahead & *try* to hit it. "

The whole point of the 3-1 day was for Coach Vo to see which pitcher could handle pressure & adversity the best.

To add to the pressure even more, Coach Vo told us that for every walk we gave up, we would have to run a lap around the fieldhouse at the end of the live matchups.

To add on top of that pressure, the lineups were "randomly picked" & somehow, the lineup I had to face had all the potential starters for the upcoming season in it, including two of the greatest hitters in Whitewater history (the centerfielder, & the first basemen).

Thank God, I *never* backed down from a challenge.

The first hitter I faced was our right-fielder (who was a left-handed hitter, & a Division I transfer). The first pitch I threw was a slider on the insider corner for strike one; which, sent a message to the rest of the hitters that "I did not care what count it was, I was going to throw *whatever* I want, *whenever* I want to." Then, I followed it up with an inside fastball that he was *very late* at swinging at. As soon as it went by him for strike three, out of my mouth came, *"this is my f@#%ing game!"* It caught everyone by surprise, including myself. As soon as I said it, all the memories I had from yelling it in high school came back up to the surface.

For the rest of the live matchups, I would yell it after every strikeout I had, & I had *a lot* of them that day. The more I yelled it, the more attention I got from the rest of my teammates. The more attention I got, the more momentum I had. Towards the end of the live matchups, it seemed like the entire team & all the coaches were watching me pitch.

Yelling *"this is my f@#%ing game!"* was a mental switch for me. From that point on, I no longer pitched scared, I pitched with conviction. I pitched *angry*.

I ended 3-1 day, allowing just two hits, giving up *zero* walks, & striking out *twelve* hitters (the *best* hitters we had).

My 3-1 day performance became a story of legend; much like the left-handed pitcher who won fifteen games in one season. It was another confirmation to my teammates, my coaches, & myself that I was there to stay. It was also a sign of things to come.

KNOWLEDGE APPLIED

Have you ever heard of the children's rhyme, "sticks & stones?" If you are one of the three people on earth who have not heard of it, it goes like this: "sticks & stones may break my bones, but your words will never hurt me."

It is a clever rhyme, but it is *crap*. The truth is, "sticks & stones may break my bones, but words will *kill* me." Especially, the words we say to ourselves.

The words we speak are like seeds that produce after their kind. Just as sure as they are planted, we can be equally sure a harvest will follow – good, or bad.

Our words are weapons of mass destruction, & too many of us are using our words to destroy ourselves.

The Bible says, "life & death are in the power of the tongue (Proverbs 18:21)." It does not say "wins & losses," it says, "*life & death* are in the power of the tongue." Too many of us are speaking *death* over our lives, & we are receiving death because of it.

Do we *really* want all the negative things we have been saying to ourselves to come true? Because that is *exactly* what is happening.

If we keep telling ourselves "I am not good enough," or "I will never measure up," guess what is going to happen? We will never be good enough, & we will never measure up. If we keep telling ourselves "I will never catch a break," then we will never catch a break. If we keep telling ourselves "I am a failure," then we are always going to fail. If we keep telling ourselves "bad things always happen to me," then bad things are always going to happen to us. If we keep telling ourselves "I have nothing to offer," then we will believe we have nothing to offer.

A couple years ago, I went to a horse show, & I got to go *"backstage"* to see some of the riders & the horses. I had never been up-close to a horse before, & I was blown away by the size of them. The closer I (hesitantly) got to them, I noticed something that was very shocking to me. These two-ton animals who are all muscle & more powerful than we can imagine, were tied up to *temporary* fences (not even drilled into the ground) by zip-ties. These horses could have *easily* escaped if they knew how powerful they were. But, they did not even try. *Why?*

There is a Greek word, called "Ochuroma," which describes "a prisoner locked by deception, or bondage" It is also used to describe "a person believing a lie, & not living their life the way that they could." *Does this sound familiar?*

Too many of us are believing the lies that we are telling ourselves – that we are not good enough, that we will never measure up, or amount to anything. Too many of us are talking ourselves out of things we deserve. Too many of us are talking ourselves out of starting, or creating, something we *need* to start, or create. Too many of us are talking ourselves into quitting when things do not seem to go our way. Worse yet, too many of us are talking ourselves out of our dream, & out of our purpose – what we have been called to do.

Every word we speak changes the direction our lives are headed. *Every* word! These words will either put us over in life, or continue to hold us in bondage. Too many of us have been held captive in our circumstances by our own words.

Despite popular belief, we cannot control what our thoughts say – remember, they come & go, just like our feelings & emotions. However, we can control what our mouth says.

The thoughts we have in our mind, will not reach our hearts, unless it goes through our mouths.

We need to be *very* aware of the words we say to ourselves. We need to be careful of what we allow to cross our lips. We need to stop giving power to the negative thoughts we have by agreeing with them by the words we speak. We need to stop describing our problems, & start declaring God's promises over our problems.

We have the authority to reject the negative thoughts we have by speaking *life* & *truth* over them.

The reason why good things happen to confident people & the reason why they always seem to succeed, always seem to date the most attractive people, & always seem to "catch a break," is because of the words they say to themselves. They *never* speak ill-well about themselves. They *never* limit their potential with their confessions. They *never* let failure become final by agreeing with their feelings & emotions. They *never* let their circumstances define who they are by professing them to be true.

Words are the most powerful things in the universe. They are so powerful that God used them to create the Heavens & Earth (Genesis 1:3) to show us how powerful they are. He created man (us) in the image of Him & His likeness, by *speaking* us into existence (Genesis 1:26-27). As a matter of fact, God never does *anything* without *saying* it first. God is a faith God. God released His faith through *words*.

To imitate God, we must talk like him & act like him. Jesus was imitating His Father (God) & was getting the same results as His Father. Jesus always spoke to the problem. More importantly, He spoke the desired results; the end results.
We would be wise to follow His example.

We need to put ourselves in a position to receive God's best for us (that He has promised) by speaking life & *truth*. We must learn to speak faith-filled words to our situations & see our lives transformed. We must learn to confess victory in the face of apparent defeat, & declare abundance in the face of apparent lack. Especially, when we do not feel like it. For as long as we say what we have, we will have what we say (Numbers 14:28). God's Word said so, & He *cannot* lie. How we feel has *nothing* to do with God being truthful.

When we tell ourselves that we are sinners, & that we are unworthy, or no good, who are we praising? It certainly is not God. Saying "I am not good enough" is not humility; it is pride. Pride says, "I can never be like Jesus." Humility says, "it is not about me, it is about Christ in me. Therefore, I can be like Him."

Many things happen to us because we *expect* them to happen a certain way. They happen because we believe it, & we *speak* it until it comes to pass. We fail sometimes because we prepare for failure - We believe it, we speak it, & then, we do it.

This is a *miserable* way to live.

I promise you, it is not the giants in our lives that defeat us. It is not the storms of life that defeat us. It is not the circumstance of our lives that defeat us. It is only *ourselves* that defeat us.

If Jesus said we can have whatever we *say* (Mark 11:23), we are best to believe Him.

I am *begging* you to audit your inner-dialogue, & take control of the words you say. If you want life, start speaking life. If you want abundance, start speaking abundance. If you want confidence, start speaking confidence. If you want victory, start speaking victory. If you want peace, start speaking peace. If you want joy, start speaking joy.

Write these declarations down, & post them everywhere you spend the most time (bedroom, office, work, car, etc.). Speak them *every* day, two to three times per day (morning & night), even, when you do not feel like it. You cannot say them enough.

You are not going to believe them, at first. They are going to make you feel incredibly uncomfortable. It is not going to feel right when you say them. But, *keep saying them!* Eventually, things *will* start to change, & you *will* start to believe what you are saying.

It is going to be hard – one of the hardest things you *need* to do. Especially, if the best example of self-dialogue you have (your parents) have spoken *death* over you & themselves your *entire* life. I know hard it is to love yourself, when your mom hates herself. I know how hard it is to be happy, when your parents are miserable. I know how hard it is to have freedom, when the house you grew up in was oppressed. I know how hard it is to have peace, when your whole life has been turmoil. I know how hard it is to break the chains of bondage, when your parents are the prison wardens.

Let me tell you something you *need* to hear: their life does not have to be your life. Their words do not have to be your words.

You can break a cycle just by changing the words you say.

"Do we *really* want all the negative things we have been saying to ourselves to come true? Because that is *exactly* what is happening."

"The thoughts we have in our minds, will not reach our hearts, unless it goes through our mouths."

@RileyTincher | #PitchingAgainstMyself

CHAPTER 9

YOU'VE GOT THE BALL

Have you ever experienced déjà vu? Have you ever had a feeling of "I have already seen this," or "I swear I have been here before?" Or, an overwhelming feeling of undergoing something strangely familiar? *I have.*

At the beginning of the second semester, of my second year at Whitewater, I moved out of my apartment I had with Zimm.

The month before, he moved to New Jersey to start an internship at a local gym as a Strength & Conditioning coach. How he found the internship, I do not know, but he needed to complete the internship in order to graduate at the end of the semester. Since he moved out, I either needed to move out, as well, or find a new roommate.

It just so happened that a couple of my teammates – our third-baseman (who I shared a birthday with), Nick, & one of the goliath pitchers I talked about it in "I'm Coming Home," Ben – had their roommate move out of their apartment, as well. They needed somebody to fill in his spot, so, I moved in with them.

They lived in a three-bedroom apartment above a bar in downtown Whitewater. I had a great relationship with both of them before I moved in with them, so I was very excited to live with them.

We had a lot of fun living together. When I say a lot... I mean *a lot*. Probably, too much fun. It seemed like every Friday night, right after practice, we would get something to eat & go straight to the bars. Then, we would follow it up again the next night.

Since we lived downtown, it was a "great" excuse for me to let go of all responsibilities, & get as drunk as possible. It was also *very* easy to get drunk as possible, because *every* bar I went to, I got free drinks.

This was also the time when my promiscuity started. At the beginning, it was just something fun to do, & then it became a game. Sometimes, it was the only reason why I went out. It seemed like every weekend there was a different girl. I did not care about who they were, who they had already been with (or who they currently were with), or what it was that they wanted. It was about what *I* wanted, & I wanted just one thing from them, & if they did not give it to me, I would move on to the next one. *It was terrible.* I would lie for personal gain. I broke hearts for selfish reasons.

This was a time in my life that I look back at in regret. I had no consideration for anyone else (especially, girls) but myself. The worst part was, my behavior was applauded. The more drunk I got, the more popular I thought I became. The more girls I slept with, the more of a man I thought I was. Sure, I have a lot of funny stories to share about those night, but I wish I did not remember them, because I *hate* reliving them in my mind.

PLANS CHANGED

There is a reason why I have written "my *first* year at Whitewater," & "my *second* year at Whitewater," instead of writing "my *junior* year at Whitewater," & "my *senior* year at Whitewater." When I transferred to Whitewater, I thought I was transferring in as a junior. With that being said, I thought my second year at Whitewater was my senior year. That was until about two weeks before the season, when I received a phone call from Coach Vo.

We had a player on our team, who had transferred from two different schools, played during the 2008 season, but became ineligible for the 2009 season, & was forced to sit out. Since year after the 2009 season was his sixth year of school, he could not participate in anything with the team until the second semester; because eligibility for Division III schools is given by semesters (every student-athlete is allowed ten semesters to participate in athletics). Since he was older than everyone else on the roster, the NCAA audited our eligibility. Unfortunately, he came back as ineligible.

That is not the reason why Coach Vo called me.

The first thing he said when I picked up the phone was "Tinch, I have great news." He went on to explain that when we got our eligibility audited, I came back as a Redshirt Junior. My immediate reaction was, *"How?"* He responded by telling me that I had been redshirted at Lincoln Trail. This added to my confusion even more, because I traveled with the team (even in the postseason), & I pitched during the season. He cleared up my confusion by explaining to me that I had pitched below the minimum inning requirement - ten percent of the season - to *not* receive a redshirt.

Of course, I was excited, but not as much as Coach Vo. I almost felt disappointed, because this would be a great opportunity for anyone else, but I did not feel like it was. I had prepared that entire year as if it were my senior year. I even took pictures with the rest of the seniors for our annual schedule posters, thinking I was a senior. Only to find out that I had another year left to play.

You may be asking yourself "why wouldn't he be excited to get another year of eligibility?"

Playing college baseball (or, *any* college sport) is tough; *especially*, playing for the Whitewater Warhawks. It is a *huge* commitment. It is a full-time job. It requires *a lot* of your time, *a lot* of your physical strength, & a lot of your mental energy. If you are going to play *any* sport in college, you better *love* it. At the time, I did not love baseball, because it continually broke my heart.

When I got the news from Coach Vo, & our phone call ended, the first question that came to my mind was, "do you *really* want to go through *all of this* again?"

I had no idea what I was going to do. I also had no idea what was about to happen to me, & what the upcoming season was going to bring to me.

NEW NUMBER

The day before Opening Day is almost as exciting as Opening Day. The final rosters are set (usually), & everyone on the team is excited for the upcoming season, & all the opportunities it would bring. This day was also the day where all the uniforms & traveling bags were handed out. It was like Christmas morning. However, this year, it was *better* than Christmas morning, because we had brand-new uniforms.

When we walked into the classroom (where we usually met) to have our final meeting before the season, all our bags were spread throughout the room. All our bags were labeled with our number, & since I knew what my number was the year before - #26 - I immediately tried to find my bag. When I found it, & opened it up, I noticed something was wrong – all the shirts in my bag were the wrong size. Shortly after, one of my teammates came up to my bag & told me that it was *his* bag. I was confused, & I jokingly asked Coach Perch, who was also in the room, if this was their way of letting me know I was cut. He laughed. Then, he told me that I had a new number this year, & that I should have checked the roster, before trying to find a bag that was not mine.

When I got to the roster that was posted on the white board in the front of the room, I found my name, & I saw that my new number was #35. At the time, I did not know the significance of it.

I went searching for my *new* bag, & when I found it, I tried everything on to make sure that it all fit.

Around that time, Coach Vo walked into the room. My back was turned toward the door, but I knew he walked in, because the whole room went silent - that is how much respect Coach Vo commanded from the team.

During the meeting, he went over what we were going to do that day at practice, & he also went over the itinerary for the next day (Opening Day) – like, what time we were supposed to be on the bus to leave for Minneapolis, what the schedule was like before the games, what time the games were at, & who we were playing.

When the meeting was over, & everyone headed out to the field house to start practice, Coach Vo had me stay behind. As soon as everyone left the room, & it was just him & I, he asked me if I knew who wore #35 before me. I did not know who wore it, so told him "no," & I asked him who it was. He responded by telling me that it was the Warhawk legend & fellow left-handed pitcher he told me about who won fifteen games in a season who wore it before me. He went on to tell me that he wanted me to wear #35, to remind me every time that I put it on, that I can win fifteen games as well.

What a *great* reminder it was.

THE START

Opening day is an exciting day for *all* baseball players. It does not only symbolize the beginning of the *greatest* time of the year. It also symbolized a clean slate, & a fresh start. What happened the year before no longer matters. This was a chance for all baseball players to start new, to have the baseball season they have always wanted to have, & accomplish things they have always wanted to accomplish.

That opening day, we were scheduled to play one game against the Augsburg College Augies in the Metrodome in Minneapolis, Minnesota, followed by a doubleheader the next day against the Hamline University Pipers.

You may have noticed a common theme that we always began the season in the Metrodome. That is because in the "Great White North," in the middle of March, there is still snow on the ground, which, makes it impossible to play baseball outside. With that being said, the Metrodome became a commodity for all baseball teams in the northern Midwest to use early in the Spring – including the Warhawks.

This year was a bittersweet year to play at the Metrodome, because after the baseball season, they were going to tear it down to build a new baseball stadium, which is now known as Target Field, an *outdoor* stadium.

Why the Minnesota Twins built an outdoor stadium? I do not know – I am sure it is great... *in the summer.*

I had so many great memories playing at the Metrodome. I remember the first time playing there in high school, & the overwhelming awe I had as I walked onto the field of a Major League Baseball stadium for the very first time. I remember looking up at the *white* ceiling & wondering how anyone caught a pop-fly there. I remember the loud echoing sound an aluminum bat hitting a baseball made when the Metrodome was empty. I remember playing the University of Washington Huskies the year before, & our second-basemen leading the game off with a homerun, & how for a moment we thought we could beat a Division I team. I also remember one of those Huskies hitting the *farthest* homerun I had ever seen – it hit the cement foundation of the second level of seating in right-field *so hard* that it bounced all the way back to our first baseman.

We wanted to make sure that we ended our career at the Metrodome & add a few more wins to the memories we had there.

On the bus ride to the Metrodome, there was a very high level of excitement & anticipation among the team. There were movies playing, but hardly anyone was paying attention to them.

There was a lot of hype among team; *a lot* more than the year before, but it was all internal. Since we had finished so poorly the year before, everyone wrote us off. The powers that be selected our conference rivals, the Stevens Point Pointers to be the Conference Champions. It only motivated us even more – we *hated* Stevens Point. Since our best pitcher the year before signed to play professionally, everyone thought our pitching was going to struggle, & that we would struggle to win games because of it. We *believed* otherwise.

We had a Division I transfer come in who was supposed to be a promising right-fielder & quality left-handed bat early in our lineup.

We had a left-handed pitcher transfer in who had all the talent to be a great starter for us. We also had *a lot* of talented freshmen come in & make the roster. Most importantly, we all were healthy… & *eligible.* This meant the return of two of the greatest Warhawk hitters – our centerfielder & our first-baseman - in the history of the program. It was not a matter of whether we were going to be good, or not. It was a matter of how good we were going to be.

The only question mark we had was our pitching; especially, our starting rotation. We had big shoes to fill with our All-Conference left-handed pitcher leaving, & three of our starters the previous year quitting. We had one returning starter – the other goliath, Jason – who was a senior, & was the only certainty in the starting rotation. The other three spots were up in the air. At least, that is what everyone thought… besides me.

There was a third lesson that stood out to me in Gary Mack's book, *Mind Gym*. This lesson was about the power of visualization. In this lesson, Gary Mack talked about Pele's (one of the greatest soccer players of all time) pre-match routine. A large portion of Pele's pre-match routine was visualization. Before every match, he would find a quiet place in the locker room, & grab two towels: one, to put his head on, & the other to cover his face. Then, he would lie down, close his eyes, & begin his "mental rehearsal."

He went through three periods of time in his mind. The first period was him playing soccer as a child, & the freedom & joy he felt learning the skills that would become the hallmark of his career. The second period was a highlight reel of his "greatest hits." He would recall all his greatest goals. He would also recall all the celebrations he had with his teammates, & the *roar* of the crowd after every goal he scored. The third & final period was the near future where he would rehearse his forthcoming match. He would visualize successful passes, & the glorious goals he intended to score. He would try to be as specific & detailed in his mind as possible. He would visualize as if he had already played his forthcoming match, so when the game came, it was like he was already there (déjà vu).

Since Coach Everson instilled the value & importance of preparation in me in high school, I immediately saw visualization as an advantage, & I started implementing visualization back in the fall, as soon as I got done reading *Mind Gym*. I visualized every start I had in the Steak Series – both of which, came to fruition.

When Fall Ball was over, I immediately started "mentally rehearsing" my first start in the season, which I visualized to be Opening Day against Augsburg. I visualized it almost every day for four months. I researched the roster & found out what starters they had from the previous season returning, & whatever holes they had in their lineup, I would fill with younger players that had some playing time, but did not start the year before. I visualized the first pitch of the game – fastball on the outside corner for strike one. Then, I would go through their entire lineup in my head, & the sequences of pitches I would throw to each hitter.

I visualized it so much, that it felt more like a memory to me, than something that I had never experienced before.

Since I was the first one on the bus, I got to choose which seat I wanted to sit in. I chose to sit in the very back (last row) of the bus, by myself, so I could have more privacy to listen to my music, read the Bible, & visualize.

I spent the first hour of the five-hour trip "mentally rehearsing" the Augsburg lineup two more times. When I got done visualizing, I stated reading the Bible. As I was reading, Coach Vo got up from his front row seat, & started walking to the back. I assumed he was walking to the back to go to the bathroom (because that is where it was), so I paid no attention to him.

As I said before, Coach Vo was notorious for not letting anyone know who the starting pitcher was going to be until about an hour (sometimes, less) before the game. So, at this point, *no one* knew who the Opening Day starter was going to be; not even some of the assistant coaches.

When he got to the back of the bus, he tapped my shoulder & signaled for me to take my headphones off. When I did, he asked me how I was feeling, then he told me, "you've got the ball tonight, Tinch." Then, he tossed me a brand-new Wilson a1001 baseball.

Our first-basemen, Jeff Donovan – J-Do, for short - was sitting in the row in front of me, & as soon as he heard Coach Vo tell me that I was the Opening Day starter, he jumped up in his seat & started congratulating me.

Soon after, the whole team joined him in the celebration.

Being the Opening Day starter is a *big* deal. If you are the Opening Day starter, it usually symbolizes that you are the Ace of the staff. I should have been more excited, but I was not, because I *expected* it to happen. I *wanted* the ball. It was what I worked for, since the end of the 2009 season.

After the celebration was over, I put my headphones back in, & pressed play on my "pregame playlist," & got ready for the game.

Fast-forward to the beginning of the first inning. I got done with my "after-warmup prayer," I turned towards home-plate, walked up the mound, covered my face with my glove, & yelled *"this is my f@#%ing game!"* for the first of *many* times that season.

The first hitter stepped into the batter's box. He was a right-handed hitter; just as I had visualized. Our catcher called for a fastball on the outside corner. I went through my windup, & as soon as my fastball released from my hand, déjà vu kicked in. Two pitches later, I struck him out; *just* as I had visualized. The second hitter stepped into the batter's box. He was also a right-handed hitter; *just* as I had visualized. I got him to ground out to our first basemen by swinging *very* late on an inside fastball; *just* as I had visualized. The third hitter stepped into the batter's box, & he was also a right-handed hitter; *just* as I had visualized. I became hysterical. I could not stop laughing. I

195

waved to our catcher to come out to me on the mound, & as soon as he got to me, he asked "what is going on, Tinch?" Then, I asked him, "Am I dreaming? Is this *really* happening?" A huge smirk emerged from behind his mask & he laughed, then said "yes, Tinch, this is *really* happening." Then, he ran back to home-plate.

I should not have done that, because I lost my focus, & I ended up giving up two hits in a row. Before I got back on the mound for the next hitter, I turned toward second base & pointed at the runner on second base & yelled at him: *"you're not f@#%ing scoring!"* Remember, I pitched *angry*, now.

The look on his face said it all – he was in complete shock, probably because no other pitcher has ever said that to him before. Just as I confessed, he did not score, because I got the next hitter out.

As soon as I got back to the dugout, our soft-spoken shortstop who was standing behind the runner on second when I yelled at him, came up to me in the dugout, & said. "you're *crazy*, man. Keep it up."

I ended my Opening Day start with five innings pitched, while giving up five hits, allowing only one run to score, walking three batters (three of the fifteen batters I would walk *all* season), & striking out four. Most importantly, we won 12-2, & our lineup proved to be as great as we had hoped it was going to be.

The joy I felt after the game was indescribable. It was a feeling like "I *finally* made it." It was also redemption for the year before. However, I knew there was more to come, but what that was, I could never have visualized, nor imagined.

KNOWLEDGE APPLIED

What are you expecting for your life? What are you *patiently* expecting for your life? More importantly, what are you *believing* in with expectation?

I believe we are not given *any* opportunities we are not ready for. Although, we may *really* want something to happen, the reason why it has not happened already may be because we may not be ready for it to happen. I would have loved to be the Opening Day starter my first year at Whitewater, but truth be told, I was not ready to be the Opening Day starter. There were *several* adjustments that I needed to make in order to grow, & I also needed to wait my turn.

The problem most of us (*especially*, myself) face is impatience. I am, by far, the most impatient person I know. When my mind is set on accomplishing something, I want it to be accomplished... *yesterday*.

Waiting is hard. Especially, if the thing we are waiting for is nowhere in sight & there are no signs of things getting better.

We have all heard the phrase, *"patience is a virtue."* Yes, it is, but it is also a fruit (as *bitter* as it may be) of the Spirit we all have been given (Galatian 5:22-23). In order for that fruit to come to harvest, we must give up control, & understand that what we want is either going to happen, or it is not going to happen – it is *not* up to us. If it does not happen, there are greater things for us (Isaiah 55:9) – that is *promised* to us. So, either way, it is going to be *great*.

It is good to have plans, & great to follow through with those plans, but ultimately, the Lord directs our steps (Proverbs 16:9).

Understanding God's plan is incredibly difficult. Somedays, it feels like it is impossible to understand. We want so desperately to "know it all," but that will *never* happen. He wants us to *trust* Him. If we knew it all, why would we ever go to Him? Why would we need to follow Him? Why would we want a relationship with Him? What would we need faith for?

The Bible says, "trust in the Lord with *all* your heart, & lean not on your own understanding (Proverbs 3:5)." It does not say, "trust in the Lord after you have figured it all out first."

This is simple to read, & comprehend, but it is not easy *(at all)* to live out. When we understand, that we are not in control, & that in all things He works for the *good* of those who love him (Romans 8:28), practicing patience becomes *easy*.

In all reality, we only have two options: be patient, or quit. What sounds like the better option to you?

Do not get it twisted, though - patience is *not* sitting around waiting for something to happen, or waiting for God to do something (He already has – *He created us*). It is *taking action* without the expectation of immediate success. Also, patience is *not* the ability to wait, it is the attitude we have while we wait.

Immense progress comes from immense patience. The *only* way to progress in anything that we do is to approach *every* day as an opportunity to get better. More importantly, to be better than we were yesterday. Notice how I wrote, "*every* day is an opportunity." Too many of us are waiting for what we think is an opportunity to finally do whatever it is we want to do, but the truth is, *every* day is that opportunity we are waiting for. It is where we are right now.

We cannot control what has happened to us, & we cannot control what will happen in the future. Yesterday is history; we cannot go back & change it. The future is unknown; tomorrow will worry about itself (Matthew 6:34). However, we can control what we do today.
We are the sum total of our todays.

The author, Leonard Ravenhill, once said "the opportunity of a lifetime must be seized within the lifetime of the opportunity." We have an opportunity of a lifetime... *today*. We can take one step forward towards what it is we want to accomplish. If we do not take action, we are going to take this opportunity for granted.

Too many of us are so fixated on who we wish we could be, where we wish we could be, & what we wish we could be doing, that we lose sight of what we can be doing *right now*.

A lot of us see the mountaintop, & it is important *(so important)* to see the mountaintop, because we need to know where we are going, & it is almost impossible to go anywhere we have not seen before. *But,* we also need to see the *steps* to get there. We do not need to see the tenth, the twentieth, the hundredth, or even the second step, we just need to see the *next* step. Every day that passes presents another step for us to take, *only if* we decide to take it.

We must not get ahead of ourselves. We cannot get to the next step, without taking *this* step. We are guided in steps, not leaps & bounds (Proverbs 20:24). There are things we *need* to do today (*this* step), to ensure that we can even get to tomorrow (next step).

What we do today is so important, because we are exchanging a day of our lives for it.

We must stay positive. We cannot take the next step, or see it, if we do not believe it is there. We cannot take the next step, if we do not believe we can take it. A lot of opportunities are missed because we believe we do not deserve it, or we think we are not ready, or we think that it is not the perfect time. The truth is, we will *never* feel ready, & it will *never* be the perfect time.

We must keep moving forward. We cannot get to the next step, if our feet are still on the last step we took. We cannot get to the next step, if we are still thinking, dwelling, or worrying about the last step.

Be careful though, what got us to this step, may not get us to the next step – we must make adjustments along the way.

We must also realize that *nothing* great happens overnight. Anything of significance, or of value, has taken a significant amount of time to manifest. Just because everyone around you seems to be "getting it" before you do, does not mean that you are never going to get it. Their timeline is different than yours.

Good things happen to those who wait. The best things happen to those who do not give up.

"We only have two options: be patient, or quit. What sounds like the better option to you?"

"Good things happen to those who wait. The *best* things happen to those who do not give up."

@RileyTincher | #PitchingAgainstMyself

CHAPTER 10

BIG MO

A s soon as we got back to Whitewater from a *very* successful trip to the Metrodome – which included not just three wins, but three wins by the ten-run rule – my roommates & I *rushed* back to the apartment as fast as we could, so we could go out to the bars *that* night.

We got back from the trip at 1:00 AM on a Wednesday night. When we got to our apartment at 1:10 AM, we did not even bother showering, because we wanted to get to the bar even earlier. We stepped into the bar around 1:20 AM. "Bar time" was at 2:00 AM, so we had about thirty minutes to drink as much as we possibly could.

Since it was a Wednesday night, that meant it was the 'all-you-can-drink" for five dollars night at our favorite bar. We all ordered *buckets* of rum & coke, or whiskey & coke, & by the time "bar time" came around, we all had finished two buckets each. Needless to say, I do not remember the rest of the night.

At the time, I thought I was celebrating my Opening Day start, & our three *huge* wins as a team to start the season, but really, I was fueling my addiction.

This became a part of my routine for the rest of the season. If there was a night that fell after a double-header, & was not forty-eight hours or less before the next game (we had a "forty-eight-hour rule" that meant we could not drink forty-eight hours before *any* games), you better believe I was drinking – even, if that meant going out *alone*.

The worst part was, I actually *believed* that going out, getting drunk, & hooking up with random girls every chance I could, *added* to my success on the field. I started giving myself the same excuses I gave my parents, like, "it's not *that* bad," or "I *only* drink on the weekends," or "I *deserve* to have some fun," or "I'm not as bad as [Insert Name]." I used alcohol & sex as an incentive, or a trophy that I earned after every game I won. The problem was, I kept winning, which only fed that belief even more.

COMPETITIVE SPIRIT

Since all three starters that pitched in the Metrodome during our opening series had *great* starts, the Ace of our staff was still unnamed.

The other two pitchers – the left-handed pitcher who transferred in, Aaron, & one of the goliaths, Jason – had better starts than I had, & as happy as I was for them, I was even more determined to have a better performance than them my next start.

There was a week between the Metrodome games, & when we traveled to Florida for our annual Spring Training trip. During that week, I made sure to beat Aaron & Jason in *everything* we did. Every sprint we ran, I tried to run faster than them. Every bullpen we threw, I tried to throw more strikes than them. Every towel drill we did, I did one more than them.

Aaron was always my throwing partner, & at the end of every throwing progression we had, we followed it up with some form of competition. One of the competitions we had measured accuracy & command. If you threw the ball to your partner's chest, where their glove was set up, you got two points. If they had to move their glove to catch the ball in front of their head, you got one point. If you threw it away (& they were unable to catch it), you lost a point. The first pitcher to score twenty points won, & they had to win by two points.

Every time Aaron & I played, we always went in to "overtime" (over twenty points) to decide who won. Sometimes, we would get into the thirties in points. We would go back & forth, hitting each other in the chest. When it got close to the end, the trash-talk would increase, which only made my focus increase. I hardly ever missed his chest, & it drove him crazy. Eventually, the trash-talk & pressure would get to him, & he would either miss a spot, or throw one away. That entire year, I only lost one game to him. He beat me early in the spring, right around the time of our first official practice with the coaches. I made sure it *never* happened again.

I carried that competitive spirit with me the rest of the season.

Jason & I eventually became the "1-2 punch" in the pitching rotation. I would start game one of the doubleheader (because I needed *a lot* more time to warm up), & he would start game two.

There were several times, I would have one of the best starts of my career, & he would follow it up with a better performance. At one point in the season, he threw a no-hitter against the University of Wisconsin – Stout Blue Devils. As we ran out to the mound to celebrate him, I could not help but be *pissed* that he threw the best possible game a pitcher could throw (besides, a *perfect* game); there was no way I could top his performance.

There was one thing I beat him in, & I will get into that later.

THE PITCHING CHART

The best thing any baseball team could ever have is *not* a loaded batting lineup, a promising pitching rotation, a hall-of-fame coach, or an unstoppable strategy. All those things certainly help teams win championships, but it is always the team with the most *momentum* that wins the championship.

There is a reason why there are so many "Cinderella teams" in baseball (at all levels), that always get hot at the right time & end up making a run for the championship. That reason *is momentum.*

If you have ever watched any collegiate, or professional baseball game, you can see which team has the momentum at any given moment, in every inning. It changes all the time. A team scores three runs in an inning, then all of a sudden, the shortstop makes a diving play, & turns a double play, & the momentum shifts. Or, it is late in the game, & the team that is behind starts scoring runs, to make it a close game, & the closing pitcher comes in & takes all the momentum away. Or, the score is tied, the starting pitcher has been dominating all game long, until he walks the leadoff hitter in the eighth inning. Now, there is a runner on first-base with no outs. The next pitch, he steals second base. Then, the hitter bunts him over to third-base. The next hitter hits a pop-fly to the centerfield, & the runner on third tags up & scores. The momentum the starting pitcher has carried the entire game is completely gone, & *he loses.*

When Coach Vo talked about momentum & the importance of having it with us, he would always portray it as this "big, beautiful lady" (his terms, not mine) who everyone wanted, but no one could keep. Throughout each game, she who would constantly go back & forth from our dugout, to the other team's dugout. The more time she spent in our dugout, the more of a chance we had to win that game. Coach Vo called this big, beautiful lady, "Big Mo."

Being the great coach that he was (& *still* is), he *knew* how to get "Big Mo" into our dugout, & how to keep her in our dugout. He knew that the biggest determining factor for what dugout "Big Mo" was going to be in, was our pitching. So, he & Coach Cally created a pitching chart that had objectives for the pitcher to accomplish every inning of each game.

On this pitching chart, there was a checklist for the following items: first pitch strikes, getting the leadoff hitter out, controlling the running game, not allowing an 0-2 (a count of zero balls & two strikes) hit, throwing a strike in a 2-1 count not giving up a 2-out walk, & putting up a zero the inning after we score.

The most important one of these objectives was putting up a zero the inning after we score, because that *kept* "Big Mo" in our dugout.

Coach Vo rarely said anything to me as I ran out to the mound in between innings. The only time that he would was right after we scored the previous inning; he would always yell, "we need a donut here, Tinch!" – referring to the zero shape most donuts make.

Coach Vo & Coach Cally talked about these objectives in this pitching chart *a lot* (almost *every* practice). Since it was important to them, I made it important to me, & it became my focus. Quite frankly, I became obsessed with this pitching chart. It was the *only* thing I checked after every game.

I am so glad that I did become obsessed with it, because I *quickly* saw the importance of them, & the results that they gave me.

This may come as a shock, but I cared more about checking those objectives off than I did about the "stat-lines" (innings, hits allowed, runs allowed, walks allowed, strikeouts) that I had. I knew that if I accomplished those objectives on the chart, my "stat-lines" would be great. I also knew that if I accomplished those objectives every inning, I would win every game.

Winning was *the most* important thing to me.

CHANGE OF HEART

One day after practice, about a week before the season started, Coach Cally & I had a conversation about the upcoming season. It was one of those conversations a father would have with a son right before the son went to college. It was also one of those conservations one would have someone right before they were about to do something *big & life-changing*. The context of the conversation was basically, "I hope you are ready for what is about to happen."

In this conversation, he wanted to see where my focus was, & what my goals for the season were. I told him I wanted to win fifteen games, & I wanted to win a National Championship. His immediate response was, "*wow*, that is impressive," then he challenged my perspective about goals, & had me shift my focus to the process of the goals, rather than the outcome. He told me that if I focused on the process, & made sure that I was *prepared* for every time I would be called to go out on the mound, that I would win every game I pitched. He used the illustration of a bricklayer building a brick wall.

Bricklayers do not set out to build a wall, they set out to lay one brick at time, until the wall is built. This translated to me that I should not focus put all my focus on winning fifteen games. Instead, I should put all my focus on trying to win every game I was called to pitch, & eventually, I would win fifteen wins.

He also checked my heart, & my intentions. He asked me *why* I had these goals in the first place. I told him what I thought he wanted to hear, & he conveyed that he thought me wanting to win fifteen games was for selfish reasons. He was right. He said, "instead of telling me first that you wanted to win a National Championship, you told me you wanted to win fifteen games." Then, he asked me, "which one do you want most?" I did not know how to respond, so I did not. He continued, "let me ask you a better question: If we won a National Championship, & you did not win fifteen games, would you be ok with that?" I emphatically said *"yes!"* Then, he asked, "How about if you won fifteen games, but we did not win a National Championship, would you be ok with that?" My instant reaction in my head was another emphatic *"yes!"* But, I did not say it, because I knew it was the wrong answer. My heart sunk deep in my chest, & I felt like he punched me right in the gut, & I asked myself, "how *selfish* could you be?" He saw how bothered I became by his questions, & he said, "If you give your team the best chance to win *every* time you go out to the mound to pitch, you can accomplish *both* goals."

THE ACE

The pitching chart was not the only thing I became obsessed with.

Before the season began, I would watch videos of Rogers Clemens & Andy Pettitte working out. In these videos, they both talked about the value of preparation, & Roger Clemens said, "the *only* easy day a pitcher should have is the day they start."

I also read an article about 2x-Cy Young Award winner, Roy Halladay, & how he prepared for each start. This article went into great detail about what he would do each day in between starts. In the article, he was quoted to say:

"Preparation is the *foundation* of my career. If I do every single thing necessary – the workouts, the conditioning, the long toss, the arm care, & the bullpens - in preparation for my next start, I can go into that day with 100% confidence knowing that I am *ready* to pitch again."

That entire offseason, I spent a significant amount of time creating a list of what I would do in between starts. I had a list of things I would do before in between my starts at NIACC, & my starts during the summer. However, I felt like I needed to make them better, because they got me to where I was, & I was not satisfied with where I was. So, I took some things from the videos of Roger Clemens & Andy Pettitte working out, & added it to my list. Then, I took some things from the article about Roy Halladay, & added it to my list, as well. It is impossible to know if something works, if it is not applied.

Once the practices started in the spring, I would try my best to apply this list in between our bullpens & live-matchups – because I treated these bullpens & live-matchups like they were my starts in the season. What made this extremely difficult to do was that I had to work around what we were doing at practice – which, we never knew what we were doing until the day of practice.

There was one thing Roy Halladay did during Spring Training, that I regretfully applied to list of things to do. He would lift heavy legs right before his starts in Spring Training, to get his legs ready for the regular Season. On the first day we started throwing live-matchups, I decided to try it myself. I lifted *very* heavy, & I threw a great bullpen. I was feeling pretty good, until we had to do conditioning that day, & my legs stopped working... *literally*. I started cramping in my calves & my hamstrings, & I could not move. To make matters worse, I could hardly get out of bed the next morning. Needless to say, I never lifted heavy legs before I pitched ever again.

When the season started, & my Opening Day start was finished, I *finally* got a chance to apply this list of things to do before my next start. The next game was in Florida against the Hope College Dutchmen, & I got the ball to start.

We won that game 5-2, & my "stat-line" was as good as my Opening Day start, but something felt *off*. I was disappointed. I walked two hitters that game, & I felt out of control. So, I took some things out of my list, & tried some different things.

Then, a wrench was thrown into my preparation plans; I was asked to come into the game in relief against the Salem State Vikings *two* days later. Even though, my arm was still sore from my previous start, & I was not mentally prepared to pitch that day, I came in & threw a great inning to close out the game.

Then, another wrench was thrown into my preparation plans.

The next day, one of the goliath pitchers, & my roommate, Ben – the one with the *hardest* fastball I have ever seen – started against the Washington & Jefferson College Presidents. The first inning, he walked the first two hitters he faced, then we committed an error, & he proceeded to give up four runs before the inning was over, which resulted in his start being over.

Guess who came in to relieve him? *Me.*

I was just as shocked as you probably are right now. I was scheduled to start two days later against this same team, & given the fact that I pitched the day before, I assumed I had absolutely *no* chance of pitching that day; I actually had my turf shoes on, instead of my cleats, so when he called my name, I had to rush to get my cleats on.

I should have known by then that *nothing* is written in permanent marker by Coach Vo.

The tone of the game was already set, so when I came in, I knew I was going to be in a fierce battle to get Big Mo back into our dugouts, & keep her there. The entire game was back & forth. We would score a run, then they would score a run. We would commit an error, then they would commit an error. In the six innings I pitched that game, I only had one inning that was clean – meaning, no hits, no walks, & no errors. It was the most challenging game I ever pitched.

Speaking of challenging, I intentionally walked a hitter for the first time (& *only* time) in my career, that game. I *hated* every pitch of it.

When Coach Vo came out to the mound to tell the catcher & I that we were going to intentionally walk the next hitter, I responded with, *"are you f@$%ing kidding me?"*
Remember, I pitched *angry*.

That anger turned into nervousness as soon we started the intentional walk. I was actually more nervous throwing that intentional walk than I was the entire rest of the game. I was so nervous that I almost threw a strike on the second pitch.

We ended up winning that game 12-8, & I learned two things that game: 1) Be prepared for anything to happen – meaning, be prepared to pitch *every* game. 2) I can handle *a lot* more adversity than I thought I could. Actually, I performed *better* when I had adversity – a runner on base – than when I did not.

That game also solidified my spot as the *Ace* of the staff. More importantly, it showed Coach Vo that he could rely on me *whenever* he needed me to pitch – It was the trust I had *desperately* wanted since I came to Whitewater.

We only had one game left for the remainder of our Spring Training trip, & I finally got the rest I needed.

Thanks to the wonderful family of our third-basemen, & my roommate, Nick, I went to Disney World for the first time in my life, & I had a *blast*. I felt like a child again. However, the thought that kept popping up in my mind the entire time we were there was: "I wish my family was here to experience this with me."

When we got back from Florida, we had two days before our Home Opener against the Ripon College Redhawks. The day after we got back, we had completely off to rest. The next day we were asked to come to Prucha field to lay more sod. This time, we were laying sod from the gate entrance to the back of the stands; it was *a lot* of sod. This was another wrench thrown in my preparation plans.

Just like every other hard, physical labor job Coach Vo asked us to do, we all hated it while we were doing it. But, as much as we hated it, it brought us all together, & it showed us that if we work together, we could accomplish *anything*.

There were two special surprises at the field that day to give us a little bit of joy while we worked. The first surprise was, our gate entrance was completed – the same brick that was used to build the backstop wall was used to build the entrance; it was *beautiful*. There was also a huge steel-cut Warhawk logo that was screwed into the wall of the entrance; it was also *beautiful*.

The second surprise was, our bathrooms & showers in our clubhouse were completed.

While we were laying sod, Coach Vo asked me to come into the clubhouse to meet with him. When I got into the clubhouse, I met him in our locker room. The first thing he said to me was something I had wanted to hear for *so long;* it was music to my ears. He said, *"I am proud of you."* Then, he told me that I would be starting game one of the doubleheader of the Home Opener the next day.

This game was very important to me, because Ripon had recruited me *heavily* out of high school, & I became very close with the assistant coach (now, head coach), Eric Cruise. Coach Cruise was from my hometown, & he always worked Coach Everson's baseball camps. *Every* time I saw him at the camps, he made it a point to come say "hi" to me & ask me how I was doing.

Of all the colleges & universities that recruited me, Ripon College was by far the hardest one to turn down, because I had a *very* difficult time telling Coach Cruise that I was not going to go there. He spent so much time recruiting me. I *hated* letting him down.

The worst part is, I did not let him down once. I let him down *twice*.

The next day was *cold* – thirty-seven degrees Fahrenheit cold. This weather is a great advantage for pitchers, because it makes the hitter's hands cold. When the hands are cold, it becomes incredibly hard to hit a baseball without the hands *stinging*, so it creates a hesitancy among most hitters to even swing the bat.

As I was warming up, I noticed another lefty warming up for Ripon, & he looked strangely familiar. I asked Coach Cally who was throwing for them, & he looked at Ripon's lineup & said "Dwyer" – The last name of who I thought it was.

Matt Dwyer pitched against me in high school for one of our rival schools. My senior year, he was always in the headlines, & it drove me crazy. As a matter of fact, he threw a no-hitter against us that season, & he was on *every* news channel that night. I was jealous.

Hearing his name only added fuel to my fire. I wanted to make sure that history was reversed, & that he remembered my name as much as I remembered his name.

That day, I threw my first complete game of the season against him. On top of that, our hitters drove in six runs against him, & we ended up winning the game 11-1.

After the game, I passed Coach Cruise in the line when we shook hands, & he stopped me to hug me, & in his raspy voice, he said, "you've come a *long* way, Tinch. The conference is *yours* to take. Go get 'em!" That is *exactly* what I did.

Four days later, I was back on the mound to start against the Marian University Sabres. I got hit around that game (& that is an understatement), giving up twelve hits in six innings, but we won, & that is all that matters.

MY ROUTINE

My next start was in eight days against the University of Wisconsin – Platteville Pioneers. Playing the Pioneers meant the start of the WIAC schedule.

At this point in the season, I was experiencing *"dead arm"* (which, I will explain later), so eight days of rest was much needed.

This was also a great time for me to get back into finalizing & perfecting my list of things to do in between starts.

Eight days later, when I got on the mound against Platteville, I felt the greatest I had ever felt on the mound before. I had excellent command of all four of my pitches, I was the most focused I had ever been, & I *quickly* got into rhythm (*a lot* quicker than usual).

We were up ten runs going into the sixth inning, so Coach Vo switched out our starting catcher, Robby Coe, for another catcher. I also had a no-hitter going into the sixth inning. Since the "ten-run rule" goes into effect after the 7th inning is complete, I only needed six outs to complete the no-hitter.

If you know anything about baseball, you know that you should *never* mess with a pitcher during his no-hitter. Pulling his catcher from the game is like breaking the law. Sure enough, with two outs in the sixth inning, the no-hitter was broken up by a single to centerfield. I do not want to blame Coach Vo, but…

The beginning of the Conference schedule meant it was going to be a *consistent* schedule for the rest of the season (barring weather postponements & cancellations) – Doubleheaders on Wednesdays, Saturdays, & Sundays.

Since I had felt the best I had ever felt before, pitching against Platteville, I decided that my list of things to do between starts was finally *perfect,* & I did not need to mess with it.

For the rest of the season, I did the same *exact* things, at the same *exact* times, *every single day.* I *never* wavered. I became so consistent with it that my coaches & teammates would know *exactly* where I was, & what I was doing at any given moment throughout each day.

Some of my teammates called it "superstition." Some called it "perfectionism." Some called it "obsessive compulsive disorder," or OCD, for short. Some called it *"crazy."* I called it *"my routine."*

I knew that every week, I would start the first game of the double-header on Wednesday, start again the first game of the double-header on Saturday, pitch in relief, or come in to close a game on Sunday, then, do it all over again the next week.

Since I had *three* days (sometimes, less) in between starts, what I did right after my start & the two days that followed were *absolutely critical* for me to be ready & healthy for my next start.

The following is a *very* detailed account of the list of things I would do in between starts - starting immediately after my start on Saturday & going all the through my next start on Wednesday. For the sake of making this easier to understand, let's just say both starts are at home in Whitewater:

After My Start - I would go right into the clubhouse, to take my cleats off, & put my turf shoes on. Then, I would go back out to the dugout to have Chad (our athletic trainer) put four bags of ice on my arm - two on the front & back my shoulder, & two on the front & back of my elbow. While I sat in the dugout icing my arm, I would "debrief" with Coach Cally & we would go over the pitching chart together - he would tell me what he saw, then he would often make suggestions of adjustments I needed to make for the next game. As soon as I got done icing my arm for twenty minutes, I would go back into the clubhouse to put a compression sleeve on over my elbow to prevent as much swelling as possible, so I could pitch the *next* day.

In Between Games – I would grab a tamp, a rake, & a bag of clay, & repair our pitching mound. *No one* was allowed to touch the mound besides myself & the other goliath pitcher, Jason. Ownership was a *very* big deal to me, & I was *proud* of that mound.

After the Second Game of the Doubleheader – I would go back into the clubhouse to text Coach Everson to let him know how my start went & whether we won, or not. If my mom was *not* at the game, then I would go for a run on the same three-mile route I *always* ran around campus. If my Mom *was* at the game, then I would go outside of the clubhouse to say "hi" to her, & maybe go out to dinner with her (if she had time). Then, I would go back to the field to run. That night, when I got back to the apartment, I would ice my arm again for twenty minutes. After icing, I would put the compression sleeve back on my elbow, & I kept it on until the next morning when I woke up.

Sunday – As soon as I woke up, I would clean my cleats & my turf shoes with *scrubbing bubbles*, while I listened to my "pre-game playlist" – which consisted of: *Trying To Find A Balance* by Atmosphere, *Dani California* by The Red Hot Chili Peppers, *Moment 4 Life* by Nicki Minaj, *Soundtrack To My Life* by Kid Cudi, *I'm a King* by T.I., & *Forever* by Drake. After I got done cleaning my cleats & turf shoes, I would drive up to Prucha Field an hour before we took batting practice, so I could run tempo sprints along the warning track of the outfield for twenty minutes. During batting practice, I would listen to my "pregame playlist" again. After batting practice, I would throw *light* long toss (also known as "airing it out"), where I would throw at about seventy percent until I reached a distance of about two-hundred feet. After "airing it out," I would go back into the clubhouse to put on my compression sleeve. Then, I would sit in my locker & visualize myself coming into the game in relief that day, for twenty minutes. *If* I came in to pitch that day, I would ice my arm again, & after the game, I would run the same route I ran the day before.

Monday – After classes, I would go to the weight room to foam roll, stretch out, & do a *light* lower body workout for about an hour. After my workout, I would go to the trainer's room to do contrast therapy – where I switched back & forth from a cold tub to a hot tub for five minutes each, for a total of thirty minutes. After the contrast therapy, I would get a deep tissue massage in my arm, shoulder, & upper back from Chad. After the massage, I would head out to Prucha field about an hour before practice, & I would run fifteen one-hundred-fifty foot sprints – all as fast as I could. Then, I would throw long toss from foul pole to foul pole; just like I did in the summer. That night, after practice, I would do an hour of Yoga, followed by thirty minutes of visualization of my start on Wednesday.

Tuesday – After classes, I would go to the trainer's room to do contrast therapy again, followed by arm care work (rotator cuff exercises with light dumbbells & bands). Then, I would head out to Prucha Field an hour before practice to do twenty ninety-foot sprints – all as fast as I could. After sprints, I would throw a 50-pitch "flat-pen" (bullpen on flat ground). After practice, I would go back to the trainer's room to ice my arm while I did stim therapy. That night, I would do my laundry & clean *all* my uniforms & under garments (we had a laundry service, but I liked doing it myself). While I would wait for the washer to get done, I would call my mom to let her know (even, if she was not going to be there) what time the games started the next day. When the laundry got done, I would neatly fold uniform & under garments, & put them on top of my travel bag, which was right next to my bed. To relax, I would play one game of MLB 2K10 on my Xbox 360. After the game, I would visualize the entire lineup of the team I was going to pitch against the next day.

This is where it gets *even more* detailed.

Wednesday (The Next Start) – As soon as I woke up, I would clean my cleats & my turf shoes while I listened to my "pregame playlist." After that, I would put on my entire uniform, minus my jersey top. Then, I would drive to the field, in *silence*, & I would park in the same parking spot I would *always* park in - one time, one of our freshman pitchers parked in *my* spot, & I had him move his car. When I got to my locker in the clubhouse, I would unpack my bag, & neatly arrange everything in my locker. Then, I would send a text to one of my friends who came to a lot of my starts & this text would always say the same thing (even, if he was not going to be at the game): "Game is at [insert time] in [insert city], see you there. Wish me luck!" After I sent the text, I would put on my jacket (even, if it was warm outside), grab my iPod, & head out to right field for batting practice. During batting practice, I would listen to my "pregame playlist" one last time. Then, I would head back into the clubhouse to put my jersey top on, & put on cleats. At exactly an hour before the game, I would find my bullpen catcher, Brandon Egnarski – "Eggy," for short - & tell him "heading out to warmup, I need you in about 15 minutes" Then, I would head down to the bullpen to start warming my body up. I would start my warmup by jogging out to center fielder. When I got to centerfield, I would tap the centerfield sign three times, & say a prayer as I ran back to the bullpen. Then, I would do the same stretches & the same amount of stretches. After stretching out, I would run ten short sprints. Right around that time, the bullpen catcher made his way out to me. When I had two sprints left, & I would tell him *"two sprints, Eggy."* After those two sprints, him & I would throw long toss until I got to about one-hundred-twenty feet away from him. Then, I would work my way back to him, & when I got to about forty-five feet away from him, I would throw a twenty pitch flatpen - same pitch sequence *every* time. By that time, Coach Cally was out there with us, & we would all head into the bullpen to start throwing off the mound. Coach Cally never said anything to me, but he was there, & that meant *a lot* to me. When I pitched off the mound, I had the same pitch sequence in the windup & in the stretch *every single time.* After I got done with my pitch sequence, Robby (our starting catcher) would come down to the bullpen, & we would face three *imaginary* hitters together; this was so he could see how each of my pitches looked (how they moved & how hard they were) that day. When the bullpen was over, Eggy was always the first to come up to me with a first bump, & he would say *"Have a day, Tinch."* Then, we all would head back into the dugout together to start the game.

That was only the beginning.

Before the game started, I would pace back & forth in the dugout like a caged lion. As soon as my name was called by our announcer, Tommy, I would sprint out to the back of the mound, where I met

Robby & J-Do to stand next to them during the National Anthem. I *loved* hearing the crowd cheer as I sprinted out to the mound.

During the National Anthem, I would say a prayer, then, I would begin to pump myself up by closing my eyes, taking deep breaths, & swaying back & forth.

To this day, no other song pumps me up more than the National Anthem. I cannot listen to it & not get goosebumps all over my body. I cannot hear it & not feel like my heart is beating out of my chest.

After the National Anthem was over, I would get on the mound & throw the same exact sequence of seven warmup pitches. Then, Robby would throw down to second, & the entire infield gathered together in a huddle, & we would all say something I cannot put in this book.

Once we broke out of the huddle, I would turn my back to home-plate, tuck my chin under my jersey, say another prayer, turn around, walk up the mound, cover my mouth with my glove, & yell *"this is my f@#%ing game!"* Then, it was time for the first inning.
My routine is *still* not over.

When the inning was over, I would run back to the dugout, where I was greeted by all my teammates. When I got to *my* spot in the dugout, I took a deep breath, set my glove down, & set my hat down on top of my glove. Then, I would sit down & wrap my entire left arm - from shoulder to wrist - with a towel, & put my jacket on over it, to keep my arm warm. The only people I would talk to in the dugout were Coach Cally & Robby, & that was only if I had something to say, or they had a suggestion of an adjustment we needed to make.

As soon as we got two outs, I would stand up, take my jacket & towel off, & set them on *my* spot. Then, I would grab my hat & start rubbing my thumb over the word "4UKING" that I wrote in sharpie underneath the bill of all my hats & on the outside heel of all my cleats & turf shoes. While I did this, I would say another prayer.

When the third out was made, I would sprint back out to mound. When I got to the mound, I would "fix" the mound with my cleats by

filling in any divots that were made by the other team's pitcher during the previous inning. When Robby got out to his position to catch, I would throw the same sequence of seven warmup pitches that I always threw. Then, he would throw down to second base, I would say my prayer, & yell *"this is my f@#%ing game!"* all over again.
I am not making this stuff up. This was my *real* routine.

I did *every little* detail of that list (& then some) for the remainder of the season, & the remainder of my career.

If something took me away from "my routine," it gave me a ton of anxiety (so, maybe it was a sign of OCD). Or, if, heaven forbid, someone tried to break me of my routine right before the game, or during the game, I would get *pissed*, & I would lash out.
The veterans of the team knew not to talk to me on game day.

For the remainder of the regular season, I won *every* game I started, because I won every game before the first inning even started.

I do not think it is a coincidence that focusing on the process - laying down one brick at a time - turned one win in to five wins in a row, which turned into eleven wins in a row.

I do not think it is a coincidence that doing *every* little thing right, to the best of my abilities, made "Big Mo" & I best friends.

KNOWLEDGE APPLIED

Momentum does not just happen. It does not appear out of nowhere. It certainly does not happen because we hope for, or wish it to happen. It is *created* by action & execution, not ideas, or thoughts. Action leads to movement, & movement leads to momentum. More importantly, it is created by doing the little things right, *all the time*. When we do this, we *always* put ourselves in a position to succeed. Ideas are great, but execution *always* wins!

Our level of success is not determined by our talent, or our strengths, or our smarts, it is determined by our discipline. With discipline, almost anything is possible. Discipline creates freedom.

Without discipline, there is distraction. Without discipline, there is discouragement. Without discipline, there is dismay. Without discipline, there is disappointment.

Discipline is *always* required.

Discipline is doing what we *need* to do – *especially,* when we do not feel like doing it - in order to get to where to want to go. Anyone can do something when they *feel* like it. It is the person who does what needs to be done even when they do *not* feel like doing it, who are the most successful.

All of us have to do things we do not feel like doing.

Jim Rohn, a best-selling author & motivational speaker, once said: "everyone must choose between one of two pains: the pain of discipline, & the pain of *regret*. Discipline weigh ounces, regret weigh tons." Pain is unavoidable. The question is not *if* we will experience pain in our lives (because, we *will*). The question is *how much* pain we will experience. The pain of discipline & the pain of regret are choices we cannot escape. The great news is, the pain of discipline is temporary. However, the pain of regret is *forever*.

We all have to pay the price of pain. We can either pay the much cheaper price now (the pain of discipline), or we can pay the infinitely more expensive price later (the pain of regret).

What would you rather have: Short-term pain for long-term value? Or short-term value for long-term pain?

Dreams *never* come true without discipline & consistency.

We are *never* responsible for the outcome; the outcome is a by-product, & it is out of our control. We are responsible to the obedience & discipline of the process. We must fall in love with the process without being emotionally-attached to the outcome.

What is the process? Doing the little things right… *all the time!*

The Navy SEALs, who I hold near & dear to my heart (because of my best friend in high school), have a quote that says, "there are two ways to do something: the right way, & *again.*"

Consistency separates the good from the great.

Do you want to be good enough? Or do want to be great?

To be great, we must focus on the process of what it takes to be great, not on the outcome of greatness.

The process is fearless.

When we focus on taking care of the little things, the big things take care of themselves. When we focus on taking care of the seconds (*this pitch*), the minutes (getting *this* hitter out), & hours (having a scoreless inning) in a day (winning the game), will take care of itself.

On the other hand, when we focus on the outcome, we become anxious, & we stress out. When we focus on the outcome, we become impatient, & we start to look for short-cuts (even though, they do not exist). When we focus on the outcome, we sacrifice the quality of our work, & that ultimately, changes the outcome.

The *greatest* coach of all-time, John Wooden, once said, "if you do not have time to do it right, when will you have time to do it over?"

Everything we do matters. From being on time, to cleaning up after ourselves, to being honest, to paying attention to the details, to being coachable, to having a great attitude, to doing more than what is required... it *all* matters.

Everything is practice. *Everything* is practice for what is to come. *Everything* is practice for achieving what we desire to achieve. *Everything* is practice for becoming who we are called to be.

How we do anything is how we do everything.

"We are *never* responsible for the outcome; it is out of our control. We are responsible to the obedience & discipline of the process."

"*Everything* is practice. How we do anything is how we do *everything*."

@RileyTincher | #PitchingAgainstMyself

CHAPTER 11

TURN THE PAGE

N ow that the regular season was over, it was time to shift gears in to the postseason. This was my first postseason with Whitewater as a starter. This was my first postseason as the *Ace* of any pitching staff... ever. This was my first *real* chance to carry my team to a National Championship.

The first step of the postseason journey towards going to the World Series was the Conference Tournament, & we had eight days to prepare for it.

After our final regular season game against the Concordia University Falcons (which, was on a Thursday night), we took the remainder of the weekend off, for much needed rest. That night, I broke my routine.

I came in to close the last inning of the second game. Since I pitched, I normally would run the same route I always ran after every game I pitched in. However, this game ended late, & it was the first "Thirsty Thursday" we could have "celebrated" all season. So, in my mind, I could not miss it – Or, I should say, I *did not want to* miss it. My priorities changed.

Instead of going for a run, & I went right back to the apartment, & got ready to go out that night.

I got so drunk that night, that I was hungover the *entire* next day. I did not get out of bed until late in the afternoon. When I finally got out of bed, I drove to the house I grew up in & spent the rest of my weekend there.

I did not do *anything* that weekend. I laid around the house watching movies, playing video games, & hanging out with my friends the *entire* weekend. I made up my mind that I would start day one of my routine on Monday, in order to get ready for my start on Friday – the first round of the Conference Tournament.

I wasted three days, that I could have used to prepare.

The *greatest* threat to future success is current success. Success creates a sense of pride, & pride leads to complacency.

The next week was finals week, so we practiced late every night.

Earlier that week, during one of our practices, we were doing bunt coverages as a team, & like always, I was at the front of the line. When I got up to the mound, I did what I *always* did whenever I was on the mound (in practice, or in a game) - I came set, took a deep breath, checked the runner, then threw the pitch for the drill. After I threw the pitch, Coach Vo stopped the practice. He walked up the mound, & stood next to me, & asked the team, "do you know why Tinch has won eleven games this season?" After a short pause, & no response, he said, "because he takes *everything* we do seriously, & he views *every* practice we have, & *every* drill we do as a chance to get better."

He was absolutely right.

I can proudly say that *every* time I stepped on the baseball field, I *never* went through the motions. I was not there to check mark a box, & say "I practiced today." I was not there because I *had* to be there. I *loved* practice. I was there because I *wanted* to be there. I was there because I wanted to get better, & get closer to my dream of being a professional baseball player.

This may be hard to believe, but I did know I had won eleven games that regular season, until Coach Vo announced it to the entire team. I knew I had won every start I had, but I did not know that the number of wins I had was *eleven.* Honestly, it came as a shock to me.

Like I said before, the only thing I checked after every game was the pitching chart. I stayed away from statistics, blogs, & message boards, because I knew it was a trap. I also knew that if I fell into it, I would become obsessed with it, & it would shift my focus from the process (my routine) to the outcome. I also knew that would take my heart away from what I *really* wanted to accomplish that season – winning a National Championship.

GET OUT OF HERE!

The day before the Conference Tournament, we had a meeting in the dugout before practice. We were all sitting in the dugout waiting, when Coach Vo walked out of the clubhouse. He was holding a piece of paper in his hand, & he started reading off it - It was a list of players who had won All-Conference awards.

Apparently, he had just gotten back from the WIAC coaches meeting where votes were made on who won each award.

We had ten players total, who were either First- or Second-Team All-Conference – the most of *any* team in the WIAC; the next closest team was Stevens Point with seven players.

As he was reading each name, we would clap & holler for every player named.

Then, he got to the major announcements – the coach of the year, the position player of the year, & the pitcher of the year. Of course, he skipped over that he had won the Coach of the Year award, & went straight to announcing that the shortstop for Stevens Point won Position Player of the Year. We all knew he deserved it (he led the conference in batting average, hits, & doubles), but we "booed" anyway. After we got done "booing," Coach Vo said, "last, but not least, the Pitcher of the Year is… Riley Tincher." As soon as he said my name, the whole dugout went nuts, & started spraying their water bottles all over me – like the scenes you see in the clubhouses of MLB teams of the players spraying each other with Champagne after they won the World Series. It was one of the greatest moments – if not, *the* greatest moment - of my entire career.

The next day was day one of the WIAC Conference Tournament. We entered the tournament as the #1 seed, because we were the regular season Conference Champions. Since we were the #1 seed, the tournament was held at Whitewater. As a matter of fact, we hosted the Regional Tournament, as well. So, the road to the World Series went through Whitewater… talk about home-field advantage.

At the time, we were the #1 team in the country with a record of 35-4. Stevens Point was the #2 seed in the tournament, & #27 team in the country with a record of 27-13. Platteville was the #3 seed in the tournament with a record of 22-18.

Since we were the #1 seed, we got to sit out the first game of the tournament. The first game was Stevens Point vs. Platteville, & Steven Points crushed them 17-6. This sent a message to us that they were not just there to win, they were there to *humiliate* everyone they played. They *scared* me.

Waiting for the first game to end, threw another wrench into my routine. I never started the second game of a double-header *all* season. I was used to being able to take my time doing my own thing before the game. Since there was a short period of time between the first & second game, I had to rush through my whole routine.
I *absolutely hate* being rushed, in anything I do.

When I finally got out to the field to start warming up, Coach Vo did something he had never done before – He walked out to me to wish me luck. Most people would have loved that their head coach would do that, but I am not most people. It pissed me off. I thought, "he has never done that before. Why would he do that *now?*" I was so angry that I could not even think straight the rest of the warmup. Coach Cally tried several times to settle me down, to no avail.

I took this anger with me into the game. Everything was going just fine, & I was able to control this anger until the second inning when I gave up a homerun to the leadoff hitter, & I totally derailed. My anger turned into *rage*.

Over the next four innings I pitched, I allowed eight more runs to score. I also gave up three walks (which, I had not done since my

Opening Day start). Worse yet, I could not field my position (a sign of things to come) - I allowed not one, not two, not three, but *four* base hits off bunts that should have been *easy* outs.

We lost that game 15-7.

I do not want to blame Coach Vo for that loss, but…

Up until that point in my Warhawk career, I had not lost a single game. In fact, it had been almost two years since my last loss at NIACC. I honestly did not remember what defeat felt like, but Stevens Point was quick to remind me. They gave me the worst beating of my career. It seemed like every pitch I threw found the barrel of *every* Stevens Point hitter's bat.

Everyone was shocked, including myself. I *never* lost, not even when I pitched against Stevens Point earlier in the season. Everyone was counting on me, the Conference Pitcher of the Year that they honored before the game, to win that game, to take us into the Conference Championship the next day. I felt so embarrassed.

Instead, we had to play again an hour later against Platteville in an elimination game. Fortunately, Aaron pitched a great game, & we won 14-0; eliminating Platteville from the tournament.

After the game, I made sure to *not* skip my run. This run was a little different than all the other runs - I cried the *entire* time I was running. I often used these runs to reflect on the game that I just pitched – going through every inning, every batter, every pitch in my head – but on this run, all I could think about was how I let my coaches & my teammates down, & how I let our fans down.

I let out *all* my emotions.

There were times during the run that I was so angry, it caused me to run so fast that it felt like I was sprinting. There were times when I felt so sad & defeated, that I could not see in front of me because tears covered my eyes.

When I got back to Prucha Field from my run, I did not feel like I was done, so I ran the route again. When I got back the second time, I still did not feel like I was done, so I ran the route *again… & again*. I ended up running the route four times before I was done. I was so exhausted, that I could hardly pick my feet up as I walked to my car.

The next day, I woke up feeling the same anger & disappointment I felt the day before. When I got to the field, I did not want to get out of my car, because I did not want anyone to see me. When I finally mustered up the courage to get out of my car, Aaron pulled up beside me & walked in with me. He asked me how I was feeling, & I jokingly asked him "how do you think I feel?"
I always masked my pain with humor.

We continued walking, & I told him, "I hope I do not have to pitch today against them, they *own* me." He stopped dead in his tracks, & turned to me & said: "Do not say that. Today is a new day. Yesterday was just one bad start… *everyone* has one. That does not mean you will never win again." He started walking away, then he stopped & turned to me again & said, "We *still* need you, Tinch."

Since the Conference Tournament was double elimination, we had to beat Stevens Point twice that day, in order to win the Conference Tournament.

The first game was a nail-biter. We were down 2-1 throughout the entire game, until the top of the eighth inning, when our bats came alive & we scored four runs. Then, Ben, came in, in the bottom of the eighth inning to close out the remainder of the game. We ended up winning 5-3, which sent us into the Conference Championship game.

In the second game (the Conference Championship game), we scored three runs in the first two innings. Our starting pitcher, J-Do, was cruising, with only one hiccup in the fifth inning, when he gave up two runs. We scored three more runs in the 7th inning. When J-Do went out for the eighth inning, he started getting a little bit wild, walking the first batter he faced, then throwing two wild pitches. As soon as the second wild pitch was thrown, Coach Vo turned to the end of the dugout, locked eyes with me, & said "Tinch, go warm up." I did not have time to think. I took my jacket off, grabbed my glove, & ran down to the bullpen as fast as I could. As I was running, I could hear Coach Vo yelling *"hurry up, Tinch!"*

Fortunately, J-Do competed & fought his way out of that inning allowing no runs to score.

I remained in the bullpen with Coach Cally & Eggy. Since we were hitting, it gave me more time to get stretched out, & warmed up. I was *very* sore from my start the day before, so I *needed* the extra time. The soreness was so bad that I kept my compression sleeve on my elbow while I was throwing to keep the pain at bay.

When J-Do went back out to the mound for the ninth inning, my warmup intensified. For every pitch he threw, I would throw two.

He got the leadoff batter out, then, he hit the second batter he faced, & walked the third batter. Immediately after the walk, Coach Vo walked out to mound, & waved me in to come in & pitch. As I was exiting the bullpen to run out on to the field, Coach Cally yelled out, "win us the Conference Tournament!"

The thoughts that popped up in my mind while I was running out to the mound were not very pleasant. Highlights (or should I say, *bloopers*) of yesterday's game were replaying in the mind. I felt as nervous as I felt my first varsity start in high school, & my first time pitching for the Wisconsin Woodchucks.

When I got to the mound, Coach Vo handed me the ball, & said "this is the *perfect* time for you to turn the page." He left the mound, & as he was leaving, he told me to *"keep the ball down."*

There was a phrase Coach Vo would always yell out every time a pitcher gave up a homerun, gave up a run, walked a batter, or hit a batter. That phrase was, "turn the page." He said it to remind us to move on from our past mistakes, & let go of our frustrations.

As you can imagine, he said it to me *a lot*, & I am glad he did. It helped me shift my focus. It was the reminder I *needed* that day, & every other day.

As I was warming up, the Stevens Point fans were yelling out: "He is *exactly* who we wanted, Coach," & "Thanks for giving us the trophy!" Believe it, or not, these comments helped turn my nervousness, into anger – Remember the huge chip on my shoulder? The more they yelled out, the angrier I got.

When I got done warming up & went to the back of the mound to pray, one of the fans yelled "you are going to need to pray more than that to stop us!" That comment put me over the top. It was like throwing a match on a pile of dead Christmas trees... soaked in gasoline. I did not even need to say, *"this is my f@#%ing game!"* after my prayer (I said it, anyway).

I threw just three pitches to close out the game - One pitch to the first hitter I faced (the third hitter in the lineup who drove in four runs against me the previous day), before he grounded out to the second basemen & two pitches to the second hitter I faced (the first-basemen, & cleanup hitter in the lineup, who I walked him three times the previous day), before he grounded out to the second basemen.

The day before, in the 9th inning, this first-basemen hit a *monster* homerun over the centerfield wall off the relief pitcher who came in after me. The second the baseball left his bat, he shouted *"get out of here!"* Then, he proceeded to run down the first base line staring into our dugout – which, we did not take too kindly to.

With that being said, I could not help but yell *"get out of here!"* the moment our second-basemen fielded the ground ball he hit. I also could not help but yell it again, once our first-basemen caught the ball to make the final out of the game. Then, our whole team decided to join in on yelling *"get out of here!"* Needless to say, he did not like that very much. He felt the need to get in the face of the instigator... me. That was not a good idea on his part. There were *a lot* of expletives exchanged between the two of us before both dugouts cleared. Luckily, some level-headed coaches & players stepped in to pull us apart, & settle us down before an all-out fight began.

To be honest, I was very reluctant to pitch that day. Actually, *scared* is a better word to use than reluctant. I wanted nothing to do with Stevens Point (especially, their hitters) after the beating they gave me the day before.

There are two greats lessons that baseball has taught me. The first great lesson is that *every* day is different. In baseball (& many other sports), any team can win on any given day. The second great lesson is that in order to be successful, at a very high level, you have to play for something *greater* than yourself... your team.

Every time I went on the mound, I *believed* I gave my team the best chance to win.

Despite my reluctance, my team needed me in that moment (just as Aaron told me), so I had to set aside my fears & my disappointment, so I could deliver for my team.

It felt *great* to hoist up that Conference Tournament Championship Trophy.

KNOWLEDGE APPLIED

Perspective is *everything*. Life is all about perspective.

If we *really* narrowed it down, we would find that in every situation that we are in, we have a choice between two different perspectives: a growth-perspective, & a fixed-perspective.

I want to remind you, though: we *cannot* control our thoughts, but we can control how we react to our thoughts. Our reaction is *crucial,* because it is what dictates the trajectory of our lives, & because perspective affects performance.

People with a growth-perspective take ownership of the process that creates success. They focus only on doing their best, in *everything* that they do. They understand that growth & development is *always* more important than a win-loss record, or a "stat-line." They *constantly* ask for & seek help, so that they can continue to learn & improve. They understand that failure is just feedback, not something to fear, or avoid. They also believe that *everything* can be better, & that *every* opportunity is a chance to get better.

It is *never* "win vs. lose." It is *always* "learn." There is always something to learn from *everything* we experience. There is always something to learn from *everyone* we encounter. These experiences & encounters do not happen accidently, nor coincidently.

It is important to know that how we perceive failure, can have a negative or a positive effect on our future. It is most important to know that our failed attempts, our mistakes, & our shortcomings do *not* define who we are.

Our ability to fail does not make us failures. We only become failures when we quit. Failing is a part of life; we all have failed, & we all will fail at something. It is a prerequisite to success.

The *greatest* coach of all-time, John Wooden (whom, I have quoted several times before), once said, "if you are not making mistakes, then you are not doing *anything*."
Making mistakes is so much better than faking perfection.

We should prefer to make aggressive mistakes, rather than passive mistakes, because passive mistakes are a result of being afraid of making mistakes, & that is a fixed-perspective.

People with fixed-perspectives are crushed by setbacks & struggles. They make excuses for their struggles, or they place blame on everybody else for their struggles. They say things like, "the reason I am not getting a promotion is because my boss does not like me," or "the reason why I did not play professionally is because I got hurt," or "the reason why I lost that game was because my Coach broke my pre-game routine by coming up to me before the game to wish me luck." *Did you catch that?*

People with fixed-perspectives also view mistakes as embarrassments, instead of opportunities to learn & get better. They avoid difficult or challenging situations. They also compromise for comfort, safety, or the "easy way out."

Prioritizing safety over taking chances is for losers, *not* champions. Anything worth doing is worth *failing* at.

The greatest & most successful people in the world have failed more times than most people have ever attempted to try.

In baseball, *the best* in the game have failed *seven out of ten* times, & they *still* were voted into the Hall of Fame.

If we fail, guess what happens? We get a free education. Making mistakes & failing are only bad, if we never learn from them.

How can we become who we are meant to be if we do not take chances? That is a *miserable* way to live. The biggest mistake we could ever make is being afraid to make a mistake. The second biggest mistake we could ever make is believing the lie that our failure is final.

Failure does not mean the game is over. The game is *never* over. There is still time – there is *always* time. There is always more to the story. The chapter we are is not the end of our story.

Too many of us get so defeated & discouraged after a loss, that we cannot pick ourselves up. I want to encourage you today to get back up there, & try again. No matter the circumstance, get back up there, & try again. No matter the cost, get back up there, & try again. No matter how you feel, get back up there, & try again. No matter what they say, get back up there, & try again. Whatever it takes, get back up there, & try again. Do not stop now, you *will* regret it for the rest of your life. Get back up there, & try again.

We will win, if we do not quit.

"There is always something to learn from *everything* we experience. There is always something to learn from *everyone* we encounter."

"Our ability to fail does not make us failures. We only become failures when we quit."

@RileyTincher | #PitchingAgainstMyself

CHAPTER 12

I WILL NOT LOSE.

After we won the Conference Tournament Championship, we celebrated like we had never celebrated before. *Everyone* went out to the bars that night. When I say everyone, I mean everyone on the team, *plus* their parents were out at the bars that night.

It was wonderful seeing all the parents, & being able to have a conversation with them outside of the baseball stadium. It was also *very* entertaining to see them enjoy themselves, & to watch the dads try to keep up with their sons.

Throughout the night, I could not stop thinking, "I wish my parents were here to experience this with me."

I was offered more free drinks & shots that night than every other night I went out prior to that night… *combined*. As you can imagine, it was yet another blurry night.

Despite the drunken stupor, it was great to see & *feel* how proud everyone (parents & fellow students) was of us that we had won the Conference Tournament. They celebrated as if they played that game, & they were the ones that won the Conference Tournament Championship. That is what beating Stevens Point brought out in everybody. The rivalry we had with them ran deep. *Everyone* hated Stevens Point. They were *always* the team that stood in our way to winning a National Championship. It was a *very* bitter rivalry between us. We were tired of losing to them, & they were tired of losing to us.

That night, right around bar time, we got the news that we were the #1 seed in the Midwest Regional Championship Tournament which started on Wednesday, at Prucha Field. We all knew we were going to be the #1 seed. What we were concerned about was what seed

Stevens Point was going to be - they ended up dropping all the way down to the #4 seed; there were six teams in the tournament. This meant that we were going to play them on the third day if we both won our first two games.

As always, they become our focus. We believed we could beat everyone else in the tournament, except them. Up until that point, three of our five losses in the season came against them; all at Prucha Field.

They had fifteen losses, & they lost to teams they should not have lost to, but every time they played us, they played their *best* baseball.

The next day, I went to the weight room to work out & to continue my routine; I knew better not to waste any more days that I could be using to prepare for my next start. Since it was early Sunday afternoon, I was the only one in the weight room… literally; it was just me & the attendant at the front desk. Since it was just the of two of us, I had him turn up the volume of the music.

While I was working out, a song came on that I had never heard before. I recognized the voice, but I did not recognize the song. It was Jay-Z, & in the middle of the song, he said this line: "I… will… not… lose." As soon as he said it, it caught my attention. I stopped what I was doing & listened to the rest of the song. A few verses later he said it again, but he added another word to it: "I… will… not… lose… *ever.*" At that moment, an emotion took over my body; one, that I was very familiar with. It was the same emotion I got when heard the National Anthem. It was also the same emotion I got when I would say, *"this is my f@#%ing game!"*

This emotion is hard to describe - it was *a lot* of confidence, mixed with intense focus, & an enormous amount of energy. Whatever it was, I knew I needed more of it.

The song came from the weight room attendant's iPod, so, I walked over to him & asked him what song it was. He told me, "it is Jay-Z's song, *U Don't Know* off his first *Blueprint* album." I asked him to play it again, "this time a little bit louder." He obliged.

As soon as I got back to my apartment, I went straight to my computer, searched for the song, downloaded it once I found it, & then, added it to my "pre-game playlist."

For the rest of the night, I played it on repeat while I studied for the last exam of the semester. I found that the more I played it, the more I was able to rap along. Every time I said "I... will... not... lose... *ever*," the same feeling I had in the weight room would surface.

Thanks to "Mind Gym," I now knew about the power of the words I said while I was rapping along to the song. So, I felt the need to add "I... will... not... lose...*ever*" to my list of declarations. But, I wanted to make it my own, so I started creating similar ones:

"I will not lose again."

"I will not lose."

"I will not lose. Period. End of story."

Then, one *finally* stuck: "I will not lose... *period*."

This became the phrase I would repeat to myself while I was visualizing my next start, while I was warming up before the game, & while I was sitting in the dugout in between innings. It also became the theme of my Regional Tournament performance.

U DON'T KNOW

There are times in everyone's life where it seems like everything is going right, or everything is going according to plan. No matter the situation, no wrong can be done, & everything seems to go our way. The Midwest Regional Championship Tournament was that time for me. What I did in that tournament in that four-day span was nothing short of spectacular. It felt like an out-of-body experience, because I was pitching out-of-my-mind. I had command of all four of my pitches. Every ball hit into play bounced our way, or went straight to a fielder. The deeper into the games I went, the better I got. No matter how many innings I threw, I did not get tired. No matter how many spots I missed, I was unhittable. I could not lose.

The first game of the Regional Tournament was against the Aurora University Spartans. They were the bottom seed (#6), but they were not to be overlooked. They had *a lot* of speed on their team - four players with over twenty stolen bases. So, the focus all week was being quick to the plate in my delivery so I could give Robby a chance to throw any runner out trying to steal a base.

Unfortunately for them, they could not steal first base, & is hard to steal any bases if you do not get on base.

They also had a pitcher who was their Conference Pitcher of the Year, so the matchup between him & I was very hyped up before the game. Unfortunately for him, he had to face the best lineup in all of Division III baseball; we hit over .350 as a team.

We won game one against Aurora, 6-1, despite Coach Vo throwing a wrench in my routine, by coming up to me while I was warming up to wish me luck *again* (just like he did the previous week before my first loss of the season). He had the *biggest* smirk on his face while he did too, because he wanted to prove to me that there is no such thing as a superstition. He was right.

I pitched seven innings, while giving up six hits, & allowing one run to score, I walked one batter (although it should have been strike three on a 3-2 (full) count), & I struck out six.

Winning game one of any tournament (especially, a double-elimination tournament) is crucial, because it makes your team's path to the Championship game *a lot* easier. More importantly, it saves your pitching. If your team loses, you have a *long* road ahead of you, playing a lot of games to "catch up;" which, requires *a lot* of arms.

Most baseball teams lose tournaments *not* because they have of a lack of talent, but because they do not have the *depth* in their pitching staff to carry them all the way to the Championship.

Stevens Point also won their first game, beating the College of St. Scholastica Saints, 12-1. They had *nineteen* hits that game, which included five doubles, & two homeruns.

Their message was heard very loud & clear from us – they were there to crush *every* team they faced.

Right after the Stevens Point game, I went for my normal post-pitching game run, but instead of listening to my normal playlist, I listened to Jay-Z's song, *U Don't Know*, on repeat the entire run. After my run, the entire team met for dinner, then headed over to the McGraw building on campus to watch a movie; McGraw had a large projection screen & theatre-type seating.

Postseason baseball was great because it was a taste of what professional baseball was like – No school at all, just baseball *every* day. However, it was also a time for temptation & distractions. It was easy to lose focus & discipline without school. That is why Coach Vo had us have dinner & watch a movie together every night during the Regional Tournament.

The next day, we played the St. Scholastica Saints. Being beat *badly* by Stevens Point the day before did not take away the fact that were a *great* team. Going into the game against us, they had one less win than us (thirty-eight). They had solid pitching, which included three pitchers who had at least eight wins. However, we had Jordan Stine (our now four-time All-Conference centerfield), who went *off* that game for four hits, which included a double & a homerun. We also had a masterful pitching performance from Jason, who lead us to a 6-2 win; eliminating St. Scholastica from the tournament.

Guess who won their second game, as well? Stevens Point. They beat the St. Thomas Tommies, 2-1. They were losing 1-0 late in the game, until everyone's favorite first basemen (*that is sarcasm*) hit a two-run homerun to put them ahead 2-1. This set up the inevitable matchup everyone circled in the Tournament bracket & was looking forward to since day one of the Tournament – Stevens Point vs. Whitewater; the winner advances to the Championship game.

J-Do got the ball to pitch against the Pointers. If you remember, the last time he pitched against them, we won the Conference

Tournament Championship. We were all confident going into that game that we were going to win. We kept that confidence until the third inning, when the wheels fell off. They scored six runs that inning to go ahead 6-2. Unfortunately, there was no way of catching them. We were *completely* deflated.

We ended up losing that game 12-4, & Stevens Point locked themselves into the Championship game the next day.

We did not have a lot of time to sit around & mope about our loss, because we had to play the St. Thomas Tommies later that afternoon. If we lost, our record-breaking season would be over.

The Tommies were the defending National Champions, & they were the favorite to win the Regional Tournament to go back to the World Series. Since they had also lost to Stevens Point, they were fighting to keep their season alive, as well.

Since we had already used our four starting pitchers in the first three games, we were forced to turn to our bullpen to pitch some innings against the Tommies.

Going into the bottom of the fourth inning, we were ahead three runs Then, the Tommies scored two runs to make the score 3-2. That is when Coach Vo brought in Ben, to "stop the bleeding," & to bring "Big Mo" back into our dugout – which, is *exactly* what happened.

In the top of the sixth inning, we scored a run, & then another run in the top of seventh inning to make the score 5-2.

Then, "Big Mo" decided to go back into the St. Thomas dugout in the bottom of the seventh.

Since Ben usually only came in to pitch one inning for us (he was our closer), & he was pitching his *fourth* inning of the game, he started getting tired & started losing his control on his pitches. He walked two batters, & gave up two hits.

While this was happening, I was in the bullpen with Coach Cally & Eggy warming up. When Ben gave up his second hit, Coach Vo walked out to the mound & waved me in to come in & relieve Ben.

My run from the bullpen to the mound was *a lot* different from the run to the mound I had going in against Stevens Point in the Conference Tournament Championship the week before. As I was running in, I kept repeating to myself, "I will not lose... *period*" over, & over, & over again.

I came into the game with one out & the bases loaded.

In that situation, my job as a pitcher was *"damage control"* – meaning, if I can get out of that inning allowing just one run to score, I did my job. However, if I can strikeout the first hitter I face, & get out of that jam allowing zero runs, that is even better (*obviously*).

Since the bases were loaded with one out, the corners (first- & third-basemen) were playing in, so they could throw home to get the force out at the plate, if a ground ball was hit to them. The first hitter I faced hit a short fly-ball (known as a "blooper") to where our first-basemen would have been playing if he was not drawn in. Another run scored to bring the game closer, & make the score 5-4. With the bases still loaded, I struck out the next hitter I faced, & got the hitter after him to fly out, & we were out of the inning.

The greatest thing about that moment was not the fact that we got out of that inning still with the lead. It was not even the fact that two of the best teams in the country had their *Aces* on the mound to close out the game. It was the fact that two of the best pitchers *in the country* were battling it out. There was a noticeable & palpable buzz in the air. I think everyone at the Stadium realized that they were witnessing something *very* special in that moment.

Their Ace, Matt Schuld, was a big right-hander (much like, Jason), who was a two-time All-American, & was *by far* the best pitcher in their program's history. He led them to a National Championship the year before by winning four games in the postseason, including two *huge* wins in the World Series.

Him & I went back & forth for the last three innings of the game. He would throw a shutout inning, then I would throw one. He would throw a one-two-three inning, then I would throw one. It was *incredible* to watch. For the first time all season, I did not sit down in the dugout in-between innings. I stood & I watched *every* pitch he threw, in awe & amazement. There were not many pitchers like Matt (there *still* are not), & it was an honor to battle with him.

We ended up winning the game 5-4, which ended St. Thomas' season. As we were going through the line to shake hands after the end of the game, I got to Matt, & stopped the line to tell him how lucky I was to share the same mound with him. He echoed the respect, we hugged, & I wished him luck in pro ball – which, was the inevitable destination for him.

After the game, Coach Vo called me, Robby, J-Do, & Ben up to his office. When we got up there, he had four packets of papers spread out on his desk, & he said "I have great news, gentlemen. It looks like you all will be playing in the Northwoods League this summer."

Those four packets of papers were contracts to play for the Green Bay Bullfrogs in the Northwoods League. Since I played for them two summers prior to that & loved being there, I knew right then that I wanted to go back, so I did not hesitate to sign the contract. Plus, I was in a hurry, because I *had to* go on my usual post-game run.

I left his office, exited the clubhouse, turned on my iPod, put *U Don't Know* on repeat, & started running.

When I got back, there were two men sitting outside of the clubhouse with Coach Vo. He called me over & introduced me to them. Come to find out, it was the Field Manager of the Bullfrogs, & his Hitting Coach. They were waiting for me to come back from my run, so they could meet me. I immediately thanked him for the opportunity to play for the Bullfrogs, he complimented me on work ethic, & asked me if I went for that run to impress him. I told him "no," & that it was "part of my routine," & Coach Vo concurred.

We then had a short conversation about how great of a season I was having, & historical it was. Towards the end of conversation, the

Field Manager asked me how I felt about my performance thus far, to which I replied, "it is not over, yet."

MOXIE

The movie we all chose to watch that night was "Secretariat." It was about a racing horse who overcame all odds to win the Triple Crown. I had *never* seen it before.

Throughout the movie, I could not help but think that I was like Secretariat. I was reminded of all the odds I had already overcome, & how far I have come to make it to this point. I was also reminded of all the struggles I had faced, all the setbacks that should have ended my career, all the lies & deceits I was told, & all the people who did not believe in me. Yet, despite all of that, there I sat, the Conference Pitcher of the Year, & the Ace of the #1 ranked team in the country.

When the movie was over, Coach Vo got up to the front of the room to talk about the schedule for the next day. As he was finishing going over our itinerary, he reminded us that we beat Stevens Point twice the weekend before to win the Conference Tournament Championship, which meant, we could do it again.

He concluded his speech by saying, "plus, we will have *our* Secretariat on the mound for us in game one." The room erupted.

That night, as I was doing laundry & preparing for my start the next day, I was trying my best to not focus on the thoughts I was having about the last game I started against Stevens Point.

Any time a doubtful thought came to mind, I would say "I will not lose... *period.*" Any time a thought about not being good enough to beat them came to mind, I would say "I will not lose... *period.*" Any time a thought about losing the game the next day came to mind, I would say "I will not lose... *period.*" Any time a thought about saying good bye to the seniors, because we lost & our season was over came to mind, I would say *"I will not lose... period."* I must have said that line over one-hundred times that night.

243

In the middle of all of it, I got a much-needed distraction. Coach Everson called me to congratulate me for signing to play with the Bullfrogs; he tracked *all* of my progress. In the conversation, I told him that I was starting the next day, & he asked me how I was feeling. I told him the truth, that I was nervous & scared, & that I did not want what happened the previous week to happen again. To which he responded, "Tinch, you would not be getting the chance to pitch against them again, if you were not capable of beating them." Then, he asked me, "Have you beaten them before?" He already knew the answer, so he continued without allowing me to answer, "then, you can do it *again*."

As our conversation continued, he reminded me to "control what I can control" – which, is throwing strikes (more importantly, strike one), pitching at a fast tempo (getting back up on the mound as fast as possible), trusting Robby, & competing. He ended our conversation with, "stop focusing on the game you lost, & start focusing on the game you won, & *why* you won it."

I *love* Coach Everson.

The next day, I showed up to Prucha Field confident, with a new perspective. Instead of being afraid to start again against Stevens Point, I was full of *moxie*.

Moxie was a word I had never heard before, until I met Coach Vo. He said it *a lot*, especially when he was describing me. Despite hearing it a countless amount of times, I had no idea what it meant until just recently when I looked it up. According to Google, moxie is defined as "a *force* of courage, or determination."

I was a force determined to beat Stevens Point that day.

The moment I started my pre-game routine that morning, I fell into a trance – you may also know it as "the zone." It was the same trance I was in when I pitched against DMACC, when I was at NIACC. I was intensely focused, & I could hardly hear anything. When I started warming up, it got even more intense. It felt as if I was not even there (out-of-body). As I was throwing in the bullpen, no thoughts went through my mind at all. It was peaceful; a peace beyond understanding. It was also really freeing to let my body go & unconsciously do what it has done *numerous* times before.

This trance continued until the end of the game. *Nothing* could break me of it. The only thing that bothered even the slightest bit was their shortstop, the Conference Position Player of the Year, because I could not get him out. We tried *everything* to get him out. There was one at-bat where I threw inside on him, & I swear the ball actually hit his hands as he was swinging, & he ended up hitting a blooper over our third-basemen's head. Instead of getting angry, I stood on the mound, & laughed, while I shook my head at him when he reached first base. He laughed as well, as he shrugged his shoulders & raised his hands in disbelief, as if he did not know how he did it either. I ended up getting the last laugh though, when I struck him out, on the hardest fastball I threw all day, to end the game. We won 9-3.

When I say that this was *the best* start of my college career, I mean it. It was not the best because I threw a complete game. It was not the best because of the "stat-line" I had. It was not the best because I threw a first pitch strike to *thirty-five* of the thirty-eight batters I faced. It was not the best because I beat Stevens Point to advance us to the Championship game. It was the best because of the feeling I had while I was pitching.

As hard as I try to find the right words to describe it, I can never find them, because there are no words to describe it, other than it was the best game of my career.

SUICIDE SQUEEZE

In between games, the Stevens Point dugout was *real* quiet. We could actually *see* how defeated they were; their body language said it all - *all of them* were walking around with their heads down. I am sure the results of the previous weekend, when we beat them twice to win the Conference Tournament, were going through their heads, & they were probably thinking, "oh no, not this again."

Right before the game started, I went up to Coach Vo in the dugout & told him I could start the second game if he needed me to. He said, "that is not a bad idea, but I already gave Jason the ball."

Jason was returning to the mound from the great start he had against St. Scholastica in game two... just *two* days before.

He showed his exhaustion in top of the first inning, when he allowed two runs to score (which, woke the Stevens Point team up), one of them coming from a *balk* (an illegal motion committed by the pitcher while a runner is on base, which is penalized by advancing the runner) he committed. Then, he, somehow, settled in.

We retaliated by scoring a run in the bottom of the first inning to make the score 2-1. Two innings later, their leadoff hitter hit a homerun to make the score 3-1. In the bottom of the fourth inning, we scored two runs to tie the game, 3-3. After that... the bats went *silent*. For the next four innings, not a single run was score. Then, the ninth inning happened.

I am not going to describe the ninth inning in great detail, because it *still* makes me mad. All I will say is they won the game on a suicide squeeze (I will let you look up what that means), & the ball was bunted less than ten feet in front of home-plate... it should have been fielded, &... the run should *not* have scored.

Two of the worst memories of my career happened at the end of that game. The first memory was watching Jordan Stine swing & miss to strikeout to end the game, & to end his career. He was *the greatest* hitter I have ever played with, or against, & I wish his career would not have ended the way it did. The second memory was watching Stevens Point dog pile on *our* field, & hoist up *our* trophy, after they won the game. That *should* have been us.

I have *zero* doubt in my mind that if we would have won the Regional Championship, & made it to the World Series that year, we would have won it all. I *firmly* believe that the 2010 Whitewater Warhawks was the best team in the country & the best team Whitewater has *ever* rostered. We just could not get past the Stevens Point Pointers - of the seven games we lost that year, five of them were to the Pointers.

I also have *zero* doubt in my mind that I would have carried "Big Mo" all the way to the National Championship game. Instead, I had to carry her to Green Bay, to the Northwoods League.

KNOWLEDGE APPLIED

If we want to live anywhere close to the way we are called to live, there must be *no compromise*. No compromise in the way we talk. No compromise in the way we walk. No compromise in the way we live our lives.

The thing about compromise is, it usually starts off *very* small in our lives. Just one sip of alcohol. Just one puff of a cigarette. Just one dip of chewing tobacco. Just one more bite. Just one pain killer. Just one hand of blackjack. Just one skipped class. Just one pornographic photograph, or video. Then, the next thing we know, everything is out of control. We never intend for it to happen… but it does happen.

These are the choices that we have made, & we must take ownership of these choices. No one forced to us to make these choices, & even if someone did force us to make a choice, no one forced us to continue to make the same choices. We are *one-hundred-percent* in control of the choices we make, & whether we like it, or not, our lives are a direction reflection of the choices we have made.

I do not believe in coincidence. So, I do not think it was a coincidence that I lost to Stevens Point after I compromised my routine for the sake of alcohol & "Thirsty Thursday." I do not think it was a coincidence that my longevity & my chances of becoming a professional baseball player dwindled, after I continued to compromise my health for alcohol & fast food.

Learning to say "no" is crucial - especially, saying "no" to ourselves. If we are not happy with where we are in our lives, then we have to start saying "no" to the things that are keeping us there.

Several times throughout every year I was at Whitewater, Coach Vo would have us all gather together around him during the middle practice. Then, he would ask us "the million-dollar question."

The million-dollar question is this: "If I gave you a million dollars to do this drill right *every* time I asked you to, would you do it?" To which, we *all* replied, *"yes!"* Then, he would always respond with: "I should not have to give a million dollars to do something right."

Let me ask you the same question, but frame it with what you may be struggling with: If I gave you a million dollars to not hit snooze, for a month, would you not hit snooze? If I gave you a million dollars to quit tobacco for a year, would you quit? If I gave you a million dollars to stop drinking for a year, would you stop drinking? If I gave you a million dollars to exercise every day for six months, would you do it? I hope that you answered "yes" to all of those questions.

If you did answer "yes" to the million dollars, but you are not currently doing what you said "yes" to, then that tells me that it is not important to you. It is not meaningful to you.

When something is not important to us, or meaningful to us, we do not make it a priority. When something is not a priority to us, we put it off. It may be something we desire to happen, but not enough for us follow through with it. It may be something we say we are going to do, but our actions are not in line with what we say.

How many more times are we going to tell ourselves, "I'm going to quit *tomorrow*," or "I'm going to start [fill in the blank] *next week*," without taking action? How many times are we are going to say, "I'm going to change," or "I am never doing that again," only to go right back to what it was that we were doing?

We *constantly* judge others for not following through with what they said they were going to do, but we never judge ourselves for not following through what we said we were going to do. We are slow to forgive others who have been dishonest, but we are quick to forgive ourselves when we are dishonest. That is called hypocrisy.

Reminder: we are what we do, *not* what we say we do. More importantly, we are what we do when we *think* no one is watching.

What we do in private is who we *truly* are. What we do in private will determine our success in public.

If we want something, we must walk like we have it, talk like we have, & live like we have it… *all the time* - especially, when we *think* we no one is watching us.

In *everything* we do, there is a choice to make, & there is always a *right* choice to make. Doing the right thing is usually not the easiest thing to do, but it is *always* the right thing to do. It is *always* the right time to do the right thing. We are *always* in the right circumstance to do the right thing. Doing the right thing should *never* be predicated on if someone is watching us, or not.

Too many of us think our struggles, & our addictions, are not significant, or "not that big of a deal." So, we keep putting off quitting these addictions, thinking we will have time to fix them later. Or worse yet, we think they are just going to fix themselves.

Our alcoholism will not just go away after college, & it will not just go away when we have kids; my childhood is a testament to that. Our pornography addiction will not just go away when we get married. Our gambling addiction will not just go away when we hit the jackpot. Our anger issues will not just go away by suppressing them. Our emptiness will not just go away when we make more money, live in a big house, drive a fancy car, & collect every other material thing we have ever wanted; my young adult life is a testament to that.

We must deal with our struggles, & our addictions *right now*, before they become worse, because they *will*. Our lives, the lives of our spouses, & the lives our children depend on this.

Wisdom is knowing the right path to take. Integrity is taking it.

"If we want to live anywhere close to the way we are called to live, there must be *no compromise*."

"If we want something, we must walk like we have it, talk like we have, & live like we have it... *all the time* - Especially, when we *think* we no one is watching us.

@RileyTincher | #PitchingAgainstMyself

CHAPTER 13

IT'S NOT ABOUT YOU

N ever would I have imagined having the season that I had my junior year. Never would I have imagined winning more than ten games (let alone, *five* games) in a season. Never would I have imagined leading the *entire* NCAA in victories. Never would I have imagined being the Pitcher of the Year. Never would I have imagined signing to play in the Northwoods League with the Bullfrogs a week before their season started.

To say my life *completely* changed in a matter of three short months, would be an understatement.

All the desires I had in high school came true. My need for attention was *finally* satisfied (or so I thought).

I was all over the news. I was all over the internet. I was in every major newspaper in the state of Wisconsin. I was receiving phone calls to do interviews on a *daily* basis. I had random people approach me in public to congratulate me & ask me for my autograph. I won just about every award a college pitcher could ever win in a year.
It *still* was not enough.

As soon as d3baseball.com announced their All-Americans awards, I checked their website expecting to see my name on the First-Team. The only question I had was if I was going to be the National Pitcher of the Year.

As I was scrolling down, I passed the National Pitcher of the Year award & did not see my name; it was Matt Schuld – who I *beat* in the Regional Tournament. Needless to say, I was a little disappointed.

I kept scrolling past the list of First Team All-Americans & still did not see my name. My disappointment grew.

I kept scrolling past the list of Second Team All-Americans, & *still* did not see my name. My disappointment grew even more.

I finally scrolled past the Honorable Mention team, & guess what? My name was not there either. My disappointed turned into *fury.*

I found their "leave a note" section on the contacts page of their website & sent them a note (anonymously, of course) that read: "How could you look past the Ace of the #1 team in the nation, who finished the season with thirteen wins & two saves?" I clicked send & slammed my laptop shut.

Soon after, I texted "are you kidding me?" to Coach Perch. He immediately called me & asked me what was going on. I expressed my frustration with not being named an All-American by d3baseball.com to him, & he responded, "that disappoints me." Thinking that he meant he was also disappointed in the award snub, I earnestly said "right?" To which he replied with, "I thought you were better than that." Immediately, my heart sunk. He continued, "we should be playing in the World Series right now, & you are more concerned about not getting an award." Guilt ensued.

The fame & notoriety that I gained throughout the season consumed me, & I wanted more of it. Thank God I had Coach Perch to challenge my intentions, humble me, & bring me back down to Earth. I *needed* that heart check.

OPENING NIGHT

Initially, my mom was not happy *at all* that I signed to play for the Bullfrogs. I was excited to tell her about this amazing opportunity hoping that she would be just as excited as I was, but instead, I got the opposite reaction. She gave me a lot of reasons why I should not play. One of them was, "what about your internship this summer?"

Earlier in the semester (before I knew I was a redshirt junior), I got accepted to intern at a local strength & conditioning gym to train professional athletes. It was a *great* opportunity, that I agreed to take.

However, it paled in comparison to the opportunity to play in Green Bay, so I had to call the owner to turn it down. Thankfully, he understood, but… my mom did not.

One of the other reasons she gave me to not play baseball that summer was her "go to" (money) in every argument we had: "how are we going to afford it?"

Since I would be playing baseball *every* day all summer, that meant I could not work. This was a *constant* argument between my mom & I throughout my whole baseball career.

I explained to her that I would live with a host family, so I had a place to stay, & every meal was provided for. She still did not get it. Money was always her main concern, & she had a hard time accepting the fact that playing baseball *is* a full-time job.

Then, the *real* reason why she was against me signing to play with Green Bay came out. She said, "I wish you would have asked me first." This escalated the argument even further. Then, it ended in her saying her most recited line, "I must be a horrible mom then," as she walked away from me out into the garage, like she *always* did.

Should I have asked her first? Yes, I should have. Would it have mattered if I did? *No.* We probably would have had the same argument, & it probably would have ended the same way.

It frustrated me that my mom did not believe in my dream as much as I did; even after all the success I had that season. It frustrated me even more that she did not want to support me, & my decisions.

Going to Green Bay was a huge step forward for me to get the recognition I *needed* to play Professional Baseball, & here she was trying to talk me out of it. I did not understand, & quite frankly, I did not want to understand. I was more than ready to leave.

A few days later – the day before the season started - I packed up my car & headed to Green Bay for the summer. As I was driving up there, I received a phone call from my "host mom," Michelle Webb. This was our first time talking to each other over the phone; we had texted back & forth the week prior. She told me about her husband, Jon, & her three boys, Tyler, Cayden, & Bryson (ages eleven, nine, & seven), & how excited they were to meet me. Then, she gave me their address, & an hour later I was there.

When I pulled into their neighborhood, I was *astonished*. The whole neighborhood was filled with *huge* houses; bigger than I had ever seen before. The town I grew up in had a few big houses, but *none* as big as these houses.

This was the same neighborhood that the head coach of the Green Bay Packers, Mike McCarthy, & several Packers players lived in.

When I pulled in to their driveway & saw their *beautiful* house, I was astonished even more. I thought, "Riley, what are you getting yourself into?"

Michelle was outside with their dog, Scout, who was the first to greet me as I got out of my car.

The first words that came out of Michelle's mouth after she introduced herself to me, were "welcome *home*;" I did not know how *impactful* those words were until later on that summer.

Her husband, Jon, was still at work, & the boys were at an after-school function, so I did not get a chance to meet them before I had to leave to go to our first practice as a team at Joannes Stadium; the home of the Green Bay Bullfrogs.

Since the Division I baseball season goes into the middle of June (late June, if you make it to the World Series), & it was the first day of June, a lot of the players on our roster were not there yet. However, the Warhawks were there, & a Pointer was there.

Stevens Point went to the World Series, & were eliminated on the third day; which only proves the point I made earlier that they played their best baseball *only* against us.

During practice, this Pointer had the courage to come up & introduce himself to all four of us Warhawks when we were standing in the outfield. We all knew who he was. He started the Regional

Championship game, & beat us two other times throughout the season. His name was Joel Delorit. He was a *very* talented left-handed pitcher, who had been a starter for the Pointers since he was a freshman.

This was Joel's second season as a Bullfrog, so it was great to hear what it was like to spend a summer in Green Bay. It was also great to hear how everything works throughout the season from someone who had gone through it all before.

Joel was not like the other Pointers (or what I *assumed* the other Pointers to be like). He was incredibly caring, & complimentary. We were very much alike. The friendship that developed between us for the rest of the season was *very* special to me. He had an inspiring story about his mom passing away due to cancer when he was a junior in high School, & how it had been just him & his dad ever since.

I also got to know his dad, Dave, because he was a very familiar face at Joannes Stadium.

After meeting Dave, it did not take me very long to figure out where Joel got his caring & kind demeanor from.

Unfortunately, three years later, Dave passed away. I was very sad to hear of Dave's passing, & I was even more sad for Joel.

In the outfield that day, I told Joel how scared I was every time I had to face his team (Stevens Point), & he laughed at me. I asked him why he was laughing, & he told me that his teammates would sit in the dugout & wait to see who our starting pitcher was going to be, & that as soon as they saw me walk down to the bullpen to start my pre-game routine, they all got scared (the *same* way I felt about them). He said, "you beat us every time before you even stepped on the mound."

Our first practice consisted of bunt coverages & batting practice, where all the hitters swung wood bats for first time since the previous summer. As a pitcher, it was very entertaining to watch them struggle with the transition from aluminum to wood. But, the entertainment was very short lived. Being the great hitters that they were, it did not take them very long to adjust.

At the end of the practice, we ate dinner as a team out on the "Leinies Deck," which was located in the right field corner. The dinner was provided by the Bullfrogs Owner, Jeffrey Royle (who, unfortunately passed away earlier this year (2017) in a terrible snowmobiling accident).

During dinner, the Field Manager introduced all of us individually to the rest of the team; there were a lot of veterans from the previous season on the team.

After dinner, he went over all the team rules. A lot of them were common sense. However, one was hysterical, & it was: "the interns are off limits" – which meant we could not sleep with the interns. I thought it was a rule to protect the interns, but really, it was a rule to give the Field Manager more of a chance with them. The funny thing, he actually ended up marrying one of them.

After he went over the rules with all of us, he told us what time we needed to be there the next day for batting practice before the game. He also announced who the Opening Night starter was going to be. *It was me.*

That night, I got back to the Webb's house a little after 9:00 PM. Jon & Michelle were outside on their back porch waiting for me. They invited out there to join them. We shared a few beers together, & we got to know each other. Jon was very high up in an international furnishing company (hence, the big, beautiful house) & Michelle was a second-grade teacher (hence, her *very* loving spirit). They were both incredibly fit, good-looking people (& so were their sons).

Throughout the summer, they were constantly prioritizing their health by waking up early *every* morning to go to the gym to workout, & by being active throughout the day. It was a rarity to see them inside, sitting down other than to eat breakfast, lunch, or dinner – they were *always* outside, playing golf, running, hanging out with friends, or at one of their son's baseball games.

They were near perfect examples for their sons to follow.

This was the first time in my life to be around a family like this. A family who made it a priority to sit down together when they ate. A family who supported each other in whatever it was that they did. A family who constantly built each other up; Michelle was *always* encouraging the boys & telling them how proud of them she was. A family who was involved in *everything* the boys did. A family who was active, & took care of themselves. A family who never held back telling each other just how much they loved each other. A family who challenged one another. A family who had high standards, & held each other accountable to them. A family who was stable. A family who did not drink two thirty-packs of beer in one weekend. A *real* family.

It was mind-blowing to me. It challenged my perception of *"normal."* To spend the summer in a *home* that was free from oppression, addiction, & poverty was extremely eye-opening.

As grateful as I was to have a *home* to live in, & how much I *loved* every minute I spent there, it also made me feel incredible grief, jealousy & envy. I never wanted to leave, because I wanted more of it, & I knew I was not going to get it at the house I grew up in. I wanted so *desperately* to have a house to call my *home*, but I could not have it, permanently.

During the first morning I lived with the Webb's, I was woken up by three smiling faces peeking through the door of the bedroom I was staying in. It was Tyler, Cayden, & Bryson. As soon as they saw my eyes open, they busted through the door, & jumped on my bed to greet me. This was my first time meeting them, because they were already in bed when I got back to their place after practice the night before.

While most kids their age act shy around strangers, especially *big, tall* strangers like myself, these boys treated me like they had known me forever. Actually, they already knew a lot about me; asking me questions about Whitewater, my baseball season, & where I was from. Unfortunately, I did not get to spend much time with them, because I had to get ready for my start that night.

When I walked into our clubhouse in Joannes Stadium, I was greeted by our Pitching Coach, Brandon Harmon. He flew in that day from Washington. At the time, he was the Director of Baseball Operations at Gonzaga University. He was a standout pitcher for the Bulldogs from 2005-2008. He instantly reminded me of Coach Cally. He had a very calm demeanor, but was very assertive.

We met that day to go over what I do for a pre-game routine. When I told him the specifics of my routine, he looked at me in awe, & said "well... I do not think you need my help."

The funny thing about that day was I got through my entire pre-game routine up until to the point of getting on to the mound in the bullpen to warmup, then it started raining. The game was postponed for about an hour.

When the rain delay was lifted, I went back out there & I went through my entire routine *again*. Coach Harmon thought I was crazy & advised me not to do so, but I knew better not to compromise my routine... *at all*. Plus, this game was a *big* game for me. It was a chance for me to show everybody in the Northwoods League, that I – a *Division III* All-American – was the *real deal*.

It was also a chance for me to start over, & redeem myself of the previous poor performances I had in this league. On top of that, it was Opening Night, & the fans of the Bullfrogs were depending on me to start the season with a win. *I delivered.*

I ended up pitching a shutout that game against the Battle Creek Bombers in front of two-thousand Bullfrogs fan; including the entire Webb family. Thank you, "Big Mo."

After the game, there were *so many* people who came up to me to congratulate me & ask me for my autograph. I had never experienced anything like it before. I felt like a celebrity.

On top of that, the boys asked Jon & Michelle if they could ride with me back home, & during the entire car ride they would not stop talking about how great I pitched.

That night, I was named the Northwoods League Pitcher of the Night (I would win that award two more times that summer).

The next day, I received a letter from the Mayor of Green Bay, with a cutout of the article they made about my Opening Night performance in the Green Bay Gazette. In this letter, he wrote:

"Riley, congratulations on your Opening Night start. We, the city of Green Bay, are proud of you. We thank you for representing the city of Green Bay & the Bullfrogs in victorious fashion. We wish you the best of luck the remainder of the season. Go Frogs!"

It was *crazy* for me to think that everyone (even the Mayor) was watching me, & depending on me to help bring the glory & recognition that Green Bay needed. After that night, no matter where I went in the city, I was immediately recognized, & congratulated.

It was no longer about me; it was about what I did for the Bullfrogs & what I did for *everyone* who was watching me pitch. However, I did not fully comprehend this until later in the season.

ROLE MODEL

As the season progressed, more of the Division I players that were on the roster started showing up. They were from all over the country - University of Washington, Brown University, University of Arkansas, University of San Francisco, University of Portland, Dallas Baptist University, Rider University, Boston College, Wichita State University, Western Kentucky University, Purdue University & Saint Mary's University; that is just a few of them. They all had different backgrounds & upbringings, but they all had one thing in common – they were *great* baseball players.

Some of them had the fortune of getting drafted in the MLB draft that summer, including Whitewater's own & my roommate, Ben.

Ben really came into his own that summer. His velocity gradually increased over the summer. At the end, right before he signed with the Mariners, there were a few times he hit ninety-six miles-per-hour on the radar gun (which helped increase his signing bonus). Although, I was sad that he was not going to go back to Whitewater the next year, I was happy for him & his family. Whitewater was a tough environment for him. For some reason, Coach Vo was always *very* hard on him.

Because we had players who were drafted, our stands were littered with professional scouts every game. This meant more exposure & more opportunities for me.

After my second start (& second win) of the summer, I was approached by a man claiming to represent the New York Yankees organization. He had a *huge* World Series ring with the Yankees Logo on his left hand, so I believed him. The first thing he asked me was if I was drafted. I told him "no," & he looked at me dumbfounded. He said "son, you have a Major League changeup, & you throw that fastball on the inside part of the plate better than most pitchers I have seen." He asked for my number, saying "I am going to call up to the organization & try my best to get you signed. Be expecting a phone call in the next couple of days."

I never got his name until two days later when he called me, & said "this is Tony Kubek with the Yankees." Tony was a legendary Wisconsin baseball player, who ended signing with the Yankees, & being their starting shortstop for a little over eight seasons. During his career, he was a four-time All-Star, & he helped the Yankees win three World Series Championships.

Tony told me that he had made some phone calls "to the powers that be," & that it was just a matter of time before they were going to send someone to watch me pitch & sign me.

I was *ecstatic.*

My dream of playing professional baseball was about to come true.

Too bad I never heard from him, nor the Yankees ever again.

Nevertheless, I kept pitching, & I kept winning. Although, I checked my phone *every* day (probably, five-times per day) for the rest of the summer, hoping I had a phone call from the Yankees & a voicemail telling me they were ready to sign me.

I went into my seventh start of the summer leading the league in victories with a record of five wins & two losses. Right before the game, during batting practice, the Field Manager called me, another one of our pitchers, Brad Schreiber, our shortstop, Brad Zapenas, & one of our outfielders, Scott Schebler, into the dugout. Initially, I was mad, because he interrupted me listening to my "pre-game playlist."

When we got into the dugout, he told that the All-Star teams were announced, & that all four of us made the team. My anger quickly went away.

As I was walking onto the mound in the bullpen to warmup for my start, I saw the entire Webb family lined up along the bullpen fence (like, they always were before every game I started). I stopped what I was doing, & I walked up to them to tell them the good news. They were so excited, & proud. Both Jon & Michelle hugged me & congratulated me. Then, Jon turned towards the stands & yelled "did you guys hear the news? My Bullfrog son is an All-Star!"

Even though the All-Star game was *the* biggest game of my life, being told that I was an All-Star was not the greatest thing that happened to me that day.

Before the top of the seventh inning began, I was doing my usual seven warmup pitches. However, this time I was *very* angry. The inning before, I gave up three runs to lose the lead we had. I carried that frustration with me into my warmup the next inning. My body language sucked, & the curse words that were coming out of my mouth were very vocal. It was so bad, that after I threw my second warmup pitch, Coach Harmon shouted out to me to get my attention. When he finally got my attention, he yelled "get over it! It is time to move in!" at me. Or, as Coach Vo would say, "turn the page."

In the middle of all of this, I noticed something out of the corner of my eye just outside of the bullpen. I looked down to bullpen to see what it was. Just outside of the bullpen fence was Bryson, my host-brother, standing there with his glove in his hand. He was playing catch with his brother, Cayden. Whenever he threw the ball, he mimicked my *exact* delivery (glove over the head, & everything).

I threw the next warmup pitch, & quickly looked back at Bryson, & sure enough, he mimicked me again.
He did this *every* time I pitched.

It was at that moment, that I had a sudden realization. I finally realized the *impact* I had on everyone around me. I finally realized there was *always* someone watching me, including little kids (like, Bryson) who wanted to be like me. The problem was, up until that point, *I* did not want to be like me. That did not matter anymore, because it was no longer about me & what I thought. It was about the people who loved & supported me. It was about me becoming a role model for these kids to follow.

The quote "play like someone is *always* watching you," did not resonate with me until that day. I had three young men – Tyler, Cayden, & Bryson – who I had immediate influence over, just because I wore a baseball uniform. They watched my every move, listened to every word I said, & looked to me for leadership, & guidance. Up until that day, I had taken it for granted.

After that day, my whole demeanor changed & I altered the way I carried myself on & off the field. I no longer wore my anger on my sleeves. I no longer allowed my frustrations to show.

If I had a bad game, the second I stepped out of the clubhouse after that game, the game was over & it did matter anymore. I no longer left the 'autograph line' early, or said "no" to an autograph, or a picture. I made it a point to go out of my way to reach out & interact with kids, if they were at our games. I also made it a point to spend every waking minute I could with the boys – playing catch with them, going boating with them, having "zombie time" with them, taking them to the Wildlife Sanctuary, & going to their baseball games.

GET READY FOR THE SHOW

For most players, the All-Star break meant three (much-needed) days off. Unfortunately (& fortunately), that was not what it meant for Brad Schreiber, Brad Zapenas, Scott Schebler, & I.

The All-Star game was on a Tuesday night, but the night before, we had the All-Star Banquet. The morning of the banquet, the field manager rented a van, & we drove over to Eau Claire, Wisconsin, where the All-Star game was being held.

On the drive over, we shared some great stories of things we have experiences (on & off the field), teammates we have played with, games we have played in, & the best opponents we ever faced. I was the odd man of the group, because my claim to fame was very new, & it was nothing compared to their claim to fame.

Brad Zapenas, played at Boston College & was the best fielding shortstop in the country (*not* an exaggeration)– he had three errors *all* season, & all three of them were throwing errors.

Brad Schreiber was illustrious for having a legendary high school career. Plus, he could throw the baseball *ninety-eight miles-per-hour.*

Scott Schebler hit *twenty* homeruns in his first year of college, & was drafted by the Los Angeles Dodgers. He was my first real-life example of a five-tool player – which meant that he hit for contact, he hit for power, he was *fast,* he threw hard, & he had a great glove in the outfield. Of the group, Scott is the only one who is now playing in the Major Leagues.

Speaking of being the odd one in the group, before we walked into the banquet, the Field Manager gave us polo shirts to wear with the Bullfrogs logo on them. Then, he talked to us about the importance of the All-Star game & how this was a great opportunity for us to get exposure. Then, he turned to me & said "except for you, Tinch... let's be honest, you play Division III, & you probably will not play professionally." To which I replied, *"f@#% you,"* then walked into the hotel where the Banquet was being held.

In the Banquet Hall, there were tables all over, with designated seating. Of course, we all sat together. While we were waiting for the Banquet to start, they had a highlight reel of everyone that was on the All-Star teams, playing on a projection screen. There were *a lot* of exceptionally-talented players there – many of which would go on to play in the Major Leagues, including Scott.

Once the Banquet started, they introduced us individually & they had a guest speaker come up to the stage & speak. It was Major League Baseball Hall-of-Famer, Harmon Killebrew.

Harmon Killebrew played in the Major Leagues for the Minnesota Twins for twenty-two seasons. He hit *579* homeruns, including the longest homerun (well over five-hundred feet) ever hit in the old Minnesota Twin's ballpark; which, is now exhibited in the amusement park in the Mall of America.

This was my first time being around a Hall-of-Famer. I was so in awe of him, that I did not hear a word he said. After he spoke, he hung around to give autographs to all of us players. When it was my turn in line, I shook his hand, & he crushed my hand with his; I could see why he hit 579 homeruns. I told him my name, & he was quick to respond: "Oh, you are the big Division III guy!" Amazed that he even knew who I was, I humbly said "yes," & he got up from his chair, looked me dead in my eyes, & he said:

"Do not let what other people say about you not being good enough to play professionally because you play Division III get to your head. None of that stuff matters. If you are good enough, you will find a way there."

I thanked him. Then, I did not just walk away from that conversation - I *floated* away.

That night, we got to our hotel, & attached to our hotel was a Go-Kart track, & an arcade. So, we all went down there with the rest of the players who were there for the All-Star game. Since we had played most of these guys pretty much every day for the last month & a half, there were a lot of familiar faces. It was nice to finally meet them though. We had *a lot* of fun that night.

The next day, we played our All-Star game at Carson Park in Eau Claire, the home of the Eau Claire Express (a team in the Northwoods League). Carson Park was famous for being the place Hank Aaron started his historic Major League career. As a matter of fact, they had a bronze statue of him outside of the stadium.

The environment of the All-Star game was spectacular. There was about five-thousand people there (the most I had ever played in front of), & there were a lot of fun games, events, & contests going on all around the ballpark.

The theme of the All-Star game was "get ready for the show." The show was in reference to the big leagues.

Before they introduced all of us to the crowd, they said "let us introduce to the *future* of Major League Baseball." When they said that, I just laughed, & recalled the comment my Field Manager had made the day before, about me playing Division III.

After they introduced us, Harmon Killebrew walked out to mound & threw out the first pitch. Then, he received a standing ovation, from the fans & the players. I can now proudly say I stood on the same field, & threw off the same mound as *the* Harmon Killebrew.

Since there were so many of us on each roster, & the managers wanted to make sure all of us got a chance to play, they split playing time up between the position players, & they designated an inning for each pitcher to pitch. My designated inning was the eighth inning.

I had no problem coming out of the bullpen in the middle of the game, but given my pre-game routine, I always preferred to start. But, it was the All-Star game, & I had to take what I could get, & be grateful for it, because they were thousands of other players who would *love* to have my spot on the roster.

When it finally came time for the eighth inning, & my name was called to come in to pitch, I ran out to the mound to begin my warmup.

This was my first time ever pitching at Eau Claire. So, when I got out to the mound I was surprised at what I saw – or, I should say, *did not see*. The way the lighting is set up at Carson Park, it makes the entire stands where the fans sit dark. There may have been five-thousand people there, but I could not see *any* of them. Given my issues of anxiety when playing in front of a lot of people, I thought not being able to see the crowd was *great*. I was still nervous though.

When I got done with my warmup pitches, I did my normal prayer with my chin tucked under my shirt. Before I turned around to walk up the mound to start the game, the shortstop ran up to me to stop me. When he got to me, he pointed at my wrist, & said "nice bracelet." As he was turning around to go back to his shortstop position, with a *huge* grin on his face, he pointed at his wrist to show me that he had the same bracelet on that I had on.

This bracelet was white & it had "He is Risen" on it – Referring to the resurrection of Jesus Christ. The significance of this moment was that I got this bracelet at a church in Whitewater during the free lunch they offered to all college students every Wednesday. I thought this church was only church that had these bracelets. I thought wrong.

I am still amazed at all the little & *big* places God showed Himself to me throughout my life – the All-Star being one of them.

I faced two hitters that inning. Both of them are now currently playing in the MLB; one is an MLB All-Star. The first hitter I face grounded out to the short stop. After the out was made, I turned to the shortstop, & pointed at my bracelet. The second hitter I faced, I struck him out with an inside fastball that blew by him & read ninety miles per hour on the radar gun (the fastest I had thrown in my entire career). I *finally* broke the ninety mile-per-hour barrier.

On the ride back to Green Bay that night, I got a text from Coach Everson asking me, "how hard was that last fastball you threw?" *Of course,* he was watching the game online. I answered with, "90," & he responded with *"by you!!!"*

BUYA

After the All-Star game, things began to fall apart for the Bullfrogs. During the All-Star break, we had several players leave to go back home & a few players leave because they signed to play professionally. This left *huge* holes in our roster.

Two of the players that left were Robby & J-Do. Them leaving was a total surprise to me. I would be lying if I said it did not upset me. I would not have minded them leaving if they had a legitimate excuse to leave. They just quit.

Before they left, they both were struggling to hit the ball, so their playing time diminished; which only made things worse. As their playing time went away, their attitudes started to change. Quite frankly, their attitudes *sucked*. It was hard to be around them, but they were my best friends & my teammates, so I cared about them. I hated seeing them give up, because I knew they were better than the way they were performing in the batter's box.

Since we had a lot of holes in our roster, we basically had to sign a whole new team.

To make matters worse, the new guys that came in would quit after a couple of games, because it was "too hard," or "it was not fun." Yes, these were actual reasons for quitting that they gave.

There was one point in the season where our roster was so low, that we only had two outfielders. One of our pitchers, & one of my favorite human beings of all time, Tim Shibuya, was asked to play in the outfield for us, & being the great teammate that he was, he gladly took on the challenge. He was an extraordinary athlete, so he actually played the outfield *very* well.

Tim had a *phenomenal* story. He grew up in Jackson Hole, Wyoming. The high school he went to did not have a baseball team, so the only baseball he played in high school was three months during the summer for his American Legion team. On top of that, he did not start playing baseball until he was fifteen years old (much like me).

Because his high school did not have a baseball team, *no one* knew who he was, so he was forced to walk on at the University of California-San Diego.

In the four years Tim played there, he earned *three* All-American awards. His junior year, he led all of Division II in victories with thirteen; the same year I led all of Division III in victories with thirteen. He finished his career as the all-time wins, all-time strikeouts, & all-time innings pitched leader in his school history. Then, he was drafted by the Minnesota Twins. Now, he is pitching in the Los Angeles Dodgers organization for their AA team.

Do you know where their AA team is? *Tulsa, Oklahoma* - the same city that I currently live in. I am so grateful that I still get to see Tim pitch whenever I want.

What stood out to me most about Tim was not all his awards, or all his success on the field. It was his energy & competitiveness. He was *a lot* of fun to be around. On top of that, I *loved* his work ethic, because I *finally* had someone to workout with who was willing to work as hard as I did. I hate to admit this, but he actually worked harder than me, which, forced me to step up my game.

One of the hard things about playing in the Northwoods League is playing with a bunch of different players who have their own agendas. A lot of the players who are there are not there to win a League Championship, they are there to get recognized & "get ready for the show." This always bothered me. No one cheered in the dugout. No one went up to home plate to greet the hitter who just hit a homerun. No one celebrated a hitter after he laid down a sacrifice bunt to move the runner over. No one picked somebody up when they had a tough outing on the mound, or they struck out at the plate. It was not a team. It was a group of individuals.

When Tim came in, the culture of our team immediately changed. His energy made being in the dugout fun again. His competitiveness made the whole team want to win.

GUILT & SHAME

Towards the end of the summer, during one of my last starts of the season, I did something that I have *always* regretted doing. I was pitching against the Waterloo Bucks, & during the second inning, I got drilled in the back of the leg with a line drive. I finished the inning, then I pulled myself from the game. I was not hurt. I was *scared.*

The last time I pitched against the Waterloo Bucks, I got hit around *badly*, & I lost. I did not want to face them again. So, when I got hit by a line drive in the second inning, I saw it as a perfect opportunity to exit the game, so I faked my injury.

That was the first time in my career that I allowed fear to dictate my decisions. Before that, whenever I started a game, I had every intention to finish it. Coach would have had to drag me off the field to keep me from pitching... even if I was hurt.

It was the most *cowardly* decision of my career.

The following Saturday, my parents came to Green Bay to watch us play. This was the *first* game they came to all summer, even though I begged them to come to *a lot* of games earlier in the season. They did not even come to the All-Star game; *the* biggest game of my career.

Keep in mind, Green Bay was less than three hours away from the house I grew up in.

Every game, we were allowed to give away five tickets to whoever we wanted. All we had to do was write down their name on the "player's list," then whoever we gave the tickets to could come pick up their tickets at the Will Call booth.

Before *every* game, I wrote down my mom & dad's name on the "player's list," just in case they did show up to a game, like I hoped they would.

The game they did decide to show up to, I did not pitch, because I was scheduled to start the next Monday. To make matters worse, they did not show up until after the game started, so I did not even get a chance to see them & talk to them before the game.

Once the game started, I would frequently peek out of the dugout to see if they were there. Every time I looked to where the Webb's seats were, Michelle would always catch me peeking, shake her head at me, & say "they are not here yet."

Around the end of the first inning, they *finally* made it, & as soon as they got there, the beer started flowing. As the game went on, the more innings that passed, the more beer that was drank. At the end of the game, my dad was drunk; not as bad as I have seen him before, but he was still drunk. I was happy that they got to finally meet the Webb family, but I was also embarrassed that they could not even go one night without drinking.

It was a late game, so before the game ended, the Webb's had to leave to get the boys to bed. After the game, I finally saw my parents for the first time all summer, but the visit was short-lived, because they "had to go, because King was at home, & he had not been let outside to go to the bathroom all day."

We got a picture together on the field together; we looked so happy… *in the picture*. I walked them out to their car, & that was it. I was *very* upset. Instead of going right back to the Webb's house, I drove around for an hour, listening to music, & crying.

It was *late* when I got back to the Webb's house. When I walked in from the garage, I saw Michelle waiting for me in the kitchen. I think she saw the redness in my eyes from crying, so she hugged me & said, "I am *so* sorry."

I have *never* felt as much shame as I felt that night.

DIET PEPSI DRINKER

On the second to last game of the season, I got the chance to cross something off my "baseball bucket list:" pitch at Warner Park in front of ten thousand fans. This was a special opportunity for me, because Warner Park was the home of the Madison Mallards, & Madison was only seven miles away from my hometown.

I grew up going to Warner Park to watch the Mallards play, & I *loved* the atmosphere of the games, as a fan. It was very much like a circus. There was always music playing, & there were a ton of clowns (drunk people). However, as a player, it was extremely distracting.

Since I was finally pitching in Madison, & it was a Sunday, I had *a lot* of people come to watch me pitch. I had to ask a lot of my teammates if I could use their "player's list" tickets, & thankfully, they all said "yes" - I ended up using *forty-seven* tickets for that game.

It was nearly impossible to go through my pregame routine before the game. There were people constantly trying to get my attention; it was very difficult to ignore them, but I had to, because I still had a game to pitch. On top of all that, was the Duck Blind. The Duck Blind was a party deck in the right field corner, where fans could buy tickets to enter & have unlimited food & drinks for the entire game. It was very similar to the "Leinies Deck" in Green Bay, except *five times* the size; it fit almost two-thousand people.

The thing about the Duck Blind was it opened an hour before the game, so by the time I started my routine (which, was in right field right next to the Duck Blind), there were already over one thousand people there, who were already drunk & were ready to heckle me the *entire* time I warmed up.

For the most part, I was able to tune it all out, until I got to the bullpen. In the bullpen, they had a water jug, & cups for the pitchers to drink from throughout the game. These cups were the Pepsi cups used in the Duck Blind. Since it was hot that day, I grabbed one of the cups to get a drink. As soon as I grabbed the cup, a man right behind me, & behind the fence between the bullpen & the Duck Blind, yelled out "there better be *Diet Pepsi* in that cup, #38!" – referring, to me being overweight. I turned around & made eye contact with him, as he was high-fiving his friends around him after making such a "great joke." I said "nope, it is just water," then I threw the cup at him, & got water all over him. He deserved it.

In the bottom of the first inning, when I ran out to the mound, the announcer told everyone over the speakers that I was the starting pitcher for the Bullfrogs. Then, he proceeded to tell them that I was a "hometown kid who was an All-American at the University of Wisconsin – Whitewater." Thanks to his announcement, I received a standing ovation from the *entire* crowd – all ten-thousand fans stood on their feet & cheered for me. It was an *amazing* sight to see.

I was so pumped up after that, that the first pitch of the game I threw was a strike on the outside corner & the radar gun read ninety miles per hour. It was one of the greatest moments of my baseball career – to hear the loud *pop* of the catcher's glove as the crowd was silent, & then hear the cheers of my section that followed when they read the radar gun display in right field.

After that inning was over, as I was running into the dugout, I saw a group of young teenage kids lined up on the fence outside of our dugout & I had a flashback of how I used to come to the Mallard's game & line up on that same fence with all my friends to watch the game, stare at the players in awe, & think about how I wanted to be them when I grew up. Then it hit me: *I finally was them.*

When I got into the dugout, Coach Harmon came up to me & said "you must be feeling good. Save some for later." Of course, I did not, & I quickly used up all of my energy.

I ended up pitching five innings, & I got hit around quite a bit; I gave up the longest homerun I have ever given up in my career – I do not think it has landed, yet. It did matter though, because I pitched at Warner Park in front of ten-thousand fans, & I was able to cross that off my "baseball bucket list."

After I got pulled from the game, I sat outside of our dugout, so I could give people I knew a chance to come up to the fence outside of our dugout to talk to me. It was great to see people that I had not seen in a while. Pretty much my entire family was there. A lot of my teammates I had in high school were there. Tommy, our announcer at

Whitewater, was there with a couple of my Warhawk teammates. Coach Diercks was there with his sons, who grew *a lot* since the last time I saw them. Even Coach Cally was there with his wife.

After the game, as I was heading back to the clubhouse from the dugout, there was a voice behind me that kept asking "hey #38, can I get an autograph?" The voice sounded very familiar, so I turned around & guess who it was? The guy who made the Diet Pepsi joke about me while I was warming up before the game.

With a big smirk on my face, I grabbed his baseball, & signed it "Diet Pepsi Drinker," & gave it back to him. The look on his face after he read what I wrote was *priceless*.

KNOWLEDGE APPLIED – PART 1

I hope you are paying attention, because I am going to tell you something that I *needed* to hear, & you *need* to hear – It is not about you. I know this is *hard* to believe, because it contradicts what everyone else is saying & teaching.

We are flooded with information about "helping ourselves." Society *constantly* tells us to love ourselves, put ourselves first, & take care of ourselves *before* we love & take care of others.
The irony is, we help ourselves when we help others.

We experience happiness when we help ourselves, but happiness is momentary. We experience joy, which is *far greater* than happiness, when we help others. We are hard-wired to experience this joy, because we *need* each other. We cannot do what we are called to do by ourselves, & without help.

It is so hard to look outside of ourselves, because we spend the most time with ourselves. I promise you though, the more you live your life thinking everything is about you, *your* desires & *your* best interests, then that is *exactly* what you will be left with - *just you.*

If every decision & every choice we make is all about us, & only for our benefit, we are going to eventually meet something that is *a lot* tougher than us, & we are going to quit, because we do not have a driving force behind what we do.

Self-fulfillment, self-promotion, self-interests, & self-reliance are roads that lead to nowhere. We all have gifts, but we are not given these gifts for *ourselves*, & *our* benefit. We are given these because other people *need* them.

When it is no longer about us, it becomes a lot easier to give (time & money), because it is not ours anyway. It becomes a lot easier to be uncomfortable (public speaking, writing a book, putting ourselves out there for many people to see), because it is not about us, it is about the message we are sharing. It also becomes a lot easier to persevere, because we understand that we cannot quit, because people are depending on us & need the gifts we have been given.

Instead of asking "what am I here for?" we should ask "*who* am I here for?" Instead of asking "what is in it for me?" we should ask "what can I contribute?" Instead of asking "how can they help me?" we should ask "how can I help them?" Instead of asking "what is best for me?" we should ask "what is best for everyone?"

The funny thing is, as much as I hated to do it, I was forced to label this book as a "self-help book," because there is an entire section in the book store called "self-help," but there are no sections in the book store called "help others."

I know that we cannot pour from an empty cup, & that we cannot help others until we help ourselves. However, when we finally figure out Who is pouring into our cups, our cups will *overflow* (Psalm 23:5).

KNOWLEDGE APPLIED – PART 2

Have you ever taken a step back & actually *listened* to *all* the different voices there are in your life? Do you know where these voices are coming from? Do you know just how many voices there are? If you *really* opened your eyes & ears, you would find that there is *constant* chatter.

On a daily basis, we interact with people who are always telling us what we should do, when we should do it, how we should do it, & why we should do it *their* way.

The truth is, it is not about how many voices there are, it is about what voices we are *choosing* to listen to, & what voices we are *allowing* to guide our lives, & dictate our decisions.

I never truly noticed just how much chatter there was around me until I was done playing baseball. I am *extremely* happy that I did not notice the chatter while I was playing, because if I had listened to it all during my career, I would not have had all the success that I had.

Now, I have a very difficult time sitting on the other side of the fence in the stands during sporting events. I never knew how many coaches there were in the stands, until I had to sit next to them.

The chatter is not just at sporting events. The chatter is all around us. Everyone has an opinion about everyone & everything, but not all of them matter. Everyone has a right to their opinion, but we have a right to *not* listen to them. If we did listen to all the chatter, we would be miserable. As a matter of fact, the reason why of some of us *are* miserable, is because of the chatter we are listening to.

One of the hardest lessons to learn in life is that there are going to be people around us who root against us. These people want to see us fail. The worst part is, some of these people are our own family members, & other people who are closest to us. They may not mean to hurt us, or cut us down with their words, but that is *exactly* what they are doing.

What they say is not even about us, or what we do. It is not even about anything we say. It is because we do not believe what they believe. We do not play for their team, & we do not play by their rules. We are stopping, or delaying them from getting what they want. This does not just happen in baseball, or any other sport. This also happens in life. We cannot take it personal. More importantly, we cannot allow it to change who we are, & what we believe.

One of the most important things we need to understand is that we can & say do *everything* right, & there will *always* be a person who is going to have a problem with us. Jesus Christ showed us that.

The other important thing for us to understand is that what people say about us, says more about them, than it does about us. As a matter of fact, what people say about us has *nothing* to do with us, & *everything* to do with them. Everything they say is just a reflection. They either see something in us that they wish they had & do not *believe* they can have (hence, the hateful, demeaning things fans say to athletes during games), or they see something in us that they hate about themselves. Plus, most of them do not even believe half of the hateful things they say.

For the longest time, whenever I was confronted by a "hater," I could not understand why they would say such hateful, demeaning things to me, & it made me miserable. Then, I realized that the reason why I could not understand why they what they did was because I am not a hater, & I cannot relate to them, at all.

Now, when I am confronted by a hater, I cannot help but have the utmost empathy for them. Honestly, I feel bad that their life is *so terrible* that they feel the need to tear others down in order to feel better about themselves. That is a *depressing* way to live.

I also feel bad for them because they usually do not know what they do (nor, the repercussion of what they do), or worse yet, being hateful is *all* that they know. They probably learned to be hateful from their parents, who were the "best examples" that they had. Unfortunately, they are just repeating the cycle.

For us, it is critical to tune out the chatter that is harmful to us. Sometimes, that means tuning out our own voice. Sometimes, that means tuning out the voices of our own family & friends. This may be hard to believe, but if they do not support you in what you do, & try to talk you out of your dream, they are not your friends, & they are not your family. Just because you share the same bloodline as them, it does not mean that you have to listen to them. Just because you do not listen to them, does not mean you are not honoring them. Sometimes, the best way to honor them is to make sure you do not have the same bad habits, & addictions that they have, so your children do not have to go through what you went through.

You may be wondering whose voice we should be listening to. We *need* to listen to the ones that have been where we want to go. We *need* to listen to the ones that care about us, & love us. We *need* to listen to the ones who support us, & want to help us.

The truth is, there is really only one Voice that provides all of that. There is only one Voice that matters, & that is the voice of God - the Holy Spirit; our Advocate who guides us & teaches us twenty-four hours per day, seven days per week, 365 days per year. When we tune into His voice, the rest of the voices we hear tune out.

Most of us view prayer as only asking God for things to happen, like a request line on a radio station. But, it not that that at all; it is a conversation, & every conversation has two parts: talking, & *listening.*

The reason why we do not hear it most of the time is because we are not *listening.* There is a reason why 'listen' & 'silent' are spelled with the same letter. The only way to hear the still, small voice of God (1 Kings 19:12), is to be still, & quiet. The only way we can recognize His voice, is to have a conversation with Him (prayer)... *without ceasing* (1 Thessalonians 5:17).

I recognize my Father's voice, & the voice of the enemy, I do not acknowledge. I hope you recognize your Father's voice, as well, because...

The voice we listen to, & believe, will determine the future we will live.

"The more you live your life thinking *everything* is about you, *your* desires & *your* best interests, then that is exactly what you will be left with - *just you.*"

"The voice we listen to, & *believe,* will determine the future we will live."

CHAPTER 14

THEIR WORLD SERIES

After the season with the Bullfrogs ended, I had to leave the Webb family, & the wonderful place they allowed me the *honor* to call *"home"* for the three months I was there, to go back to the house I grew up in for the remainder of the summer to get ready for my senior year at Whitewater.

There was about two weeks left of summer, but I did not get to enjoy them very much, because there was *a lot* I needed to get done before the school year started.

Since I left Whitewater the day after we lost the Regional Championship & went straight to Green Bay, & had been playing baseball all summer, I never had a chance to go & look for an apartment to live in my senior year. So, I had two weeks to find a one-bedroom apartment, sign a lease, & move all my stuff from the house I grew up in back to Whitewater.

Fortunately, on the day I went back to Whitewater to look for an apartment to live in, the very first place I went to had a one-bedroom apartment available. It was the *only one* they had available, so I took it, without hesitation.

A week and a half later, I moved in.

While I was moving all my stuff into my new apartment, I was greeted at the front entrance of the apartment complex I lived in by J-Do. He was living there as well (on the floor above mine), & moved in the same day I moved in.

I did not want to live by myself because I *hated* being by myself, so I was very excited to have someone close to me that I could hang out with whenever I wanted. It was an added bonus that it was J-Do.

The next day, Coach Vo asked Robby, J-Do, & I to meet him in his office at Prucha Field. J-Do & I rode together, & met Robby in the parking lot. Despite my animosity for them leaving me & the Bullfrogs that summer, it was *great* to be together again.

Shortly after we arrived at the field, Coach Vo showed up. As we were walking from the parking lot to the clubhouse, we all caught up & talked about how our summers in Green Bay went. Coach Vo acknowledged his disappointment in Robby & J-Do for quitting, & I agreed with him.

When we got into the clubhouse, he let us know that we had been voted by the team to be this year's Captains. This was a *huge* honor. He then went over what he expected from us as leaders of the team. He also talked about how Fall Ball was going to be laid out, & the excitement he had about all the freshmen & transfers we had coming in; he had a *very* busy summer recruiting.

After our meeting was over, I stayed behind because I had a question to ask him. This is when another one of the biggest regrets of my baseball career happened.

During the summer, all the Division I pitchers talked about how they took Fall Ball completely off to rest their arms – meaning, they did not pitch, or even throw, *at all* in the fall.

They planted is seed in my ear, & it festered, & grew. I thought that since I pitched *way more* than they did, that I deserved a break as well. In all reality, I probably did need the rest. I threw over 180 innings that year; almost more than double what any other Warhawk pitcher threw.

That is why I stayed after with Coach Vo – to ask him if I could get a break from pitching. He was very reluctant (& rightfully so), for a lot of reasons. One of the reasons was, no one had ever done it before in Whitewater history. Another reason was, I had *a lot* of momentum going for me, & he did not want that to stop. Another reason was, he did not like me missing two months of opportunities to get better. The final reason was, I was now a captain of the team, & as a captain, I led the way, & the rest of the team followed my example.

That is exactly what happened, & part of the reason why I regret making this decision.

As soon as some of the other veteran pitchers heard that I was not going to pitch during Fall Ball, they decided that they were going to rest as well. I could not say anything about it, because I was the one that started it.

The major reason why I regret making this decision was that as soon as Fall Ball started, & I *chose* to sit out of all the scrimmages, I got *lazy* (according to my standards), & my body started falling apart because of it. I started having injuries that I would never completely recover from, no matter how much therapy I did, how much ice I used, or how many cortisone & lidocaine shots I had injected (*thirteen* total injections throughout the year – *seven* injections during the three months of my senior season). This is when my addiction to ibuprofen & other pain killers started.

My body was not the only thing that started falling apart.

HIS LOVE AFFAIR WITH WHITEWATER

On the second day of school, I was walking the hallway of the Williams Center between classes when I crossed paths with Coach Mills. The conversation we had that day laid the foundation of my senior year. What he said was going to happen to me the rest of the year came true.

On Wednesday, March 9th, 2016, Coach Mills passed away after a long bout with cancer. The amount of influence this man had on my life is *immeasurable*. I could never repay him for what he had done for me. I could not think of a better way to honor him than to immortalize him in this book. With that being said, here is my tribute to Coach Jim Miller:

Coach Jim Miller was known by many names but the one that he was affectionately referred to as the most was "Mills." We celebrated Mills' life in his home that is known as the University of Wisconsin -

Whitewater, in the only way he would have wanted it to be done, surrounded by his friends & family.

Mills was born & raised, & he lived & died in Whitewater, Wisconsin. Mills was *"Mr. Whitewater."* He devoted his *entire* life to his home, & it is what it is today because of him.

At Whitewater, we have a saying called "Powered by Tradition" - It is our mission station. Many believe that this statement refers to the National Championships Whitewater has won, the Conference Championships Whitewater has won, & the amount of All-American athletes that have played there, but that is not what it refers to.

The saying "Powered by Tradition" is about loyalty, love, family, & constancy; every core value that Mills represented. Simply put, Mills is the tradition that we are powered by. He was a *true* Whitewater legend. No one loved UW-Whitewater & Warhawk Baseball more than Coach Mills; he lived & bled purple!

There were many attributes & characteristics to admire about Mills. He was a Hall of Fame Baseball Coach. He won four-hundred games, & has the second most wins in UW-Whitewater history. He was a great communicator & teacher. He was a *constant*. He was incredibly generous with his time & money. He never said any bad things about anyone, or anything. He was diligent. He had amazing attention to detail. He was a hard worker, & he instilled his great work ethic in all his coaches & players. Above all, he valued friendship & relationships more than *anything*, until the day that he died.

Despite of all those wonderful things, what I admired most about Mills, was his love for his wife of *fifty* years, Carol. I will never forget the day he hired Jordan Stine & I to come over to his house to do yard work. I was amazed to see him drop *everything* he was doing to greet Carol with a hug & kiss when she came home from work, & I remember telling myself, "I want a love like that someday."

There are so many things I want to thank him for. The time he spent teaching me the game. The things he taught me about facing hitters. The conversations we would have about life. Mills was the one that taught me to always have a plan. Mills was the one that taught me to stay the course. Mills was the one that taught me to be content with what I have accomplished, but never be comfortable.

I will never forget the conversation I had with him in the Williams Center hallway on the first week of school my senior year. He congratulated me on a great season & summer in the Northwoods League, & he asked me what I wanted to accomplish my senior year. As the conversation was ending, he put his hand on my shoulder, looked me in the eyes, & said:

"Tinch, you have a *huge* target on your back now. Pitcher of the year is a *great* accomplishment, & you should be proud of that. But, be ready, because every team you pitch against this year is going to face you like they are playing in their World Series. Do you know how you can make sure they never beat you? You must outwork them."

I am a better man today because of my association with Jim Miller. I am a better man today because of his influence on one of the greatest influences of my life, my Head Coach, **John Vodenlich**.

I am so honored to have played a part in the building & inauguration of his Stadium, Prucha Field at James B. Miller Stadium. I am so honored to have been a part of his day when we retired his number & officially named the stadium, "The Mill;" I still have his bobblehead on my shelf in my office.

I do not think it is a coincidence that on that day, my Senior year, I pitched one of the best games of my life.

Every time I pitched at The Mill, he was there, right at the gate by our dugout, either talking to Coach Vo, yelling "come on, Tinch," or... yelling at the umpires. The strike zone was never good enough for him, & I thank him for that; for always wanting the best for us.

I miss you, Mills. I hope to leave a legacy as legendary as the one you have left. I hope to love people as much as you loved them. I hope to make as great of an impact as you have made.

WAKE-UP CALL

At the end of Fall Ball, we had our annual Steak Series. This was the first Steak Series I did not play in. I had a *very* hard time excluding myself from it. I still think about it in regret, & ask myself "why would you voluntarily opt out of your last chance to play in the Steak Series?"

As I mentioned before, the Steak Series was one of the greatest times of the year, where the environment was intense, the teams were extremely competitive, & the best players on the team got their chance to prove who was better than who. My senior year, I had to enjoy it as an umpire.

It just so happened that the week of the Steak Series (which, was also the week of Initiation) was on the week of Homecoming. On top of that, the day of the Homecoming football game was on Halloween. This meant that the Initiation Party was on the Friday before *the biggest* party of the year in Whitewater (Homecoming). This also meant that it was going to be a blurry, *disastrous* weekend for me.

I would explain how the weekend went, but I cannot remember *anything* from the middle of the Initiation Party on Friday night to waking up Sunday morning. I cannot tell you if I had fun. I cannot tell you how I felt during it. I cannot tell you who I was with during it. I cannot even tell you where I was at during it. It was all a blur to me. I was *black-out* drunk Friday night, all day Saturday, & Sunday morning.

On Sunday morning, I woke up in a place I had never been before, next to a girl I had never met before. This was the first time this ever happened to me… & *the last*.

I snuck out of what I assumed was her apartment without waking her up, figured out where I was, & I walked home.

During my walk home, I quickly figured out why they called this the *"walk of shame,"* because that is *precisely* what I felt. I was embarrassed.

As I was trying to recollect what I did the night before & figure out how I got to that apartment, with that girl, a still, small voice popped in my head, & it said: "if you are upset with your parents drinking, imagine what your kids are going to think of you drinking."

My heart sunk the most it had ever sunk before.

I was not living "the college life," I was repeating the cycle of alcohol abuse in my family.

From that moment on, I stayed sober the rest of my senior year.

DEATH OF A KING

A few weeks later, I received a phone call from my mom in the middle of the week, asking me to come back to the house I grew up in that weekend. I told her I would, so on that Sunday, I drove there.

When I walked into the house, I knew immediately something was wrong. I cut straight to the chase, & asked my mom what was going on. She told me to sit down (which, confirmed that something was wrong), & she said, "we need to talk about King."

King was thirteen years old at the time, & in the past month, or so, his health started to rapidly decline. He was pretty much blind in both eyes. Because he had so many ear infections throughout his life, he was partially deaf in both ears. He also had bad arthritis in his hips, which made it hard for him to get up & down.

King *loved* walks, & that is an understatement. *Every* night, around the same time, he would whine to go for walks. We could not even mention "going for walks," or even say the word "walk" around him, because he would go crazy with excitement. For a while, we had to spell it out, "W-A-L-K." Then, he figured that out.

During the summer while I was away, that excitement he had went away, & he hardly ever wanted to go for walks anymore. That is when my mom knew something was wrong. She did not have the heart to tell me (& I do not blame her) until that weekend I went home.

I was forced to make *the hardest* decision of my life to put him to sleep.

Before I left for school every year, I wrote King a "see you later" letter. These letters always contained the best memories I had with him that summer, & they expressed my love for him, & how much I would miss him, & what I wanted to accomplish that year *for him.*

That night, with tears in my eyes, I wrote my last "see you later" letter to King; it is now framed in my office. I am not going to share the entire letter with you, but I will share an excerpt of the letter with you just to show you how much I *loved* him:

"Never in my lifetime, did I think, or want this day to come. I never thought about my life without you, but now I have to live it. I never wanted to write this letter, but unfortunately, here I am, writing it. One letter is not even large enough to express the love that I have for you, King. Instead of mourning your death, I am going to celebrate your life. You are more than a best friend to me. You are even more than family to me. You made it so easy to love you unconditionally every day of your life, because you loved me the same way. There will never be a dog, or person that will have the same impact on my life as you have had, King. You are irreplaceable."

He slept right by my side that night... like *always*.

The next morning, we called the Veterinarian to come over to euthanize him. I held his paw as he took his last breath, then, I carried his lifeless body out to the Veterinarian's car, & just like that, his life & our *inseparable* relationship was over.

As the letter said, King was more to me than a best friend, or a family member. He was a part of me. *Everywhere* I went, he was there. If I had a bad day (& there were *a lot* of them), he would *always* cheer me up.

I looked forward to the walks as much as he did, because I would use these walks to vent my frustrations & disappointments to him, & the whole time, he would walk right beside me, looking up at me, as if he was listening to me.

After I moved away, King was the only thing I looked forward to when I came back to the house I grew up in, & he was the only reason why I called my mom & dad - to see how he was doing.

Now that he was gone, things at the house I grew up in *never* were the same. I hardly ever came back as much as I used to, & the routine phone calls my parents & I had become less frequent.

HIGHWAY 26 & COUNTRY ROAD N

The death of King took *a lot* out of me.

I was also struggling with the responsibilities of being a captain (I felt like I was the *only one* leading) to a young team who seemed to not want to listen to me. Add the *enormous* pressure I felt to have a repeat performance of the best season of my career on top of that, & soon after, the depression I felt after my first year of college came back, but this time stronger than ever. I no longer wanted to go to class. I no longer wanted to go to works out. I no longer wanted to be around *anyone*, including my coaches & my teammates. I just sat around my apartment, playing video games, & watching movies.

Living by myself only made matters worse, because isolation leads to destruction. When we are in isolation, issues always seem bigger than they are, & solutions are almost impossible to find.

Since I felt like my depression was *never* going to get better, I started having suicidal thoughts for the first time in my life.
I wanted to end it all.

I began to believe that if I killed myself, no one would miss me. Worse yet, I believed that if I killed myself, their lives would be *better off* without me.

I know this is crazy to comprehend, given all the success I had on the field & all the accolades & praise I received off the field that year, but this is what I was dealing with.

On the surface, my life was *great.* I was an All-American. Everyone on campus & everyone in the town knew who I was. People treated me like I was a celebrity. I received the royal treatment; I hardly ever had to pay for meals, or drinks. But deep down, I was miserable, I felt so *alone*, & I no longer wanted to live anymore. The pressure was too much, & I was *beyond* burnt out.

On the last weekend before finals week, I kicked all the "underagers" (younger that twenty-one years of age) on our team out of the bars. It was a serious problem among the team, & the coaches caught wind of it, &

told the captains to make sure it never happened again. I followed through with their request without *any* support from Robby & J-Do, or the rest of the veterans on the team.

The text messages I received that night from the "underagers" I kicked out were malicious, degrading, & downright, *hurtful*. Here I thought I was doing them a favor, by keeping them out of trouble (they were breaking the law by being in the bars), then they treated me like I was a monster, & I had stolen their most precious thing from them.

That night sent my depression over the top. I could not handle it anymore, & I began to question if all the pressure, all the anxiety, all the stress, & all the backlash was worth it.

The next week, the night after my last final exam, I drove back to the house I grew up in for Christmas Break. While I was driving down county road N, my mind became consumed with suicidal thoughts. I began to think, "if I drove my car off a bridge, or if I got hit by a semi, all of this could end." These thoughts continued, "All of this pain I am feeling. All of this loneliness I am feeling. All of this shame I am feeling. All of this pressure I am feeling could quickly go away if I end my life tonight."

I started agreeing with these thoughts, & I made the decision that at the next intersection, I would drive my car out in front of a semi-truck.

At about midnight, I got to the intersection of Highway 26 & country road N. Since it was late at night, there were no cars around. So, I waited at the stop sign, for what felt like an eternity, for a semi-truck to come driving down Highway 26. I kept looking to my left & to my right, until finally, I saw a semi-truck in the distance approaching the intersection; it was about a mile away.

As the semi-truck got closer, tears began to fill up my eyes & roll down my cheeks. I was holding on to the steering wheel so tightly that I lost feeling in my fingers. When the semi-truck got even closer, I closed my eyes, & I slowly let off the brake pedal in my car, & I began to roll out onto the highway.

I braced for impact.

For about five *long* seconds, I thought "this is it. this is *the end.*" Then... *nothing* happened. I did not get hit. I opened my eyes to see that I was in the middle of the highway. Then, I looked to my left where the semi-truck was approaching from, & I saw that he had pulled off to the side of the road less than one-hundred yards away from me. He was honking his horn at me, because he probably thought I fell asleep.

I was so embarrassed, & so ashamed. I quickly peeled off that highway, & I drove back to the house I grew up in as fast as I could.

I *never* told *anyone* about what happened that night, so I carried that embarrassing moment around with me in the back of my mind for the rest of my senior year.

I became an *expert* at wearing a mask. I portrayed a man who loved & cared for everyone. I portrayed a man who exuded passion for the game of baseball, & for helping all his teammates. But on the inside, I *hated* myself. On the inside, I was *screaming* for help, but I never had the courage to ask, because pride got in my way. I thought:

"I am the senior, I am the captain, I am the All-American, I am the Pitcher of the Year, & I am the man everyone looks up to. I cannot let them know that I tried to kill myself. I cannot let them see that I am having serious, *life-threatening* issues. I cannot let them see that I am *weak.*"

PEAKS & VALLEYS

My senior season started the same way my junior season started... with a win as the Opening Day starter. However, that win did not happen in the Metrodome. If you remember, the Metrodome was no longer around. Since it was no longer around, we had to travel south (to warm weather) for Opening Day.

We ended up playing a doubleheader against the Washington University Bears at their home field in St. Louis, Missouri. I pitched game one of the doubleheader, & we won that game, 11-1. Statistically, I pitched great, but I *felt like crap.*

Before the season started I was diagnosed with plantar fasciitis, which is *excruciating* pain in the heal of your foot. It was the same foot as my busted ankle. Coincidence? *Definitely not.* It also did not help that I was overweight, which put a lot of pressure on my feet.

The pain was so bad that I could not run (sometimes, even walk), because I could hardly put *any* weight on it at all. It was always the worst in the mornings. When I woke up, I had to hop on one leg from my bed to the bathroom just so I could soak my foot in hot water, because that was the only thing that seemed to help subdue the pain.

We tried *everything* to fix it, but *nothing* got rid of it, until I finally got custom inserts made for my shoes *after* the season was over.

For the first part of the season, I basically pitched on one leg. That was until I discovered that the more Ibuprofen I took, the less pain I had.

My second start of the season was in Florida on our annual Spring Training trip. We played a doubleheader against the nationally-ranked St. Olaf College Oles, & I started game one. They were from Minnesota & they played in the same conference as St. Thomas.

This game did not go as planned. We were tied 2-2 going into the bottom of the last inning. I gave up a hit to the leadoff hitter, then I was pulled from the game. The reliever who replaced me proceeded to give up three hits in a row, including a walk-off single with the bases loaded & we lost the game, & I lost my second start of the season.
It was also my second loss of my entire Whitewater career.

After that walk-off single to end the game, St. Olaf celebrated like they had won their World Series. *Coach Mills was right.*

To say that the loss devastated me would be an understatement. I had such high hopes going into that season, & immediately those hopes washed away with that loss. I finally succumbed to the pressure of trying to repeat the performance of my junior year.

Coach Cally could see how upset I was, so when the second game of the doubleheader started, he took me down to the bullpen to talk to me. When we got to the bullpen, he asked me how I was feeling, & I told him about how my performance on the field upset me, & how angry I was that we lost. He stopped me, & said "I did not ask how you felt about your performance, I asked you how *you* felt." After a long pause, I told him about the pressure I was feeling & how I hated it.

I *really* wanted to tell him that I was depressed & suicidal, but I could not muster up the courage to do it.

His response to me talking about the pressure I was feeling, was not what I had expected to hear from him. He asked me, "What is pressure?" I did not know how to answer him, so I did not. He went on to say, "At the end of the day, this is *just* a game." I looked at him confused because baseball was more than *just* a game to me – it was my *life*. He continued, "This is not a matter of life & death. This is not real pressure. Real pressure is what you went through in your childhood."

As soon as he said this, I had flashbacks to moments in my childhood that I wish I did not remember. One of them was when I was probably 8 years old, & rode in the back of my dad's truck, as he drove my brother & I home *drunk* from the races we went to every Friday night. We were on the highway, going well over fifty miles-per-hour, & he would swerve back & forth laughing, as my brother & I cried in terror. The other one was when I was ten years old, & I walked into my parent's bedroom, to find my mom passed out on the bed. I panicked & jump on the bed, & started shaking her to try to get her to wake up. I started crying thinking she was dead. Then, I grabbed the phone to call 911, & all of sudden, she woke up... to stop me from calling 911.

What Coach Callahan said to me that day in the bullpen forever changed my *perspective* of pressure. The pressure I was feeling was nothing compared to the pressure I felt when I was a kid. More importantly, the pressure I was feeling was *nothing* compared to the pressure, my friend in high school, the Navy S.E.A.L. probably feels as he risks his life to defend our country & our freedom.

The rest of Coach Cally & I's conversation was filled with jokes about Rickey Henderson, & stories about our childhood dogs. In the midst of that conversation, he said something that I will never forget, & it was this: "In life, there are going to be a lot of peaks & valleys, just make sure there are more peaks than valleys."

My senior season proved that quote to be true.

KNOWLEDGE APPLIED

I cannot even begin to imagine the pressure you may be feeling right now, nor how long you have been feeling it, but I do know that you are not crushed by it. You would not be able to read this book right now if you were. I also know that you are not alone – *all* of us deal with pressure, in one way, or another.

I want to ask you the same question Coach Cally asked me – What is pressure? How you answer that question will ultimately determine how you handle pressure.

Pressure is a matter of perspective – meaning, when we change our perspective, the pressure we feel changes. We can either view pressure as a bad thing, or we can view it as a good thing (which, it is). We can either avoid pressure, or we can embrace it. We can either succumb to pressure, or we can rise above it & overcome. We can either let pressure beat us down, or we can take advantage of it, & use it to succeed. We can either let pressure burst our pipes, or we can use it to create diamonds.

We must put pressure in its place. We must reframe how we perceive pressure. If we continue to perceive it as negative, we will continue to associate it with negative thought processes like "self-doubt" & "unbelief." If we continue to give in to it, it will blind us, & make us feel alone & helpless. If we perceive pressure as positive - better yet, if we perceive it as a *privilege* (because, it is) - our performance & our lives *will* become better.

We *love* to exaggerate. We love to make things bigger than they really are. We love to make our successes & our accomplishments better than they really are. We love to make our problems much worse than they really are. We love to make the pressure we feel more immense than it really is.

Often times, we are the ones that *create* the pressure we feel.

We must see pressure as what it is, & not make it what it is not. The pressure we may be feeling is nothing compared to the pressure the majority of the rest of the world feels. I am not trying to downplay the pressure you are feeling right now, but it is nothing compared to the pressure some families feel trying to figure out how they are going to eat their next meal. It is nothing compared to the pressure some families feel about having to "pull the plug" on one of their loved ones who has been staying alive because of a ventilator for the last three months. It is nothing compared to the pressure some of our military men & women feel when they have to tell a family that their loved one died fighting for our country, & for our freedom. It is nothing compared to the pressure David felt before he fought Goliath. It is nothing compared to the pressure Jesus Christ felt while he was praying *for us* to God in the Garden of Gethsemane right before he was betrayed & gave Himself up to be crucified - He was feeling so much pressure that he was sweating drops of blood (Luke 22:39-46). We do not have to do what we do. We *get* to!

When we *finally* realize how *fortunate* we really are, *everything* changes. When we *finally* realize who we *truly* are – beloved, called, equipped, anointed, empowered, & blessed beyond measure – & how much power we have been given, pressure becomes *a lot* easier to handle. When we *finally* realize *why* we are here, & *why* we are called to do what we do, burn out no longer exists. When we *finally* realize Who has our back, we have peace beyond understanding, because we *know* God is greater than *any* problem we will *ever* face, & He is greater than *any* pressure we will *ever* feel.

The next time we are feeling pressure, we need to remind ourselves of a few things. The first thing we need to remind ourselves of is that it is not the first time we have experienced pressure, & it will not be the last time either. The second thing we need to remind ourselves of is that just like before, we will be delivered from this pressure again. The third thing we need to remind ourselves of is that we are not *that* important, & what we are facing is not a matter of life, or death, & the outcome of our circumstance will probably not matter a year from now. The forth thing we need to remind ourselves of is that we are *better* under pressure, because pressure reveals treasure. *It is not about the pressure we feel; it is about what we do with it.*

If you are currently going through depression, or you are having suicidal thoughts, please have the courage to ask for help – I am *begging* you. The self-doubt & the self-destructive thoughts you are having right now are not *real*. You are under attack, & since you are being attacked, that means that you are *valuable.*

Do not believe the lie that you are going through this alone; just because you feel that way does not mean it is true. There are *a lot* of people around you who *love* you, care about you, & *want* you in their life, & they are willing to do *anything* to help you.

There is also a phone number you can call *right now*, for *immediate* help. That phone number is: 1-800-273-8255.

I know just how hard it is to keep going, when you feel like you are drowning, & everything around you is *dark*, with absolutely zero light in sight. But, that does not mean that the light is not there.

You have a million reasons to live right now, & if your perception is so distorted that you can only think of *one* reason to live, then hold on to that reason as tightly as you can.

If you think that you do not matter, & that you do not make a difference, you are *wrong.* As long as you have breath, you have *hope,* & you have a purpose that is far greater than yourself. Please do not make a permanent solution to a *temporary* problem. We *need* you.

I promise it *does* get better; I am *living* proof of this.

"When we *finally* realize who we *truly* are, & how much power we have been given, pressure becomes *a lot* easier to handle."

"It is not about the pressure we feel; it is about what we do with it."

@RileyTincher | #PitchingAgainstMyself

CHAPTER 15

BIG PUMA

The third start I had during my senior season was on the last day of our Spring Training trip to Florida, & it was against the Minnesota Twins. Yes, you read that correctly... *the Minnesota Twins.* Every year for Spring Training, we would play a Major League organization (not, the actual Major League team though). For my senior year, we played the Twins.

Getting the chance to start against a Major League organization, with *professional* hitters, was a *very* big deal to me. On top of that, Ron Gardenhire (the manager of the Twins, at the time), & Hall of Famer, Paul Molitor (the current manager of the Twins) were in the stands watching the game. I saw this start as an opportunity to prove to everyone that I deserved the right to play professionally, & to prove to the Twins that I deserved a spot on their roster.

Have you ever heard the phrase, "do *not* meet your heroes?" Paul Molitor was that hero for me, & he proved that phrase to be true. He was a former Milwaukee Brewer great, that I grew up admiring, because my dad talked about him like he was a god. When I finally got the chance to meet him after the game, he was a complete jerk to me; he did not even shake my hand when I reached it out towards him.

Although it did not count (statistically), my start against the Twins that day was the best start I had all year. I had a no-hitter going into the sixth inning, until it was broken up by the leadoff hitter hitting a line drive straight to my shin. As soon as the ball hit my shin, I went down immediately. I instantly lost feeling in my foot, so I thought my leg was broken. I could not bear to look at it, so when our third-basemen came over to me while I was laying on the ground, I asked him if it was broken. He looked at it, & with a *giant* smirk on his face, he said, "na man, you are a good." Then, he helped me off the ground, & I tried "walking it off."

It took walking around the mound several times & a few pitches off the mound before I regained the feeling back in my foot. I finished the inning, & my start was over.

I spent the rest of the game, laying in the bullpen with my foot elevated & a bag of ice on the spot I was hit in the shin. It reminded me of laying on the ground after I busted my ankle in Captain's Practice my sophomore year.

We ended that game in a tie, 1-1, because it was an exhibition game, & we did not want to use up more pitchers than we had to. We *should* have beat them.

After the game, we lined up to shake hands, & the hitter that lined one off my shin gave me a *big* hug, & in his thick Hispanic accent, he said "I thought I broke your leg, man." I never felt so *tiny* around someone else before, until he hugged me; it felt like he swallowed me whole. His name was Miguel Sanó, & at the time, he was only *seventeen* years old. Now, he is twenty-four, & he is the designated hitters for the Minnesota Twins & is considered one of the best prospects in the Majors.

Once we got done shaking hands with the Twins, we met with Coach Vo in the outfield to talk about the game, our Spring Training trip, & what we needed to work on to ensure we would have a successful remainder of the season.

In his post-game speech, he said something about me that would become *the greatest* compliment I have ever received, but I will not share it with you until later.

SIC 'EM BEARS

On the van ride from the game to the airport, I sat "shotgun" in the front seat next to Coach Perch as he drove. For the Spring Training trip, we had rented a few fifteen-passenger vans to drive the team to & from the airport, & to & from our games.

While we were on our way to the airport, I checked my emails on my phone, because I had been (impatiently) waiting to hear if I had been accepted into Graduate School at Baylor University for the following school year.

Before the season started, both Coach Perch & Coach Cally encouraged me to further my education right after my baseball career was over. They believed it was going to be over after my senior season, but I was in denial, & I did not want to believe that to be true.

Coach Perch & I spent a significant amount of time together trying to figure out what I wanted to get my Master's degree in, & what graduate school I wanted to go to. He taught a class at Whitewater that I had taken called "Sports Pedagogy" – which, is "the art & science of teaching sport skills." It is also a fancy word for "coaching." I *loved* the class, so I decided I wanted to get a Master's Degree in it.

There were only a few universities who offered a Graduate Program in Sports Pedagogy, & Baylor University was one of them. As a matter of fact, it had *the best* Sports Pedagogy Graduate Program in the county. So, I applied there.

Part of the application process was taking the Graduate Record Examination (GRE) & writing a "personal statement of purpose." Since I had decided to go to Graduate School pretty late, & our season was about to start, I did not have much time to study for the GRE. In fact, the night I decided to go to Graduate School, I signed up to take the GRE the *next* morning. I took the thirty-question practice exam, & that was all the studying I did (it was just like when I took the ACT).

Writing my personal statement of purpose was when I first fell in love with writing, because I was *finally* able to write about what I believed in, what I loved, & what I was passionate about.

Coach Perch helped me through the *whole* process. He edited & revised my personal statement of purpose, *several* times. He wrote an *amazing*, heart-warming letter of recommendation for me; I cried reading it. He also helped me get other letters of recommendation from other prominent people.

It was *so great* to be able to sit right next to him as I opened the email I received from Baylor with my acceptance letter in it, & to share that moment of jubilation with him as I read it out loud.

EXPAND THE ZONE

When we got back from Florida, our home-opener was a doubleheader against the Ripon College Redhawks, & just like the previous season, we swept them in the doubleheader.

I was back in the win column.

That following weekend, we started our Conference schedule, by playing a four-game series at The Mill against the University of Wisconsin – Superior Yellowjackets. Since I started (& won) against Ripon just two days prior this series, my next start got bumped back to game one on Sunday.

It was a dark, cloudy, rainy day on Sunday. It was so dark, that we actually had to turn on our lights in the middle of the day. Plus, it was cold (like, it *always* is in early Spring in Wisconsin). It took me *a lot* longer than usual to warmup.

For the first pitch of the game, I threw an outside fastball that was literally *six* inches off (no exaggeration) of the plate, & the umpire called it a strike. As soon as the umpire called it a strike, Robby's eyes lit up with excitement, & he actually started laughing under his mask. He was so hysterical that he bounced the ball back to me.

Robby & I never had this home plate umpire before, so being the *great* catcher that he was, Robby wanted to test if strike one was legitimate, & he also wanted to see just how big the strike zone was going to be that day. So, the next pitch, he set up a little bit further outside, & the ball crossed the inside line of the opposite batter's box (further than six inches away), & the umpire called strike two.

It was at that moment, that Robby & I realized it was going to be a *very long* day for the Superior hitters.

Towards the end of my career at Whitewater, umpires *loved* me, even though the feeling was not mutual *at all*. Since I did not waste any time in between pitches, it made the games go by *very* fast; which, umpires loved. I also commanded all my pitches better than most pitchers in the country, so I threw *a lot* of strikes; which, umpires also loved. Like clockwork, during each game I started, towards the end of the game, the batters would always try their best to break up my rhythm by frequently calling time, & stepping out of the batter's box. Then, they would take as much time as they could to get back into the batter's box. When they did this, I *never* stepped off the mound. I kept standing there with my glove in my face, ready to deliver the next pitch. It was almost guaranteed that as soon as the umpire figured out what the hitters were trying to do, he would quickly stop letting them call time to step out of the batter's box. This caused a disruption in a lot of the hitter's pre-pitch routine, & I took great advantage of this.

I ended up throwing a shutout that game, & we won, 3-0. I also struck out a career-high eleven batters.

After the game, the home-plate umpire came up to me in our dugout, shook my hand, & said "it was such an honor to umpire you today, & witness the legend I have been hearing so much about."

SHOOT 'EM, MARCUS!

Our next conference matchup was against our conference rival, Stevens Point, in Stevens Point. As always, it was a highly-anticipated series; one that we had looked forward to for months.

In my opinion, the Pointers were a much better team (talent-wise) my senior year, as opposed to my junior year; regardless, both teams were *very* talented. They had *a lot* of players returning from the previous year. They had a *solid* lineup from beginning to end. They had a *great* pitching rotation, which included Joel, & another pitcher who was an All-American. They also had a few players who ended up playing professionally.

Unlike the previous year, I was not afraid to pitch against them. I was excited. However, my excitement was not because of the game, it was because the Webb family was coming to watch me pitch.

After I got done warming up in the bullpen, & I started walking back to the dugout, Tyler, Bryson, & Cayden came running up to the fence next our dugout to see me. They were all wearing the Whitewater Baseball shirts I got them for Christmas, & the athletic tape necklaces I made for them on my last night I lived with them the previous summer. I hugged them over the fence, & shortly after, Jon & Michelle walked up behind them & I hugged them as well.
It was *so great* to see them again; it was a breath of fresh air for me.

They were staying in the same hotel we were staying in, so after the game, we all went to the hotel pool & spent more time together.

The start of this game was unlike any other. Normally, after I got done with my warmup pitches, Robby would throw down to second to simulate throwing out a runner trying to steal second. However, this time, after I got done throwing my warmup pitches, I guess I did not get out of the way in time, & Robby threw the ball right into my back; I think I *still* have a bruise.
When this happened, the Stevens Point fans erupted.

I picked the ball up off of the ground, shook my head at Robby, & stared at him as I threw it to second base.

To make matters worse, he came out to the mound to see how I was & to see if I was hurt, & he interrupted my prayer behind the mound; he knew better than to do that. Before I even opened my eyes, & lifted my chin from under my jersey, I told him, "you better get the f@#% back behind home-plate."

Our dugout had a great laugh at the situation, by yelling "shoot 'em, Marcus!" I do not know where that phrase came from but we always yelled it whenever Robby threw down to second in between innings, or whenever he threw a runner out, or picked a runner off; which, happened *a lot.*

This was only the beginning of things "going wrong" that inning. I gave up a hit to the leadoff hitter. Then, the second hitter (the previous year's Conference Position Player of the Year) laid down a bunt, & in a feeble attempt to field that bunt, I committed an error. This was not just any error. This was an error you would see on ESPN's *"not* top 10." The bunt was down the first base line, & I tripped on my own feet trying to field it. Then, once I recovered & picked it up, I tried underhand tossing it to J-Do at first base, but I ended up losing control of it & "bowling" it past him into right field. Our right fielder then picked up the ball & threw it away, which caused a run to score.

The next hitter I faced reached on an error, as well. So, with a runner on first & second base & zero outs, they bunted again, & again, I could not field the bunt in time, & all runners were safe, leaving me with the bases loaded & *still* zero outs.
It felt like all the wheels had fallen off.

Then, unlike any other time before, Coach Cally came running out to the mound for a mound visit. This was the *only* time in my career that Coach Cally came out to talk to me on the mound; it was always Coach Vo every other time.

When he got out to the mound, he waved off Robby & the other infielders from joining us on the mound. We stood there in silence, while I caught my breath. Then, he said one phrase to me, & left the mound. That phrase was: "slow the game down."

One of the first things I learned about baseball, was as I began to climb the ranks, from youth to high school to college, I realized the game got faster & faster. At every new level, the athletes were faster. The ball moved faster out of the hand & off the bat. Plays & coverages unraveled faster. The pressure to be perfect was *a lot* higher. The games seemed to *fly* by. The score & the outcome of the game could quickly change, if I allowed it to. That is why it was so important to remember that the game is the same regardless of the speed of the game. The objectives & fundamentals are *always* the same.

We are the ones who have to slow the game down in our minds, & understand that there is absolutely no need to rush *anything*. Just because the game is faster, does not mean we have to move faster.

When we try to rush things, we tense up, & it is nearly impossible to throw, or hit a baseball to the best of our abilities, when we are tense. It is also nearly impossible to make quality decisions when our minds are going one-million miles-per-hour & we are thinking about a million things all at once.

I *needed* that reminder from Coach Cally.

Thanks to his reminder, I got out of that inning only allowing three runs (damage control). Then, I shut them down the rest of the game, by not allowing a single run to score for the next eight innings.

We came back & ended up winning that game, 5-3.

P? F? P?

I was *infamous* for not being able to field my position. I am surprised more teams did not play more small ball (bunting) against me. It was like I was completely allergic to the ball as soon as I pitched the ball & it left my hand. On add to my inability to field my position, if the ball was hit *hard* to the right side (first-base side) of the infield, & the first-basemen was drawn off the bag, which forced me to cover first base, it was a *guaranteed* hit for the batter.

It was hard for me to get my *big* body moving in that direction.

My inability to field my position was so bad that it was funny. Coach Vo gave me the nickname of "Big Puma" as a joke.

One good thing came out of it: every time I started, his son, & our bat boy, Sam, would wear his puma shoes to bring me "good luck."

Our dugout was *very* vocal, & that is an understatement. We had several chants & phrases we would yell out throughout the game, depending on the situation. Whenever a pitcher fielded a ground ball, fielded a bunt, or covered first-base, the dugout would yell "P… F… P!" – referring to "pitchers fielding practice."

However, whenever I fielded the ball, or covered first base (which, was a *rarity*), there was always a hesitation, & they would yell it out in the form of a question: *"P?.. F?.. P?"*

Fortunately, for me, my inability to field my position did not hinder my success on the field, & that is because I was surrounded by some of the best fielding infielders in the country. We also had one of the best – if not, *the best* - lineups in the country, & we scored *a lot* of runs, which took the option of small ball (bunting) away from most opposing team we faced.

I would not have won as many games as I did, without my team.

I would not have won all the awards I won, without my team.

KNOWLEDGE APPLIED

Everyone needs team. Not *just* athletes… *everyone.*

Life is not meant to be lived alone. We did not get to where we are, on our own. We will not get to where we want to be, on our own, either. Simply put, we need people - *we need each other.* Without people, there are no victories. Without people, there is no growth. Without people, there is no fulfillment, nor joy.

God uses people to grow people.

There are certain things that we are not good at, or strong at, & there are certain things that we cannot do. That is normal.

The goal is not to strengthen our weaknesses. The goal is to amplify our strengths & surround ourselves with people who can do what we cannot do, & people who are better than us at what we do.

Our lives become better when we realize that we do not have to know everything, & we do not have to be good at everything. Our lives become better when we realize we do not have to pretend like we know everything, & pretend like we are good at everything.

Real life change happens in relationships. If I were to ask you to list the top five books, messages, or videos that changed your life, it would take you a *long* time to come up with that list (or, you might not be able to come up with five). However, if I asked you to list the top five most influential *people* who changed your life, you would be able to list them off *immediately*.

In order for that *real*-life change to happen, we must have the courage to ask for help. I know it is incredibly vulnerable, but the depth we are willing to be vulnerable shows the true measure of our courage. We cannot allow pride to keep us in what it brought us into.

The problem is, we all love to pretend that we have it all together, which makes us want to fix things on our own terms, because we do not want to tell anyone our secrets.

Worse yet, we pray & we ask God to help us, but we get hung up on *how* He wants to help us. We ask God to heal us, & but we get hung on *how* He wants to heal us. We *all* want God to intervene, but we want Him to do on *our* terms, not His, because His terms often reveal our shortcomings, which makes us uncomfortable.

I know that a familiar captivity can feel more comfortable than an unfamiliar freedom, but these secrets, & these issues that we like to hide are too heavy for us to carry on our own.

I know that it is *a lot* easier to offer help that it is to ask for it, but we all need help, because we *all* struggle & we *all* have shortcomings.

If we want to live a better life, & turn our dream into reality *faster*, we must get around people who are playing the game at a higher level than we are. *Proximity is power*. Surrounding ourselves with people who are already successful in an area we want to be successful in allows us to model a behavior that is *proven* to work.

If we want to become wise, we need to start walking with the wise.

We cannot do life alone, *but...* we must be very careful about who we do life with. We are only as good as the company we keep. The quote, "show me your friends & I will show you your future" is true.

It is almost impossible to live the right life with the wrong people. Bad company *always* corrupts good character.

Here is a hard pill to swallow: The people in our lives who are closest to us may be the ones who are holding us back from being who are a called to be. I have experienced this myself, & I have witnessed it happen to my teammates, my friends, & the athletes I have had the privilege of mentoring, too many times.

There were two transfers who came in my senior year who completely changed the culture of our team... for the *worst*. Not only did they drink (which, pretty much everyone on the team did), they also did drugs, & they *blatantly* broke the rules.

The worst part about these two was that they had significant influence over our younger, impressionable teammates, who made up the majority of our roster.

Over the course of that year, I witnessed these young, talented kids lose their focus, change their priorities, & ultimately, lose their chance of having a career they could have been proud of.
All for what? For short-term fun? To fit in?

Sadly, they all play the "what if" game, or the "should have, would have, could have" game now.

Too many of us are spending our most valuable resource – our time - with the wrong people, in the wrong environment, making the wrong choices. Because of this, we are not where we want to be in life, & we wonder *why?*

We see so many people who get in trouble hanging out with similar people that we hang out with, in similar environments we are in, making similar wrong choices that we make, but we fail to see the direct correlation in our own lives.

This does not just apply to breaking the law, or making legal mistakes that cost us our actual freedom. This also applies to spending time with small-minded people who cost us our mental freedom, because we start believing the same doubts they believe, & we start having the same fears they have. If we do not become aware of this, we *will* be in the same bondage they are in.

Who are you spending the most time with?

Who are your friends?

Who is on your team?

I do not care how strong you think you are. I do not care how confident you think you are in your beliefs & values. You *will* develop the same characteristics, mindsets, & habits as the people you spend your most time with. It is only a matter of time.

Think about the habits your parents have. Do you have some of them? If you do, it is not by chance. It is because we have spent the majority of our time on Earth with them.

Here is an example: my parents never wore their seat belt when they drove, so when I started driving, I never wore my seat belt. Here is another example: my parents were constantly worrying about money, so when I grew up & moved out on my own, I was constantly worried about money. I actually had a *serious fear* of being homeless.

This happens to all of us. I am not special. You are not special. I am not exempt from it. You are not exempt from it.

The saying "you are the sum total of the five people you spend the most time with" is not just a quote, it is the truth.

You owe it to yourself & to your future to make the right choice - have that hard conversation with your parents, or your friends, & let go of that relationship that you *need* to let go of.

The right choice is not always the easiest choice to make, but it is *always* the right choice to make, & it *always* worth making.

HONOR

There is no such thing as a "self-made" man.

If we are going to stand alone, we are going to fall alone. If we are going to take all of the credit for all of our wins, then we better take all of the credit for our losses, as well.

There is absolutely no way that I could have accomplished what I did (the awards, the victories, etc.) during my baseball career, without my teammates. For the rest of this chapter, I want to thank the three teammates I had who had the biggest impact on my career at Whitewater, & give them the honor they are overdue.

WOBBY

You are *the greatest* catcher I ever had; that is saying something, because one of them is playing in the MLB right now.

Not every pitcher is given the blessing of having the same catcher *every* year that they are at a certain school, but I did, & I am so grateful that it was you. You were there for every start. You were there for every bullpen. You were there for every mound visit; as unpleasant as some of them were – I am sorry for swearing at you.

The chemistry we had is indescribable. There were points at the end of our career that we knew what each other was thinking without even saying a word.

Trust is *big* thing for me, & being able to go up on the mound & *completely* trust you as my catcher every single pitch, was liberating. There was only *one* time I shook you off (which, I will talk about later in the book), & I *still* regret it.

I have never seen a catcher who picked off as many runners as you did. I have seen a catcher throw as *hard* as you did - Actually, I did not just see it, I *felt* how hard you threw when you hit me in the back at Stevens Point. I have also never seen someone drink as many Red Bulls as you drank, & eat as many skittles as you ate.

You are one of a kind, Robby. Thank you for being my catcher. I did not win thirty games in my career... *we* did.

J-DO

You were *the best* overall athlete I ever played with; you were great at *everything* you did. You were my best example of Bo Jackson.

You accomplished things on the baseball field, & on the football field, that *no one else* will *ever* be able to accomplish.

What you did on the mound & in the batter's box the last month of our senior year was nothing short of miraculous (which, I will talk about later in the book). I never really paid attention to our hitters when we were hitting, but when you were up the plate, I *always* paid close attention, because I did not want to miss history being made.

Above all of that, I valued our friendship more than anything else; I am disappointed that we have drifted apart, but I guess that is what time & distance does. You forced me to elevate my game in so many different areas; I had to grow just to be around you. You forced me to grow as a baseball player. More importantly, you forced me to grow as a Christian. You challenged a lot of perspectives by opening my eyes to so many truths, & allowing me to be enlightened.

Thank you, Jeff, for being a *bright* shining light during one of the darkest periods of my life. Thank you for introducing me to your *wonderful* family, & *moosh* - my good luck charm. Thank you for being you, despite everyone else telling you not to be.

EGGY

You were *the greatest* teammate I ever had.

I never played with someone as selfless as you.

You were the one that started every chant in the dugout. You were the one that always "woke up" the bats. You were the only voice I heard when I was pitching – I *loved* when you yelled, "Can I help you? No thanks… *Just looking!*" after every batter I struck out looking. You were the one who made sure I was ready for every start I had.

Thank you is not enough for being as consistent as I needed you to be, & for being as superstitious as I was. You may not have had the career you wanted (statistically), but you were *exactly* what our team needed, & what *I* needed.

I am so sorry for bruising your most precious jewels.

"Life is not meant to be lived alone. We did not get to where we are, on our own. We will not get to where we want to be, on our own, either."

"It is almost impossible to live the right life with the wrong people. Bad company *always* corrupts good character."

@RileyTincher | #PitchingAgainstMyself

CHAPTER 16

KEEP THE BALL DOWN

Have you ever had, or do you have a fear that is so *ridiculous* that you are too embarrassed to tell anyone about it? I have – I should say, *had.* That fear I had was *wind* – also known as anemophobia. Now, before you start judging me, please let me explain.

Ever since I was a young kid, anytime I was outside & the wind started picking up speeds, I would suddenly get *a lot* of anxiety. I do not know why, but it *always* happened. I never had a negative experience with wind (or at least, none that I can remember) that caused trauma.

I actually loved storms, *especially,* thunder storms; I would sit on our couch in our living room & stare out of our front window, watching the skies light up with each lightning strike. *But,* if the storms caused the wind to pick up, I had to go down into my basement in order to calm down. I am not just talking about fifty+ miles-per-hour winds. I am talking about twenty+ miles-per-hour winds; which is an average windy day in the Great Plains - & the irony of all of this is I have lived in Oklahoma (one of the windiest states in the United States) for five years now.

During my childhood, I spent *a lot* of time in my basement

This fear (anemophobia) stayed with me throughout college, & it was intensified every time I stepped out on to the field.

At first, it was not that bad. Then, I got to NIACC, where the wind blew hard *every* day.

On game days, whenever I was the starting pitchers, the first thing I did when I pulled up to the field was check the direction the wind was blowing by looking at the American Flag hanging on a flag pole behind the outfield fence. If the flag indicated that wind was blowing out (which, it *always* was), the anxiety I felt as a child whenever the wind picked up would quickly come back, & my mind would become consumed with thoughts of giving up *many* "wind-aided" homeruns.

When I got to Whitewater, I started checking the flag less frequently… until my senior year; more specifically, my seventh start of my senior year.

THE GOLDEN CHILD

After my started against Stevens Point, I carried "Big Mo" with me to my next start against Platteville. I *always* had "Big Mo" with me when I pitched against Platteville. In my career against them, I had a record of four wins & zero losses, with twenty-six innings pitched, twenty-one strikeouts, & a 1.38 earned run average (ERA); my lowest ERA against any other opposing team I faced.

We beat Platteville 5-1 that day, & I went deep into game, pitching eight innings. I was mad when Coach Vo pulled me from the game, because I *always* wanted to finish what I started. At least that was my mentality *until* my next start.

After that game, my record improved to five wins & one loss. Things were looking up. I was finally back in a groove, & pitching the way I *expected* to pitch.

My next start came against the University of Wisconsin –Stout Bluedevils, at their home field in Menomonie, Wisconsin. It was our longest trip of the year (a little over four hours), & since our game was at noon on Saturday, we left Friday night.

Saturday was very rainy in Menominee, so they pushed the games back until Sunday. This threw a wrench in my routine.

I loved being able to hang out with my teammates at the hotel all day, but my mind & my body was ready to pitch *that* day.

To make matters worse, I woke up the next morning with a sore throat & a *terrible* cough. There was not an inning I pitched that day that I did not have *at least* two cough drops in my mouth. As a matter of fact, I choked on one of them when I gave up my first homerun.

When we got to the field that morning, I checked the flag in the outfield & it was blowing out. It was not a slight breeze, either. The wind was blowing so hard, it looked like the flag was going to blow right off the flag pole. My anxiety sky rocketed.

Despite the wind, I still had a little bit of hope. If the wind was blowing out, that also meant good things for *our* hitters, & I will take our hitters over any others, *every* day.

I also had a little bit of hope because prior to my senior season, the NCAA completely changed the way aluminum bats were made.

The new bats were known as BBCOR bats. BBCOR stands for "Batted Ball Coefficient of Restitution."

Without getting into too much physics & biomechanics, the difference between the aluminum bats we used the years before, & the BBCOR bat that we used my senior year was how hard the baseball bounced off the bat. The baseball bounced much harder off an aluminum than it did a BBCOR bat.

The BBCOR bats were much like wood bats; which, is one of the reasons (other than pitcher's safety) why they made the switch from aluminum – to simulate what it would be like to play professional baseball, where a hitter is only allowed to swing a wood bat.

As a pitcher, I *loved* the switch. I thought it brought more authenticity to the college game. There was no longer such thing as a 160-pound middle-infielder being a power hitter – which, was the case for my junior year's Conference Position Player of the Year (Steven Point's shortstop), who hit .400 & had twenty-nine extra-base hits (including seven homeruns) the year before the switch, then hit below .300 & only had five extra-base hits the year after.

Plus, the switch helped decrease my ERA, because I did not give up as many extra-base hits as I did the year before... excluding my start against Stout.

Everything was going great during my start until the second inning. There were two-outs with a runner on first-base, & #9 hitter (very bottom of the order) was up. On the second pitch of the at-bat, I got him to hit a pop-fly to centerfield... or so I thought.

Like I always did, I pointed my finger to the sky & yelled "up" to indicate a popup was just hit. Then, the ball kept carrying, & carrying, & carrying... until it finally went over the fence, just over the glove of our center fielder. That was homerun #1.

In the fourth inning, it got out of control. I gave up another pop-fly homerun to the first hitter I faced that inning. That was homerun #2. Then, I gave up another pop-fly homerun to the fourth hitter I faced that inning. That was homerun #3. Finally, I gave up a *legitimate* homerun to the sixth hitter I faced that inning. That was the homerun #4; the final homerun I gave up that day.
I got out of that inning giving up four runs, which, were all homeruns.

After that inning, I did not want to be out there anymore. I was sick, & I did not want to give up any more homeruns. However, Coach Vo kept sending me out there.

I had a clean (zero runs) fifth & sixth inning, & we were tied 7-7... until the seventh inning, when the wheels came off. I gave up a hit to the first two hitters I faced, then the reliever who came in after me gave up a three-run homerun to the first hitter he faced. Then, he proceeded to give up four more runs that inning. We ended up losing that game, 14-8. I did not see the end of the game.

About an inning after I got pulled, Coach Vo walked up to me in the dugout, & looked me up & down. I had *poor* body language (head down, shoulders slumped, avoiding eye-contact); partially, because I was sick & I *hate* being sick. After looking me up & down, he said "your acting like your dog just died." At the time, he did not know that my dog (King) *actually* died a few months before that.

I do not know why he said that, but I am guessing it was to remind me not to take us losing so seriously.

Nonetheless, I was immediately filled with rage. I saw red & I clenched my fists. Before I could even step one foot forward towards Coach Vo, Coach Cally grabbed my arm, pulled me back, & told me to follow him.

He took over to a soccer field that was right next to the baseball field, & he made me run sprints (probably, to help me blow off steam).

In between my sprints, he asked what I thought about the game (how I felt physically, what I wish I would have done differently, etc.).

After one of the sprints, he asked me "why do you think you gave up so many homeruns?" Without thinking, I answered, "because of the wind blowing out." He stopped me before I could say any more, & he told me, "that is just an excuse, Tinch. Excuses are like losses, everyone has them... *except* for Champions." Then, he asked me, "can you control the wind?" I felt like it was a trick question, so I cautiously said, "no..." He responded, "then, stop using the wind as an excuse."

I ran a few more sprints. Then, he asked me, "what *can* you control?" To which I respond, "my command (location of my pitches)." He enthusiastically said, "that is right!" & continued by asking me another question, "what is the best way to reduce the chances of giving up homeruns?" Before I could even answer, he said "keep the ball *down*."

After I got down running sprints, we went back into the dugout to eat our between-game snacks. While we were eating, Coach Vo called for our attention, then he said:

"We need to turn the page & regroup for next game. You guys are acting like the world is about to end because Tinch, our Golden Child, got hit around, & lost. That just goes to show you that even the best get hit around sometimes. He will bounce back... just like we will bounce back in this next game."

He was right. We did bounce back & we won the second game, 13-8. Then, we swept them the next day, to win the series.

Unfortunately, it took me a little bit longer to bounce back.

KEEP YOUR HEAD UP

My next start came against the Concordia University – Chicago Cougars. This was a highly-anticipated matchup. At the time of the game, we were both nationally-ranked; we were #10 in the nation, & they were #25. We had a record of 20-5, & they had a record of 20-4. Plus, we both had *solid* teams. However, they had two players that would later on be drafted in the MLB draft that summer, & we did not.

There was only one game that year that Coach Cally could not be there to watch me warm up (because of his other job), & it was this start against the Cougars.

Everything about my warmup was off. I could not get my arm loose, I was all over the place with my command, & I had a hard time focusing. Because of this, I got *really* frustrated, & I carried my frustration out to the mound with me.

Much like my start against Stout, everything was going smoothly until the second inning. I gave up three hits in a row to make the bases loaded with no outs. I though, "oh, *great*... This is Stout all over again." Then, fortunately, I got the next hitter to ground into a double-play. I did as much "damage control" as I could, & I got out of that inning allowing just two runs to score, to tie the game up, 2-2.

The next inning, I gave up a homerun to give them the lead; This homerun was *not* a wind-aided at all, it was a *"no-doubter."* As soon as it left his bat, I knew it was *gone*.

As he was running the bases, the doubts & disbeliefs engulfed my mind; I thought, "Here we go again..."

I then proceeded to give up a double, followed up by a *deep* fly-ball to centerfield, which, our centerfielder caught at the warning track, to end the top of the fourth inning.

In the bottom of the fourth inning, we scored a run, to go ahead, 5-4. Then, I went back out to the mound in the top of the fifth inning & gave up *another* double to the leadoff hitter, & after that double was hit, my start was over.

As soon as I saw Coach Vo walking out to the mound to pull me, I turned my back to him, hoping he would go away. When he got to the mound, I turned back around, did not make eye contact with him at all, & I held on to the ball until the relief pitcher got to the mound. When he finally got there, I slammed the ball so *hard* into his glove that I forced him to drop it. Then, I walked off that mound with my head hanging so low I could have dragged my chin on the ground.

I do not know what frustrated me more. Getting hit around so badly two games in a row? Or not even making it past the fourth inning (I maybe did that three other times in my *entire* career)?

At that point in my career, I not only *expected* to win *every* game I started, but I also expected to throw a complete game *every* time I went out there. Anything less, outraged me.

Fortunately, we won that game, 7-6. The relief pitcher (whom, I will talk about later) *finally* shut down the cougar hitters, & we scored two more runs in the bottom of the sixth inning to secure the win.

After the game, I was *still* frustrated & disappointed, even though, we won. I hardly said a word to anyone. I kept my head down the entire time I fixed the mound, & cleaned up my locker, & I did not acknowledge *anyone*, not even the coaches.

Shortly after everyone left, I received a text message from Coach Vo, & it said: "Keep your head up! The sun comes up tomorrow!"

As soon as I read the text, the water works started, & I began to cry, uncontrollably - luckily, there was no else in the clubhouse that saw me crying. The reason why I cried was because in that moment, I was having a *very* hard time believing that my struggles were going to get any better. I seriously thought that my career was over, & that my "streak of luck" had finally come to an end.

It is *amazing* how one simple gesture - a text message encouraging me to "keep my head up" - could make such an impact on me.

Fortunately, my "streak of luck" did not end. My next start came against Platteville, & we all know how that ended.

AUTONOMOUS

After beating Platteville, my next start was scheduled against the University of Wisconsin – Oshkosh Titans (the other school in the WIAC that highly-recruited me) that following weekend.

To give me some much-needed extra rest, I did not start until game one on Sunday (as opposed to my usual game one start on Saturday).

The rest of the conference was thinking that I was going to start on Saturday, so they hyped up the matchup between Oshkosh's Ace & I. He was also a left-handed pitcher, & he too had been dominating hitters in our Conference all season long.

Unfortunately, for the people that eagerly awaited our matchup, they had to wait a little bit longer until the Conference Tournament to see us pitch against each other.

Their Ace ended up beating us game one on Saturday, & we lost game two as well. We had not been swept in a doubleheader by Oshkosh since my first year at Whitewater. Needless to say, Coach Vo was frustrated with us, but he was not frustrated because we lost both games; he was frustrated because we *beat ourselves* - we committed *seven* errors, & allowed nine free passes (walks & hit-by-pitches) that day; which, we *never* allowed to happen during a doubleheader before. We *needed* to hit the reset button.

When we showed up to the field on Sunday, the wind was blowing straight out to left field at forty+ miles-per-hour (if not, *more*). It was *the* windiest day I had ever played a baseball game in before.

Obviously, I was incredibly nervous before the game. Not only because of my fear of wind, but I also had memories of my start against Stout swirling around in my head.

Thank God, Coach Cally was there to calm me down throughout my warmup. Every pitch I threw in the bullpen before the game was preceded by him reminding me to "keep the ball down."

I carried that phrase with me into the game, & before every pitch, I would recite it, repeatedly.

Wind blowing straight out is not necessarily a bad thing for me. Throwing toward home-plate, against the wind, added wind resistance to my pitches, which, increased the movement of my pitches.

When I threw my first slider that day, it moved *at least* two feet (not an exaggeration). The look on Robby's face after he caught it was the same look he gave me after I threw the first fastball six inches off the plate against Superior, & it was called a strike. From that slider on, we used the wind & the movement of my pitches to our advantage.

It was a *very* long day for the Oshkosh hitters, just like it was for the Superior hitters.

It was quite the opposite day for our hitters. We ended up scoring *nineteen* runs that game – seven of those runs scoring off the bat of *four* homeruns. In fact, we scored eight runs in the first inning.

During the middle of that inning, I had to go back down to the bullpen to throw to keep my arm warm.

The wind was not the only crazy thing that happened that game. If I were to ask you how many pitchers Oshkosh used that game in which they allowed nineteen runs to score, you would probably guess that they four, maybe five different pitchers, & if you did guess that, you would be *wrong*.

Oshkosh used only *two* pitchers that game, & the first pitcher they used only faced the first five hitters in our lineup; he only got one out, & allowed four runs to score, before he was pulled. That means the pitcher who came in after him threw the remaining 8 2/3 innings, while allowing *fifteen* more runs to score.

In baseball, this is known as a pitcher being "hung out to dry."

On top of the fifteen runs he gave up, he also walked seven hitters. I did not count how many pitches he threw, but it had to be close to two-hundred pitches; almost double the amount of pitches a starter normally throws in a game.

The worst part was, this pitcher received no sympathy from his head coach. He was on his own. What he had to deal that day was *abuse.* I felt *terrible* for him, but at the same time, I also felt overjoyed that I chose to go to Whitewater, instead of Oshkosh, because this was not the only time he *abused* pitchers.

I pitched a complete game that day, winning 19-2; this was my third complete game of the season. My record improved to seven wins & two losses. More importantly, I was back on a winning streak, & I had "Big Mo" back on my side, & she would stay with me through the end of the regular season.

My final start of the regular season came against the University of Wisconsin – Lacrosse Eagles. This start was on a very special day - the day we dedicated to Coach Mills & renamed Prucha Field, James B. Miller Stadium - or, "The Mill" for short.

Whenever I look back at my baseball career, & think about all the starts that I had, two starts always come to mind, because they were the best starts I had. The first one I think of is my start against Stevens Point in the Regional Tournament my junior year, & how "in the zone" I felt. The second start I think of is my start against Lacrosse my senior year, & how "in control" I felt.

In order for you to understand how I felt during my start against Lacrosse, I want to give you a brief lesson in motor learning. Simply put, motor learning is the (internal) process of improving motor skills through coaching cues & practice.

There are three stages of motor learning most athletes go through. The first stage is the cognitive stage, where the athlete develops an overall understanding of the skill they are trying to learn. This is where they learn the objectives of the skill, but have a hard time completing the objectives without help - for example: a baby learning to walk by holding their parent's hand.

The second stage is the associative stage, where the athlete begins to demonstrate a more refined movement of the skill they are trying to learn. In this stage, they can begin to do the objectives of the skill on their own, but they still need help, or correction from time to time -

for example: a toddler transitioning from the walking to running stage; they can do it, but they still fall down sometimes.

The third & final stage is the autonomous stage, where the athlete can perform the skill automatically, & *without* thinking about it - for example: a grown-adult no longer has to think about the objectives needed to perform the skill of walking. Depending on the skill being learned, it takes *years* of practice to get to this stage. Most athletes *never* get to this stage. Fortunately, I did.

During my start against Lacrosse, every pitch I threw I could *feel* the ball coming off my fingers tips, & I knew *exactly* where the pitch was going to be the moment I released the ball. It was *the greatest* feeling I ever had pitching, & it is almost impossible to explain. I am incredibly grateful I got to experience it at least once in my lifetime.

I only made three mistakes that game, two of which, were homeruns. The funny thing is, I knew they were going to be homeruns the moment the ball left my fingers. The third mistake I made was a wild pitch I threw in the ninth inning, when I bounced a slider two feet in front of home-plate; I am sorry, Robby.

We won that game by a score of 10-4, & I finished the regular season with a record of nine wins & two losses. We went on to win that series against Lacrosse, & we finished the season with a record of thirty-one wins & nine losses. We also finished the season ranked in the top-ten nationally. However, we were not the only WIAC team in the top-ten. We were accompanied by our biggest conference rivals, Stevens Point, who won the regular season WIAC Conference championship. This meant that the Conference Tournament was going to be held at Stevens Point the next week.

KNOWLEDGE APPLIED

We *love* control. We love being in control. We love when we think we have control. We love the idea of controlling the outcome of our lives. We love the feeling we get when we think we have control.

We love to be the King. Too bad, we all are *lousy* Kings.

The thought of having control & being in control of our lives is often an illusion. The *truth* is, we are hardly ever in control, & we hardly ever have control.

This is hard to *fully* comprehend (almost impossible), but there are only a *few* things we actually can control – our attitude, our words, our effort, & our focus. That is it.

Despite what society teaches us, we cannot control the outcome of what we are trying to accomplish; remember, we are only responsible for the obedience to the process. Furthermore, we cannot control the people in our lives; even though, we *desperately* want to control how they feel (especially, about us), what they say, & what they do. We cannot even control our own thoughts, but we can control our behavior, & our actions.

We all try to control things we cannot control. I am guilty of it. You are guilty of it. We are all guilty of it.

Instead of trying to control what happens to us, we should control how we *respond* to what happens to us. That is where all the *power* is.

We cannot let what is out of our control hinder the things we *can* control. If we continue to worry about things we cannot control, we are setting ourselves up for a lifetime of misery & frustration. Plus, worrying about something that we cannot control is *not* going to change the fact that we cannot control it.

The problem is, we all try to figure out things that simply cannot be explained. Even if they were explained, our *tiny, finite* brains would *never* be able to comprehend it all. This bothers most us.

Knowledge *is* power, & we should try to gain as much knowledge as we can. We cannot have wisdom – *the greatest* of all riches (worth more than any amount of gold, silver, or diamond) – without knowledge. *But*, we must realize that there are things we *never* will gain *true* knowledge of, & there are things we will *never* understand – at least not during our time here on Earth.

Control stems from expectations (& vice-versa) – Expectations we have of other people, & expectations we have of what we think should be happening. Expectations *always* lead to disappointment. Expectations are the reason why most arguments occur, & why many relationships fail. It is impossible to simultaneously have expectations of someone else, & have empathy for them. It is only when we drop all expectations we have of other people, that we have peace, & peace is one of the greatest feelings (besides, love) we will ever experience.

Jesus Christ did not have any expectations of us before He gave up His life. He did not say "you must follow these rules, before I save you," nor "you must do this behavior, before I forgive you of all of your sins." Jesus forgave us because He *loves* us. If He did not have any expectations of us, why do we have expectations of each other?

Jesus offers the peace that we *need*, but it comes at the expense of control, because we cannot save ourselves. If we want this peace, if we want the freedom He promises (John 8:36), & if we want the rest He *desperately* wants to give us (Matthew 11:28), we must surrender control. He *has* to be King!

The world tells us to "try harder," but Jesus tells us to "give up;" give up control of what we *think* we have control of.

True faith comes from surrendering control. *True* peace requires us to surrender our delusions of having control. Surrender means giving up trying to figure out what only He knows. Surrender means giving up what we think *should* be happening for what is *actually* happening. Surrender means not allowing our lives to be guided by our feelings, & instead by *His Word*. Surrender means trusting the One who is in complete control.

It was only when I realized that I cannot control the wind, that He took my fear of it away from me. It was only when I surrendered to it, that I finally had control over it.

It is not about what happens around us, or what happens to us.
It is about what happens within us & through us.

"If we continue to worry about things we cannot control, we are setting ourselves up for a lifetime of misery & frustration."

"It is not about what happens around us, or what happens to us.
It is about what happens *within* us & *through* us.

@RileyTincher | #PitchingAgainstMyself

CHAPTER 17

CALL TO THE BULLPEN

L ike every other season, we had *very high* hopes going into the postseason. The expectation of our program was *always* to compete for & win a National Championship, & justifiably. Every year under Coach Vo's leadership, we were contenders. Since 2004, we had been to the World Series three times, & we won it all in 2005, just six years prior to my senior year. However, *I* had never been to the World Series as a Warhawk.

In my first two years at Whitewater, we lost in the Regional Championship game; the game that decides who goes to the World Series, & who does not.

The previous year's (my junior year) loss to Stevens Point by a suicide squeeze left a *very* bitter taste in my mouth (that is still there), & I was not the only one.

Before the season started, us Robby, J-Do, & I (the captain) called a meeting with the entire team. Before the meeting started, I wrote "G2G" on the whiteboard in front of the classroom we met in.

In this meeting, we talked about the upcoming season & what expectations we had for the year.

At one point in the meeting, I gave a speech that explained what "G2G" was an acronym for – "Good to Great."

We had a young team, with *a lot* of new faces, because we had five seniors graduate, seven players quit, & one player sign to play professionally, the previous year.

Since we had *a lot* of new faces, not many of the players on our roster knew about our previous years' struggles, & not many knew that we had lost in the Regional Championship game each of those two years. So, to bring awareness to it, I described our previous two years as being *"good* enough," & I added that in order to win a National Championship that year (which, we all agreed that we wanted to) we needed to be great at *everything* we did.

YOU REALLY *ARE* GOOD

The first step we took towards going to the World Series was the WIAC Conference Tournament. Since we did not win the regular season conference championship, we did not get to host the tournament; Stevens Point hosted it, since they won.

We went into the tournament as the #2 seed. The #3 seed team was Oshkosh. Stevens Point, being the #1 seed, sat out the first game, while we played Oshkosh.

A lot of people expected me to start game one, but I did not, & neither did J-Do. I did not why then, & still do not know why now, but my best guess is that it was to give both J-Do & I more rest (which, was *always* needed). Instead, one of our spot starters (a pitcher who started a game on occasion, if we needed) started the game; it was his fourth start of the year, & his first start in over two weeks.

He did what most pitchers in his position would *not* be able to do. When his name was called (unexpectedly), he came in, & he pitched like he had been one of our top four starters all season. Because of his performance, we won game one. This win set up the matchup everyone was looking forward, Stevens Point versus Whitewater - the winner advancing the Championship game.

We played them the very next game that day, & again, J-Do & I did not start. Instead, our #3 starter, Justin Lambert, pitched.

Justin was the relief pitcher who came in after me against the University of Concordia – Chicago Cougars – the one whom I slammed the ball so hard into his glove that he dropped it.

Justin had an *incredible* story. His story was very similar to Matt Millar's story. He was actually Matt's teammate in 2005, & just like

Matt, he was also kicked off the team. Prior to the 2005 season, he fell hard into alcohol abuse, hardly ever attended classes, & eventually, ended up failing out of school before the season even started.
Because of Matt, Justin got back up on his feet & cleaned up his act.

Prior to the 2011 season, he had been working two jobs: one in a factory, & the other as an alcohol distributer (how ironic). With a slight push from Matt, Justin applied to go back to school, got accepted, & rejoined our baseball team.

He was the "old man" of the team. At the time, he was a twenty-six years old sophomore; at least seven years older than the rest of the sophomores on the team.

Everyone *loved* Justin. He was a quirky guy, who had a ton of energy - he *loved* sugar about as much as Robby did. He also had a lot of great stories to share.

His pitching delivery matched his personality - it was *effective*, but not very consistent. One pitch, he would throw a fastball in the upper-80's on the radar gun. Then, the very next pitch, he would throw that same fastball that barely touched 80. One pitch, he would throw a sharp-breaking curveball. Then, the very next pitch, he would throw a curveball that would just spin & not break at all.

His performance against Stevens Point matched this inconsistency. He dominated the first inning, then, the next inning he gave up two runs. He dominated the fourth inning, then, the next inning he gave up three runs. Then, he did something he never did before; he made an adjustment (I do not know what), & he became *lights out*. More importantly, he became consistent.

He did not allow another run to score the rest of the game, & he carried this consistency with him through the end of the season.

Unfortunately, we did not recover from the initial six runs he gave up. We lost the game, 6-5. This loss set us up for a rematch against Oshkosh the very next day at ten in the morning. This also set us up for the matchup *everyone* wanted to see – me versus Oshkosh's Ace.

After Coach Vo told me that I would be starting the next day, on the bus ride back to the hotel, I called my mom to tell her. Since the game was at 10:00 AM on a Saturday, I assumed her & my dad would not come, since my dad worked Friday nights. I wanted to ask anyway. She told me that "she would try to make it," & that there was "*no way* dad would make it.*" Even though I assumed they were not going to be able to make it, I was still disappointed to hear it.

The next day, at the field, while I was warming up, another wrench was thrown into my routine. I was on the mound in the bullpen, when they called my name to go to home-plate. At first, I *refused,* because I had a game to warm up for, & I *never* broke my routine for *anything...* or *anyone*. Then, they called me name again, & I *still* refused. Finally, they sent one of our pitchers down to the bullpen to grab me; that poor pitcher looked *so scared* coming up to me in the bullpen to tell me that I needed to go to home-plate.

When I *finally* got to home-plate, I was met by the WIAC commissioner, & he had a plaque in his hand. Then, an announcement came over the speakers that said that I was the 2011 Max Sparger Scholar-Athlete Award winner; this award was given to the best scholar-athlete in the conference. At first, I was excited, & then, I was angry. I realized that because I won this award, it meant that I did not win a consecutive Conference Pitcher of the Year award – Oshkosh's Ace, Luke Westphal, took it away from me, even though I had a better record than him. This only added fuel to my fire, & I wanted to prove to the voters that they chose the wrong guy.

The highly-anticipated matchup between him & I was all that it was hyped up to be. It reminded me of the matchup I had with St. Thomas' Ace, Matt Schuld, the year before.
Luke & I went back & forth the *entire* game.

It was a shutout baseball game, until our freshman centerfielder hit a solo homerun in the top of the third inning to make the score 1-0. We held on to that lead until the bottom of the sixth inning, when I gave up a run-scoring triple that tied the game 1-1. Then, we both settled in even more, until the bottom of the ninth inning.

With two outs, & a runner on third base, Oshkosh's hitter did the unexpected. He laid down a two-out suicide squeeze bunt - this is when "Big Puma" showed up to the game. I got to the ball too late, & threw to first base but the runner was already safe. This allowed the runner on third to score, & the game was over. They won, 2-1, on a walk-off *two-out* suicide squeeze. I was humiliated.

Before the bottom of the first inning started, as I was warming up on the mound to begin my start, I heard a man in the stands behind home-plate yell "rooster!" The voice of the man sounded *very* familiar, & "rooster" was the nickname my dad gave me when I was a child; which, evolved from my original nickname, "Riley Roo." I looked to see where the voice was coming from, & I found my dad standing next to my mom behind the fence behind home-plate. As soon as I made eye contact with him, I was instantly filled with joy.

This was the first game my dad came to see me pitch since my redshirt-freshman year at NIACC.

For whatever reason (there were so many that they gave), he was "not able to" come to see me pitch the year before (my junior year); *the best* year of my career. He also was "not able to" come see me pitch in the Northwoods League; not even, when I pitched in the All-Star game – *the pinnacle* of my career. He also was "not able to" to come see me pitch on Sundays during the summer, when I pitched for a local home talent team. The sad thing about it was, the field we played at was less than five miles away from the house I grew up in.

Since my dad was *finally* there to see me pitch, I had *zero* time to feel sorry for myself in the dugout after our loss. I had to quickly suck up my embarrassment, so I could see him for the first time in *months*.

The first thing my dad said to me was, "Wow! You really are good, bud." Notice, he did not say "you are *really* good." He said, "you really *are* good," as if he was *surprised* to see me pitch so well.

GRADUATION

The day after our loss to Oshkosh, Stevens Point ten-runned them to win the Conference Tournament Championship. In doing so, they received an automatic bid to the Midwest Regional Tournament.

Because we lost, we had to wait to receive an "at-large" bid into the Regional Tournament.

Since we were nationally-ranked all season – top ten, the majority of the season - we had no doubt that we would receive the bid. Plus, we were hosting the Regional Tournament again; which, added to our certainty. The only thing we did not know was what seed in the tournament we were going to receive.

Later that night, after the Conference Tournament Championship had been decide, we received the bid we had expected, & we were named the #2 seed in the Tournament; Stevens Point was the #1 seed.

Since there were only six teams in the Tournament, that meant our first matchup would be against the #5 seed team. The #5 seed team was our regular postseason foe, the St. Thomas Tommies.

On the first day of the tournament, the first game that was played was Stevens Point versus Aurora (the #6 seed). Their game went into extra innings, & Stephens Point beat Aurora the same way they beat us in the Regional Championship game the previous year; they laid down a suicide-squeeze bunt to win the game.

The second game of the day was our game against St. Thomas. For this game, Coach Vo had a *different* strategy to save J-Do & I's arms for later in the tournament. He had J-Do start, since he had not pitched in over two weeks. Then, he had me come on in relief after J-Do. The plan to save our arms worked... *for J-Do.*

J-Do pitched the first three innings, & came out of the game when the score was tied, 1-1. Then, I came into the game in the top of the fourth inning, & the first batter I faced, I gave up a homerun, which allowed them to take the lead, 2-1. Fortunately, that would be the *last* run they scored that day.

In the bottom of the fourth inning we scored a run to tie the game, & then we scored another run in the bottom of the sixth inning to take the lead, 3-2.

I was settled in, & pitching great, until the top of the eighth inning, when I gave up a single to the leadoff hitter in typical "Big Puma" fashion; I could not field a bunt. Then, I was done.

That day was a *very* special day for me. I beat one of the best teams in the nation to earn my tenth win of the season. We won the first game of the Midwest Regional Tournament; which, is critical for *every* team trying to win the Championship. It was also Graduation day for me. Since I was unable to attend the Graduation Ceremony the weekend before (because we were playing in the Conference Tournament), we had an on-field Graduation Ceremony just for me after the game. During this Ceremony, I received my diploma from the Athletic Director, the Provost, & the Chancellor of the University. One of the best parts about the Ceremony was that I was surrounded by my coaches, & my teammates, who had been there for me through *every* win, & *every* loss. Even better than that, I received my degree on the very field I had spent *countless* hours on, practicing & playing. It was another amazing milestone accomplished on that field.

It was also great to see how proud my Mom was of me... *that day.*

DEAD ARM

There are different periods throughout the year when pitchers experience what is called "dead arm." The symptoms of dead arm are: your velocity goes down a little bit, the hardness of your fastball goes away (it seems to have no zip), your breaking ball just spins & has no break, & your changeup has no pull.

Dead arm is unavoidable. It is guaranteed to happen to *every* pitcher.

For me, dead arm always happened four times throughout the season: a couple of weeks before spring training, during spring training, in the middle of the season, & during the conference tournament. The later I got in my career, & the more I pitched, the more frequent I had dead arm, & the worse it was for me; even after taking Fall Ball off, & not throwing for five months.

Dead arm can ruin a pitcher's season; even, his career. Dead arm can also show a pitcher's character, & show his ability (or inability) to compete. They say only the great players rise to the occasion. I say the great players rise to the occasion when they do not have their best stuff; for example, Michael Jordan's Flu Game.

When my name was called, & I ran out to the mound, it was my game, & no one else's game. I did not care if my arm was dead. I did not care if every pitch I threw in the bullpen was off target. As soon as that first pitch was thrown, good luck trying to take me out of the game. Even at my worst, I *believed* I gave my team the best chance to win whenever I was on the mound.

If there was one thing I was good at, it was competing. I never gave in, despite the circumstance. I just kept pitching, even if my arm was in excruciating pain.

My senior year was when my addiction to Ibuprofen (& other pain-relievers) really took off.

What I did not mention before was how I added taking Ibuprofen into my routine. As soon as I woke up the morning of a start, I would take three two-hundred milligram pills of Ibuprofen. Then, when I got to the field right before batting practice, I would take three more pills. Finally, an hour before the game, right when I was about to head out to the field to begin my warmup, I would take three more pills. That was my routine my junior year.

My senior year, I increased my dosage from three to five pills (sometimes, *more*) every time I took them (when I woke up, right before batting practice, & right before my start). Then, about half way through the season, I got introduced to Tylenol-3, & I started taking it right before I went out to warm up, in addition to the five (or more) pills of ibuprofen. I took it right before I went to warmup because I did not want the drowsiness side effect from the codeine to set in before I started pitching.

All the pain-relievers I took may have alleviated the pain I felt (short-term), but they did not take away dead arm.

After my relief appearance against St. Thomas, dead arm set in, & I never truly recovered.

DRIVE THE STAKE IN

The next day we played the #3 seed in the tournament, the Hamline University Pipers. Justin got the start. We had the lead, 6-3, going into the bottom of the of seventh inning, then, my name was called to come on in relief, after the second hitter hit a single up the middle. I managed to get out of that inning, allowing zero runs to score. However, the next inning was a *much* different story.

Since I did not have my best stuff that day, I had to resort to throwing *a lot* of off-speed pitches to try to keep the hitters "off-balance," but it did not work. In the top of the eighth inning, I gave up three straight hits to the first three hitters I faced; which, loaded up the bases with zero outs. Then, I was pulled from the game. Those three runners eventually came in to score, to tie the game, 6-6.

With the score still tied after the ninth inning, we went into extra innings. In the top of the tenth inning we scored a run, to go ahead 7-6. Then, Robby, who was our *brand-new* closer, closed out the game in the bottom of the tenth inning, to advance us to the third round of the Regional Tournament; which, was the next day.

Just like the previous year, the third round of the tournament was against none other than the Stevens Point Pointers. However, this year, the Pointers lost in the second round to the #4 team, the St. Scholastica College Saints.

Because they already had one loss in a double elimination tournament, we had an opportunity to end Stevens Point's season early, just like they ended our season early the year before.

On the day of our game against Stevens Point, Coach Vo asked us to meet him & the rest of the coaches at the Van Steenderen Softball Complex (Whitewater softball field) to hit in the batting cages right outside of the field.

When the team got done hitting (I did not hit... *ever*), Coach Vo had us stick around until one of our assistant coaches showed up with a *huge* bag that was full of *something*.

As we all stood there wondering what was in the bag, Coach Vo delivered a speech. To be honest, I do not remember much of what he said, because my mind was fixated on what was in the bag.

When our assistant coach *finally* opened the bag, he revealed to us that in it was a bunch of wooden stakes. Coach Vo told us to each grab a stake, then he proceeded to tell us about how Stevens Point was our vampire who constantly drained the life out of us. He concluded the speech by saying, "today, we are going to drive these stakes through their hearts, & we are going to kill them *once & for all*." Then, one by one, he had all the seniors come up & drive their wood stakes into the ground with a bat. The last senior he had come up to the front was J-Do, & after J-Do drove his stake into the ground, Coach Vo told him that he was going to be the starting pitcher that day, & J-Do went nuts, & we all joined him.

I have *never* been as pumped up for a baseball game as I was after that speech & after J-Do brought us all together.

As soon as the game started, Stevens Point came out swinging. They roughed J-Do up pretty badly the first inning. They got three hits off him, including a run-scoring double. Even the outs he got that inning were hit *hard*.

Somehow, J-Do managed to escape the inning allowing just one run to score; which, was the *only* run they would score that day.

After J-Do got out of that first inning, only allowing one run to score, I knew right then & there, without a shadow of doubt, that we were going to win the Regional Championship.

Now, you may be asking yourself, "How could he know that they were going to win the Regional Championship in the third round of the Tournament?" Let me tell you, it was because this game *the* championship game for us. All the preparation we did before the season & during the season, led us up to *this* game. Everyone else in the tournament besides Stevens Point *did not matter.* The Pointers were our *only* competition.

The year before, we lost seven games all season, & five of them were to the Pointers, including the Regional Championship game. This season was a split as well, & there was no way that we were going to let them finish on top again.

I have had the fortune of watching J-Do pitch *several* times, & I had *never* seen him make adjustments & compete the way he did that day. After the first inning, he threw *sixty-percent* breaking balls (more than *double* the average percentage of breaking balls thrown in a game) the rest of the game, & that is not an exaggeration.

When the final out was made, we celebrated like we won the Championship, because that was our Championship, & now, the only thing that stood in our way from dog-piling, lifting up that Regional Championship Trophy, & going to the World Series was St. Scholastica. *They did not stand a chance.*

After we got done celebrating, we lined up to shake hands with Stevens Point players, & the joy I felt went away. In the line, I crossed paths with Joel Delorit, & my heart *broke,* because I realized that his baseball career *just* ended. I hugged him & told him what an honor it was to be able to watch him pitch, & how grateful I was to be his teammate. It was tremendously hard to hold back the tears.

NOT AS I HAD VISUALIZED

To my surprise, my parents came to the game against Stevens Point; their *second* game in a week, & *forth* game in my entire college career. They came to the game because that day was my birthday.

They also came to the game hoping I would start; instead, they got a much better show watching J-Do pitch.

I had no idea they were there until after the game, when they came over to the dugout, to wish me a "happy birthday," before they left. We played that game early Friday afternoon, which was just early enough for my dad to watch it before he had to go to work.

After they left, I went back into the dugout to grab my equipment. While I was in there, Coach Vo came up to me & told me: "Tinch, you've got the ball tomorrow... Lead us to the World Series." With a *huge* smile on my face, I emphatically said "yes, sir!"

That night, while I was going through my routine to get ready for my start, I could not stop thinking about the game the next day; I was *so* excited. This was the game I had prepared the entire year for. I visualized it *so many* times – I saw myself striking out the last hitter to win the game, then throwing my glove up in the air, while Robby tackled me to start the *infamous* dog-pile. This moment replayed in my mind an *immeasurable* number of times that year.

Because of the excitement, I did not sleep much that night before the game. When I woke up the next morning, my body was *tired*. Also, my shoulder was *throbbing*; it hurt so bad that I could barely lift my left arm up to put my hat on just before I left to go to The Mill.
I doubled down on the pain-relievers that day.

When I got to The Mill, it was very dark & gloomy outside; there was no sign of the sun peeking through the clouds at all. It almost felt like a night game, even though the game was scheduled to start at 2:00 PM. It was so dark that we had to turn our stadium lights on.

Since we had not yet lost a game in the Regional Tournament & it was a double-elimination tournament, St. Scholastica not only had to beat us once that day, but they had to beat us *twice* in order to advance to the World Series; which, is almost an impossible task.

When I started warming up for the game, it took me a little longer than usual to get loose. To "help" me loosen up more, I had Eggy bring me more ibuprofen when he came down to throw with me; they did not help. Once I started my warmup, *nothing* about it seemed right; despite all the pain-relievers I took, my shoulder *still* hurt, & because it still hurt, all the pitches I threw in the bullpen seemed "forced" – like I was muscling the ball to the catcher. Regardless, I did not let it bother me, because I had experienced warmups like this before (some of them, even worse), & still won the game.

Despite how *off* I felt, when it came time for the game to start, & my name was announced as the starting pitcher, *I was ready*. I ran out to the mound to start the game, & immediately, my adrenaline took over, & I was on *fire*. Unfortunately, a fire that burns as I bright as I was burning, fizzles out *very* fast.

When the first inning started, I was throwing the hardest I had thrown in a while, & my off-speed pitches were better than they had ever been before; it was the exact opposite of my pre-game bullpen. Of the first seven batters I faced in first two innings, I struck out *four* of them. Then, my fire burnt out.

I went out to the mound in the third inning, & the first fastball I threw was so slow that it looked more like my changeup. I thought maybe it was just a fluke thing, until it happened again the next fastball I threw. Then, I started to worry, because I thought maybe I injured my shoulder - if I did injure it, I would not have felt it, because all the pain-relievers I took.

It became so apparent that my velocity had *significantly* decreased, that the St. Scholastica dugout noticed, causing the heckling & the chants to arise. Good thing I knew how to compete, which helped me get out of that inning without allowing any runs to score, despite giving up three hits.

I could feel the game & *the moment* I had visualized so many times before slipping away from me.

The rest of my start was "damage control." I gave up hit, after hit, after hit, & I tried my best to not to let any runs score.

In the top of the sixth inning, we were losing 1-0; I gave up a run in the top of the fourth inning. The first hitter I faced, I drilled right in the back, on the first pitch of the at-bat. Then, the very next pitch I threw to the next hitter ended up being a double (the fourth double I gave up that game) to right centerfield. It was deep enough to score the runner from first. Then, out to the mound walked Coach Vo.

Just like that, my Regional Championship start was over, & *the moment* I had visualized so many times before was wiped away.

As soon as I got back to the dugout, my eyes began to fill with tears, but these were not tears of sadness, they were tears of frustration. The moment I had worked for, hoped for, & imagined over & over again in my mind, slipped away from me, & there was *nothing* I could do about it. I felt like a failure.

I could not watch the game, & I did not want any of my teammates to see me crying so I walked all the way down to the bullpen, sat down on the mound, & covered my face with my hands.

After we got out of that inning allowing only one more run to score, I had an unexpected visitor come to the bullpen. It was Danny Putman - a fellow senior, & our All-American right-fielder.

When he got to the bullpen, he sat next to me, put his arm around my shoulders, & said, "we are going to win this game because of you. You have gotten us this far, & you are going to take us further, but we *need* you right now… in the dugout." He stood up, then he helped me up, & we walked back to the dugout together.

We scored two runs in the bottom of the sixth inning to make it a one run game (we were down 3-2).

Something else also happened that inning, St. Scholastica's starter, who threw a *twelve-inning* complete game three days prior, ran out of gas, & they were forced to pull him from the game.

To make matters worse for St. Scholastica, they did not have *any* reliable pitchers left, so they were forced to use some pitchers who had hardly ever pitched prior to the Regional Tournament.

In the bottom of the seventh inning, Danny scored the tying run. Four hitters later, with runners on first & third base, our designated hitter hit a three-homerun to put us ahead, 6-3. We held on to that lead for the rest of the game.

That moment I had visualized so many times throughout my senior year came to fruition, but it was not me who brought it to fruition. It was Justin Lambert. He was the relief pitcher who came in to replace me, & he proceeded to throw four shutout innings to win us the Regional Championship, & send us to the World Series for the first time in three years.

Even though I was not the one who made the final out, & even though I was not the one who was tackled by Robby, being a part of the dog-pile that happened after the final out was made *still* was the one of *the best* moments of my baseball career.

KNOWLEDGE APPLIED

Sometimes, things do not go as we planned them to go. Actually… *often times*, things do not go as we planned them to go.

It can be terribly frustrating. We plan, & plan, & plan. We visualize the plan succeeding, over, & over, & over again. Then, we sharpen our axe (prepare). When it *finally* comes time to start chopping down the tree, it falls the opposite way we planned it falling. Or even worse, we get to the tree & it has already been chopped down by someone else.

We *need* to change our perspective. Regardless of if we were the ones that chopped down the tree, or if it was someone else who chopped it down. *The tree still got chopped down.*

One of the greatest lessons sports teaches us is that we are always playing for something bigger than ourselves – the team, & a Championship. When we are playing for something bigger than ourselves, that means we must set aside our egos, & suppress our need for attention, praise, & glory.

We may want to be the ones who lead our team. We may want to be the ones who are featured in the headlines. We may want to be the ones who receive all the awards & accolades. We may want to be ones who make the final out of the game. *But*, if we are not meant to be the ones leading & receiving all the attention, then we have to accept it.

Not everyone is meant for "the spotlight." If we are not meant for it, that does not mean that we do not have gifts. It also does not mean that our gifts & the roles we play are not important. They *are* important; so important, that your team *needs* them.

We *all* are on the same team, & we *need* each other. When one of us succeeds, we *all* succeed. We must learn to celebrate our teammates' success. When we do this, it does *not* diminish our own success, it *elevates* it even more.

Despite popular belief, we are *not* in a competition with one another. Someone else's victory is not our defeat. There is *always* enough success & abundance to go around.

Competition only leads to comparison. Constantly competing against & comparing ourselves to others only takes away from our contentment. When we focus on our competition, we lose sight of who we are, what we have, & what we can control.

If we cannot stand to see the success of others, we will *never* experience our own success. Celebrating others is extremely hard to do; especially, when it seems like everyone around us is achieving what *we want* to achieve, while we continue to struggle. When we celebrate ourselves, we experience happiness. When we celebrate others, we experience joy. Joy *always* trumps happiness.

We all struggle with jealousy & envy. We must fight them *every* day.

Jesus Christ *commanded* us to "love your neighbor as you love yourself (Mark 12:31)." This is not just a command, it is also an observation: "how you love your neighbor *is* how you love yourself. *When we portray jealousy & envy, our insecurities are revealed, & it tells everyone around us that we do not love ourselves.*

"We all are on the same team, & we *need* each other. When one of us succeeds, we *all* succeed.

"When we celebrate ourselves, we experience happiness. When we celebrate others, we experience joy. Joy *always* trumps happiness."

@RileyTincher | #PitchingAgainstMyself

CHAPTER 18

BRACING

E very young baseball player dreams of one day playing in the World Series. Whether it is playing catch in the backyard, or playing whiffle ball with the neighborhood kids, the "go-to" situation is *always* "game seven of the World Series, bottom of the ninth, two outs, bases loaded, & a full count."

Unfortunately, for most young baseball players, this "go-to" situation never happens, because their dream of playing in the World Series does not come true… but, mine did.

There is nothing like the College World Series (even, the Division III World Series). Prior to going, I had heard *so many* great things about it from my formers teammates, & other players that I have played against who have had the fortune of playing in the World Series. However, none of their comments meant anything to me until I actually got to experience it myself.

It was one of the best – if not, *the* best - experiences of *my life.*

I have played *hundreds* of baseball games, against the some of the best players & teams in the world, but *none* of them compared to the three games I played at the World Series my senior year.

The World Series is *the* pinnacle of the season; quite frankly, the pinnacle of anyone's *career.* It is *the thing* everyone works so hard to get even get a change to go to.

Being able to hear your name announced over the speakers as you run out onto the field in front of ten-thousand cheering fans, & play against the best teams in the country is something only a few people get to say they have done in their lifetime. I was *very* fortunate enough to be one of those select few.

ANOTHER SNUB

The Division III College World Series was held in Appleton, Wisconsin at the Fox Cities Stadium – the home of a Minor-League baseball team, the Wisconsin Timber Rattlers. The stadium was only a little over two hours away from Whitewater, so instead of having to hop on a plane & travel across the country, like the other teams in World Series had to do, all we had to do was take a short bus trip there. We had home field advantage.

We left for the World Series two days before our first game. When we got to Appleton, we went straight to our hotel to get checked in. The hotel we were staying at was the Radisson Paper Valley Hotel in the heart of downtown Appleton.

Throughout my baseball career, I stayed *a lot* of hotels (hotels & buses were like my second home), but none of *fancy* as this one; they had Sleep Number beds in *every* hotel room.

Shortly after we got checked in & settled in to our rooms, we met back down in the hotel lobby, & got back on the bus to head to Fox Cities Stadium for team photos & for the scheduled practice we had on the field that day.

When we got to the stadium, Coach Vo handed out our World Series "swag" – a duffel bag, a half-zip jacket, a pair of shorts, a t-shirt, & a hat (all with the "2011 Division III College World Series" logo & the Warhawk logo on them). It was like Christmas morning. After we received our "swag," we got off the bus & we walked into the stadium together.

The Fox City Stadium is a *gorgeous* stadium; you can see why they host the Division III College World Series every year, the moment you walk into the stadium. It reminded a lot of the stadiums I played at in the Northwoods League... but *way* better.

Prior to our scheduled practice, we took team photos on the field. The seven other teams who also made it to the World Series also took team photos the same time we did. These seven other teams were from all over the country – the Buena Vista University Beavers were from Iowa, the Chapman University Panthers were from California, the Kean University Cougars were from New Jersey, the Keystone College Giants were from Pennsylvania, the Marietta College Pioneers were from Ohio, the Salisbury University Sammy Sea Gulls were from Maryland, & the Western New England University Golden Bears were from Massachusetts.

After the photos were taken, we were the first team scheduled to practice on the field; it was *weird* having the other seven teams watch our entire practice. We only had thirty minutes to practice, so all we did was throw, take groundballs, & go over bunt coverages & other game-situations with runners on base. Because of time constraints, we were not even allowed to have batting practice. So, after our time limit on the field was up, we hopped back on the bus & drove down to Oshkosh to hit in the indoor batting cages at the University.

After we got done hitting, we had to rush back to the hotel to get ready for the Awards Banquet that night.

On the bus ride back to the hotel, I tapped J-Do on the shoulder (he was sitting in the seat in front of me), & when I got his attention, I asked him if he thought *we* were going to win another All-American award this year; he was an All-American the previous season, as well. He told me that he "did not know," but he said it in a way that meant he knew the answer, but he did not want to disappointment me.

Coach Vo gave J-Do & I crap *all* year, by telling us that it is "easy to win an All-American award *once*," but "winning it twice means you are a *true* All-American." At the time, Coach Vo was one of four Warhawks in the history of the program to win two All-American awards, & he made sure we knew all about it.

I *desperately* wanted to join him, & the other three.

That night, for the Awards Banquet, we all got dressed up; it was *shocking* (but, also nice) to see some of my teammates wearing something other than our uniforms, or athletic gear.

After the banquet started, & after we ate one of the *greatest* steaks I have ever had (even better than the Steak Series steaks), it was time for the All-American awards to be announced.

Going in to the World Series, I was ranked third in the country in victories, with ten. I was also ranked in the top ten in innings pitches (95.1 innings), as well as fewest walks allowed per nine innings (1.17). On top of that, I was the Ace of a team in the World Series; one of the best teams in the country.

Earlier that week, I was named to the First-Team All-Conference team, & the First-Team All-Region team for the second year in a row. I thought I was a *shoo-in* for another All-American Award, & so did everyone else at the table I sat at during the banquet; they all turned towards me & acknowledged me as soon as the host of the banquet announced that they were going to begin naming the All-Americans.

They started announcing the All-American Award winners with the Third-Team All-Americans. My name was not announced. Then, they moved on to the Second-Team All-Americans. My name was *still* not announced. At this point, it felt like my heart was beating out of my chest. I felt *extreme* excitement & *utter* disappointment were at the same time, because either I was going to be a First-Team All-American, or I was not going to be an All-American at all.
I played it off to the people at my table like I did not care.

After announcing a few of the First-Team All-Americans, they announced J-Do's name as a utility player. He was awarded for his performance both on the mound & in the batter's box throughout the season. I was *super* excited for him (we all were), but at the same time, I was also eagerly waiting for them to call my name, so I could join him up on the stage.

After they said, "that concludes the All-American awards," my heart sunk, & instantly, my excitement went away, & my disappointment took over. Doubt & negative-self talk came shortly after. I thought, "you *fool!* why did you even think you deserved to win another All-American award? Your season was *not* as great as you think it was."

Thank God, shortly after the banquet, I was reminded of why *we* were there - To win another, much more important award.

INSIDE FASTBALL

Our first game of the World Series was against the Buena Vista Beavers. We played them in the night game on day one of the World Series. Since it was a Friday night (after work), the stands were filled with Whitewater fans, which made it *very* hard to stay focused to warmup before the game.

So many people I knew were at the game, including two of my Bullfrog coaches, who came down to the fence outside of the dugout to see me, Rob, & J-Do. Since Green Bay was less than twenty minutes away from Appleton, the Webb family was also there, & they also came down to fence outside of the dugout to see me; it was my first time seeing them since my start against Stevens Point in the regular season. It was great seeing them, but it was also very distracting. J-Do got the ball to start that game, but I needed to be focused & ready to come in out of the bullpen.

The game was *full* of emotion from start to finish; mainly, because of the amount of Warhawk fans that were at the game.

We went back & forth the entire game. They broke the shutout in the bottom of the second inning by scoring a run. Then, we scored two in the top of third inning. Which, they followed up with scoring another run in the bottom of the third inning to tie it up. Then, the very next inning, they took the lead, & held on to that lead until the top of the ninth inning, when we scored two more runs to tie the game, 4-4. When we tied up the game, I was in the bullpen warming up.

With two outs in the bottom of the ninth inning, & runners on first base & third base, Coach Vo went out to the mound & waved me in to come in to pitch.

Since the bullpens were in center field (much like many Major League Stadiums), the run from the bullpen to the mound felt like I was in running into a Major League game. Plus, when the fans found out it was me coming in to pitch, they all stood to their feet & gave me a standing ovation; I still get goosebumps thinking about it.

When I got to the mound, Coach Vo handed me the ball, & told me to get us back in the dugout to hit. Then, he turned around & walked back to the dugout. I asked Robby to stay on the mound with me. Then, I put my arm around his shoulders, put my hand on his chest, stared him in the eyes, & said "Robby... you have got to trust me to throw inside."

In pressure situations, or if there were any runners in scoring position, Robby had a tendency to rely *heavily* on the fastball on the low outside corner, & rightfully so - it is one of the most effective pitches to induce a ground ball. But, since I did not throw very hard (especially, my senior year), every hitter I faced expected me to throw on the outside corner.

What separated me from most pitchers like me was my ability to command the inside part of the plate, & sometimes, Robby forgot that. So, I felt the need to remind him... even though it was pointless.

Robby called an outside fastball for the first pitch of the at-bat, & I just stood there staring at him; we had a system where if I liked the pitched he called, but I did not like the location to which he called the pitch to be thrown, instead of shaking him off, I would just stare at him until he changed the location.

After a long stare down, he called for an inside fastball. I threw the pitch *exactly* where he had his glove set up, & the batter hit it up the middle for a walk-off single.

I (not we) lost the game, 5-4.

I was so humiliated, that after the game, I walked straight to the bus with my head down without acknowledging anyone... not even the Webb family, & not even my mom.

GOOD WRENCH

Do you remember me telling you how important it was to win the first game of a double-elimination tournament? Well... now that we lost the first game of the World Series (an *eight-team* double-elimination tournament), we had to win four games in a row to even get to the Championship. If I would have not shaken off Robby, & we would have won, we would have only had to win two more games to get to the Championship.

Our backs were now against the wall, & we had to fight to survive.

The next day, we played the Western New England University Golden Bears. Justin got the ball to start the game, & like I said earlier, "Big Mo" continued to be on his side.

Despite how great Justin was throwing, I had a very hard time watching; I *always* had a hard time watching.

If I was ever pitching in the game, I was calm & confident, because I felt like I was in control - I admit that I am a control freak. If I was not pitching in the game, I was pacing back & forth in the dugout, covering my eyes with my hands, because I had no control over the outcome of the game.

Here is a better example of how much anxiety I had when I was watching (those of you reading this who know me well, will understand): When I was pitching in the game, I never rocked when I sat down in the dugout. When I was not pitching in the game, I could not stop rocking back & forth when I sat down in the dugout.

We had a three-run lead going into the top of the fourth inning. Then, Justin got into a little bit of trouble, & allowed two runs to score, to make the score 3-2. After those two runs scored, I sat in the corner of the dugout with my head buried in my hands, praying, "please God, do not let last night's game be my last time I pitch in my college career." I repeated this prayer for the rest of the game.

My mind was eased when we scored three runs in the top of the seventh inning, to increase our lead, & make the score 8-2. We only gave up one more run the rest of the game, & we won to survive & move on to the third day of the World Series.

On the bus ride back to our hotel, Coach Vo made an announcement that we would be playing the loser of the game between the Marietta College Pioneers & the Chapman University Panthers. Then, he said "regardless of who we play tomorrow, we will have our Ace on the mound, & he *will* beat whoever we face." The whole bus erupted in excitement.

That night, as I was going through my routine to get ready for my next start the next day, I had a wrench thrown in the middle of it… but it was a *good* wrench.

My hotel roommates (two sophomores) & I got into a discussion about pitching mechanics. Specifically, we talked about one thing that I had struggled with my entire career (mostly, before I came to Whitewater) - "bracing." Simply put, bracing is keeping a strong, stiff front leg when it lands on the mound while the pitching delivery is being finished. In a very respectful way, they both interrupted my routine & told me that I was struggling with bracing again. I am so glad they told me, because they gave me hope again.

They told me that in my four previous times pitching (my appearances in the Regional Tournament & my appearance in the first game of the World Series), I had a weak front leg, & I was collapsing, which caused my fastball velocity to go down, & my ball to become "flatter." When my front leg was strong & braced, I pitched like I was 6'3" (my *actual* height). When my front leg was weak, & collapsed, I pitched like I was 5'7." Instead of the ball releasing out of my hand at a downward angle, it was releasing out on a straight line, which, led to me getting hit around every time I pitched. I blamed it on dead arm, but that was not the only reason why.

Instead of visualizing my start the next day, like I normally did, I spent the remainder of the night repeatedly going through my delivery with my roommates, trying to fix my "bracing problem."

The next day, I started bracing more, & guess what happened? My velocity went up.

As I was warming up in the bullpen, I could hear the ball hitting the catcher's glove - I had that *"pop"* again. I had not heard that sound in long time. It was so loud that a crowd of kids began to form on the deck that surrounded the bullpen. One of the little kids, probably about ten years old, that was on the deck right behind me turned to his friend, & said, "Wow! This guy must be a Major Leaguer!"

During the game, I threw the hardest I had thrown in almost a year. If I had made the *easy* choice to *not* listen to my hotel roommates, because, they were underclassmen, or because I was going through my routine, I would not have made the necessary adjustments for that game, & my velocity would not have gone up.

Unfortunately, my "bracing adjustment" was all for nothing.

KNOWLEDGE APPLIED

There is *always* something to learn in *every* situation we are in; every situation presents an opportunity to get better. Also, there is *always* something to learn from *every* person we encounter; *everyone* we meet knows something we do not know, even people who are younger than us & may not have as much experience as us.

We must *never* stop learning. The day we stop learning is the day we stop growing. The day we stop learning is the day we stop winning. The day we stop learning is the day we stop living.

One of my favorite stories of "never stop learning" is about Teddy Roosevelt, the twenty-sixth president of the United States, & one of *the toughest* human beings to ever live. He died in his sleep at the age of sixty years old, & when they found him in his bed the next morning, he had a book in his hands.

The saying "we learn something new every day" is true… *if* we are paying attention & we are actively seeking things to learn. This only happens when we realize that we are students for life.

Knowledge is power, but awareness is *much* more powerful.

It does not matter what we do, what level we are at doing what we do, how long we have been doing what we are doing, or how great we are at doing what we do, we *never* know enough to stop learning, & we are *never* good enough to stop making adjustments.

Author, Brian Herbert, once said: "the capacity to learn is a gift; the ability to learn is a skill; the willingness to learn is a choice." When we have a willingness to learn, we *will* learn.

"We must *never* stop learning. The day we stop learning is the day we stop growing. The day we stop learning is the day we stop living."

"Knowledge is power, but awareness is *much* more powerful."

@RileyTincher | #PitchingAgainstMyself

CHAPTER 19

OUTLIVE YOUR LIFE

The day I had been trying to avoid ever since the beginning of my senior year had arrived. Actually, this was the day I had been trying to avoid ever since I ran out into left field to play my first ever baseball game when I was fourteen years old. This was the day my baseball career ended. This was the day my life ended.

There is no better word to describe this day than "ominous."

When we got on the bus to head over to Fox City Stadium for our game, Coach Vo let us know that we were going to play the Chapman University Panthers that day. We did not know much about them, other than the fact that they had a *stud* left-handed pitcher of their own, who was a two-time All-American & the National Pitcher of the Year the season before. He had pitched two days early, & apparently got hurt, so he was no longer our concern.

The bus ride to the stadium was *eerily* silent. The way everyone sat in their seat, not saying a word, was almost like they knew about the impending doom we were about face, & that we were about to play the last game of the season.

When we got to the field, we stepped off the bus into the dark, cloudy, & cold weather outside, & all of us walked into the stadium like we were walking into a funeral.

Two hitters in to the first inning, our shortstop got the first base hit of the game. Then, two hitters later, he was picked off at second base by the catcher. This was a sign of things to come.

In the bottom of the first inning, I struck out the first hitter I faced – if you can recall, I was throwing the hardest I had thrown all year. Then, I got the second hitter to swing late & hit a fly-ball to left field.

I was thrilled. I thought I was in for some smooth sailing that game, until I walked the next hitter with four straights balls; something, I had not done since the *intentional* walk I threw during Spring Training Trip my *junior* year.

After I threw ball four, one of the fans (one of our player's dad) in the stands yelled "you have got to be kidding me, Tincher."

The next hitter, I gave up a single to right field, & just like that, there were runners on first & third base. Luckily, we got out of the inning unscathed.

When I got back to the dugout, I sat next to Coach Cally & he looked at me like he wanted to say, *"really?!"* Without him saying a word, I responded to his look by saying, "you know me. I love pitching with a little adversity."

That is *exactly* what I had to do for the rest of the game.

The next inning, J-Do hit a leadoff single which *finally* woke up our dugout. A few pitches later, he was picked off at first-base by the pitcher for our second picked off runner of the game. Our dugout went right back to being *silent.*

In the bottom of the second inning, the first Chapman hitter I faced hit a slow groundball up the middle (I probably should have put a glove on it, but remember... "Big Puma"). Our second baseman was in perfect position to field the ball, then the ball hit the base & bounced in a completely different direction, & the runner was safe. The next hitter got a base hit, which put runners on first & second base with zero outs - *the perfect* bunt situation. On the second pitch of the at-bat, the hitter laid down a near perfect bunt between me & the third-basemen & for the first time in a long time, I *pounced* on that ball & threw the runner out at first base. A *much-needed* strikeout & a groundball to first-base later, we got out of that inning unscathed.

In the third inning, it was three up, three down for both sides. This was not the case for the fourth inning. Our leadoff hitter, Danny, started the fourth inning with a base hit up the middle, which woke up our dugout again. Then... he was picked off at first-base by the pitcher for our third picked off runner of the game. Our dugout went right back to be *silent... again.*

I wish I could say the same thing happened to the Chapman hitters in the fourth inning, but it did not. The first hitter of the inning reached base on an error. Then, the second hitter hit a groundball up the middle. This time, our shortstop was in a perfect position to field the ball, & this groundball hit the base as well, bouncing in a completely different direction; it was déjà vu.

With runners on first & second base with zero outs, it was another perfect situation for a bunt. This time though, I did not field it. It was bunted directly to our third-basemen & he could not field it cleanly; which, was the *second* error in the inning.

While the play was developing, I crouched down to avoid the throw, then I turned toward first base & I waited for the ball to be thrown, to no avail. When *their* crowd & dugout erupted in celebration, I *knew* something bad happened.

With the bases now loaded & zero outs in the inning, I had to do as much "damage control" as I possibly could.

The fourth hitter I faced in the inning flew out to centerfield, which, allowed the runner on third-base to tag up & score. The fifth hitter I faced in the inning hit a groundball to J-Do, & he threw to second-base to make it a runner on first & third base situation with two outs. It was the wise thing to do, because he was pulled off the bag & there was *no way* I was going to be able to cover first-base in time to get the hitter out; remember... "Big Puma." The sixth & final hitter I faced in the inning, grounded out to our shortstop, & we got out of the inning only allowing one run to score.

In the top of the fifth inning, our first hitter led off the inning with a base-hit, which again, woke up our dugout. Then, the next hitter hit into a double play. This completely deflated us, & our dugout went back to being *silent*, yet again.

After our third hitter flew out to center field, it was time for us to take the field for the bottom of the fifth inning.

Chapman's first hitter got a base-hit up the middle, but that was not the end of the story. Our sure-handed centerfielder (whom, I had seen make numerous amounts of diving catches) went to field the ball, & the ball went right under his glove; this made me reminisce of the error I made in left field, in eighth grade. The hitter advanced to second-base on the error. On the first pitch to the next hitter, I threw a wild pitch to advance the runner on second base to third. He then tagged-up & scored the second run of the game, when that hitter hit a pop-fly to centerfield. The next two hitters hit infield pop-flies, & we got out of the inning with the score now 2-0, in Chapman's favor.

The Chapman pitcher made *quick* work of our hitters in the top of the sixth inning with *another* three up, three down inning.

In the bottom of the sixth inning, the first Chapman hitter lined out to our right fielder, Danny; when I say, "lined out," I mean he hit a *rocket* to Danny - I have no idea how Danny saw it, because it was moving so fast. The next hitter hit another line drive to the outfield, but this time, no one was there to catch it. The ball ended up going to the deepest part of the outfield (left center field), & the hitter got a stand-up triple. On the very first pitch of the next at-bat, the hitter laid down a suicide squeeze bunt to score the runner on third - we had no idea it was coming, so we were not ready for it.

Oh, the irony. I was *so* angry about our previous season ending by way of a suicide-squeeze bunt, & yet, here I was in the World Series, fielding the *second successful* suicide squeeze of the year off me.

With two outs in the inning, I got the final hitter to hit a ground-ball to J-Do, who stepped on first-base for the final out of the inning... & the final out of my start.

When I got back to the dugout, Coach Vo walked up to me, shook my hand, & told me that I was done for the day. It took *everything* in me not to cry.

The next inning, our first hitter - our shortstop - hit a single to left field. Two batters later, J-Do hit the *furthest* homerun I had *ever* seen him hit. He hit it to opposite field (left-field, because he was a left-handed hitter), & it would have gone over the scoreboard in left center field if it did not continue to hook. His two-run homerun cut the Chapman lead down to one run by making the score 3-2. Unfortunately, we never got a hit the rest of the game & those two runs were the only runs we scored the entire game.

After J-Do's homerun, I spent the rest of the game sitting in the corner of the dugout with my head buried in my hands, *praying*.

When our time came to hit in the top of the ninth inning, I did not lift my head from my hands until our final hitter. When the "ping" sound of his bat hitting the ball was made, I looked up, & I watched the ball hit the ground & go straight to the second-basemen. Then, I watched the second-basemen field the ball & make the throw to first base to get the final out of the game… & the final out of my career. My heart *shattered*.

That was not how I wanted my senior year to end. That was not how I wanted my baseball career to end. I was supposed to win the National Championship game, hoist the trophy above my head, & ride off into the sunset that is known as professional baseball.

Everything I had worked for, & prepared for came to a sudden stop. All my hopes & dreams disappeared, in an instant. No one told me that this was going to happen. No one told me that there would come a day where I would no longer be able to play the game that I loved *so dearly*. No one told me that there would come a day where I would no longer be able to play with the men whom I loved *so dearly*; the same men who I made so many sacrifices with, & the same men who I shed blood, sweat, & *tears* for, day after day, for the last three years of my life.

With heavy hearts, & tear-filled eyes, we lined up to shake the hands of the Chapman players. When we got done shaking their hands, each of us were called up to a table they had set up behind home-plate. On this table, they had miniature World Series trophies for every player who participated in the World Series.

They were *not* the trophy we there to win.

After we all received our "participation trophies," we got a standing ovation from our fans in the stands. Up until that moment, I was able to hold back most of my tears. But, as soon as I saw the fans, I could not hold back my tears any longer. I realized that, that would be the *last* standing ovation I would ever receive, & the *last* time I would ever play in front of those Warhawks fans.

Since there was a game that was scheduled to be played right after ours, we did not have time to stand around on the field, so we had to quickly grab our stuff out of the dugout & leave the field.

As soon as I got to the top of the steps, I was greeted by my dad & mom who were there *again* to see me pitch. We all hugged, & my mom cried as we were hugging, but I did not. My sadness turned into bitterness, & I thought to myself, "why are you both sad? You *hardly ever* came to see me pitch."

We walked over to the concession stands together, & I had them buy me a couple of World Series shirts, a World Series poster with pictures from the games we played on it, & a framed picture of all the Seniors together on the field.

While we were waiting in line for the poster to be made, I got a tap on my shoulder. I turned around & it was J-Do. As soon as I turned around he wrapped his arms around me & *we both lost it*. I became cathartic, & I could no longer control my emotions.

J-Do & I were best friends & we had been through *so much* together - three years of *countless* wins, championships, losses, practices, games, workouts, bus rides, hotel rooms, meetings, camps, drunken nights, heartaches & heart breaks, challenging conversations, & *hours* spent in fellowship together were wrapped in *this hug*. I did not want to let go of him, & he did not want to let go of me.

THE *LONGEST* BUS RIDE HOME

I was the last one out to the bus. When I finally got out there, the whole team was outside of the bus conversing with each other & with our fans, & some of the Warhawk parents. That moment was a blur to me, because *so many* people came up to me when I got there to congratulate me on my historic, & highly-decorated career, including people who had been to *every* game I pitched in, & even some people whom I had never met before.

After Coach Vo told us it was time to board the bus & head back to Whitewater, Coach Cally gathered up all the pitchers, & took us aside. We all wrapped our arms around each other & formed a circle. He told us how proud he was of us, & how we carried the team to the World Series. Then, he concluded his speech by saying:

"I hope you all realize how *lucky* you are. You all were fortunate enough to play with one of the *greatest* Warhawk pitchers of all time. Tinch did *everything* the right way. He worked his ass off *every* day. He battled through things, on & off the field, that *no one* should ever have to go through. He took what he had, & he made the most of it. We all can learn something from him & what he was able to accomplish during his career here at Whitewater. There will *never* be another one like Riley Tincher."

I thought I did not have any more tears to shed after hugging J-Do, but I was wrong.

When we finally got on the bus, as the bus was leaving, Coach Vo had all the seniors stand up & give a speech to the rest of the team about our Warhawk legacy & how we wanted to be remembered. Since I sat in the back of the bus, I was the last one to give a speech. I stood up, & I thanked all the coaches first; more specifically, Coach Vo, Coach Perch, & Coach Cally. Then, I turned my attention the rest of my teammates, & I said, "I hope I showed you all how to do everything the right way. I hope I proved to all of you that if you work hard enough, you can accomplish *anything*," then, I sat down.

For the rest of the bus ride back to Whitewater, I kept thinking about my legacy as a Warhawk, & I kept asking myself the question: "how do you want to be remembered?"

My entire career, replayed in my mind – from the moment I ran out to left field to play my very first baseball game in eighth grade to the final out that was made in the World Series. I thought about all the games I won, & all the Championships we won. I thought about becoming an All-American, & playing in the Northwoods League All-Star game. I thought about the start I had against Stevens Point in the Regional Tournament, my junior year. I thought about the dog-pile we made after we won the Regional Championship to go to my first ever World Series, my senior year. In the midst of my nostalgia, I also thought about my start against the Minnesota Twins. Thinking of that game reminded me of the postgame speech Coach Vo gave to us after we tied them. In the middle of his speech, he said something about me that at the time, it did not mean much to me, but now, it means *everything* to me. He said, "I do not want my son, Sam, to grow up to be like Paul Molitor, or any other Hall of Famer. I do not even want him to grow up to be like Derek Jeter, or any other Major Leaguer. I want him to grow up to be like *Riley Tincher*."

Wow! I *still* get chills thinking about it. It is actually hard for me to believe that Coach Vo - one of the greatest influences on my life - said that he wanted his son to grow up to be like *me*.

When the bus got back to Whitewater, we all exited the bus, hugged one another one last time, & said "see you later" to each other.

As I was hugging Coach Perch, he told me some shocking news; he told me that he was not going to coach at Whitewater the next year. I had a feeling something was up, because he had been acting very different for the last month – however, the news still surprised me.

He then proceeded to tell me that him & his family were moving to Eau Claire, Wisconsin, because his wife got a new job there at the University. I was happy for him & his family, but I was also sad that he was stepping away from the Warhawk family, & stepping away from something he was *very* good at.

There is *no one* else like Coach Perch.

As we hugged good-bye, I could not help but think about the memories I had with him, & how much he helped me come to UW-Whitewater, & later, help me get into graduate school at Baylor University. *I cried again.*

That night, I received text messages from Coach Hergert & Coach Everson, telling me how proud they were of me, & how fortunate they were to have coached me. However, I believe it was the other way around; it was an honor to call them "coach." I had several men in my life who *pretended* to be coaches, but very few *actual* coaches – Coach Hergert & Coach Everson were two of them.

The next day, I packed up my apartment & made my rounds of "good-byes." First, I stopped at the trainer's room (my second home) to say bye to all the athletic trainers, & to thank them for all that they did for me - Athletic Trainers do not get paid what they deserve for all the hours they spend doing what they do. Then, I had lunch with Coach Cally, & during the lunch, we talked about our future – what he was going to do, & what I was going to do; I played it off like I knew *exactly* what I was going to do, even though I had no clue. Finally, I met with Coach Vo & the five other seniors at a bar to have one last beer together. At the bar, we shared memories of the past, & stories from the season. When it was all said & done, we said our final "good-byes," & we parted ways. I left Whitewater that night.

I had *no idea* about the misery & pain I was about to endure.

KNOWLEDGE APPLIED

How do you want to be remembered? What is the legacy you want to leave behind? How do you want people to *feel* when they think about you & what you have done? When you die, what do you want people to say about you at your funeral?

I want you to make time to think *very carefully* think about these questions, because I want you to have absolute clarity as to what legacy you want to leave behind. The truth is, we are going to leave a legacy, regardless of whether we are intentional about it, or not.

We have *one at-bat* at this life; *one* chance to do whatever it is we want to do, & be whoever it is we are called to be.

Too many of us are living like we are going to get another chance; like we are going to get another at-bat. *We are not!* Too many of us are living like we are promised tomorrow. All we are promised is *this* moment. Too many of us are wasting our time pursuing the wrong things – we were not born to go to school to get the job, work the rest of our lives, pay the bills, retire, & die, but we have been conditioned to believe that.

If we understood how *precious* our life is (before something tragic happens), we all would totally change what we do on a daily basis, & totally change the way we view things.

If we knew how *lucky* we are to be alive, we would not be walking around with our heads down.

Do you know what the odds of becoming a human being are? One in four-hundred-trillion – Let me spell that out for you just so you can see the degree of *rarity* it is: 1 in 400,000,000,000,000.

I used to think that I was not significant; that I was made in an assembly line of people just like me, & that there was *nothing* special about me. That was the *biggest lie* I had ever been led to believe.

It was not until I started reading the Bible & soaking in God's Word that I started seeing how significant & valuable I really am. God created *me*... He fearfully & wonderfully created *me* (Psalm 139:14). He knew me before I was even born. He counted the very hairs on my head; even though, that number is going down as my age is going up. He also created *you*, & he gave you unique gifts for *His* purpose.

If we fully comprehended how loved, treasured, & precious we are to *Him*, we would not be treating ourselves the way that we do.

If we understood how *protected* we are, we would not be living our life *scared*, & we would take more (necessary) risks.

If we realized how much we have been given & entrusted with, we would not be wasting our lives, dreading Mondays, working for the weekends, & only thanking Him for Friday.

If we comprehended that this life is setting us up for the next life (Heaven), we would treat each other *totally* different.

If we recognized that He is in control, & that His plans are far greater than ours, we would willingly get out of His way. It is our job to do the natural, & allow Him to do the supernatural.

My life is a testament to this truth.

My kindergarten teacher would not believe you if you told her that the same kid who got in trouble on a daily basis, the same kid she thought was autistic, would eventually earn a Master's Degree from Baylor University.

My fourth-grade teacher would not believe you if you told her that the same kid who had dyslexia, the same kid who could not read until fourth-grade, would eventually write *this* book – Thank you so much, Mrs. Albers for having patience with me & making the time to teach me how to read.

My eighth-grade baseball coach would not believe you if you told him that the same kid who thought he was a left-handed catcher, & could not hit a baseball if it was set up on a tee, would eventually receive a scholarship to play college baseball.

My first coach in college would not believe you if you told him that the same kid who was his "oh shit" pitcher, would eventually become an All-American. He would laugh at you, if you told him that this kid would also lead the *entire* NCAA in victories.

I know the phrase "anything is possible" sounds so cliché, but it is cliché because it is *true*. Jesus said so (Mark 9:23).

Too many of us are taking whatever we can get, because we believe that is all we deserve. Too many of us are allowing bad things to continually happen to us, because we do not know what we want. Too many of us are waking up like it was an accident.

Everybody ends up somewhere, but very, very few end up somewhere *on purpose*.

We will very likely overestimate what God will do *through* us in the short term, but we will *immensely* underestimate what God will do *through* us in a *lifetime* of faith.

Unfortunately, we cannot live forever, but we can create something that does.

At Whitewater, we had a list of standards - not rules, *standards* - that we all had to follow. One of those standards was, "always leave something better than when you arrived."

It is our responsibility to leave this Earth better than when we arrived. It is our responsibility to leave our families better than when we arrived. If we do this, we will outlive our lives, & we will leave a legacy that will be remembered *forever*.

We get to decide what legacy we want to leave behind. Once we know what we want that legacy to be, *every* choice & *every* decision we make from this day forward must be in line with the legacy we want to leave - Every single choice, & every single decision!

It is *so easy* to get caught up in the mundane day-to-day "grind," & became unaware of the fact that our most valuable resource - our time – is slipping away from us.

What we do *today* matters. What we do in *this moment* matters. *All* of it plays a *crucial* role in the legacy we want to leave behind. *There are sixty-six books in the Bible, your book is the sixty-seventh. What is your book going to say?*

"If we knew how *lucky* we are to be alive, we would not be walking around with our heads down."

"What we do *today* matters. What we do in *this moment* matters. *All* of it plays a *crucial* role in the legacy we want to leave behind.

@RileyTincher | #PitchingAgainstMyself

CHAPTER 20

EXTRA INNINGS

E very athlete dies *twice*. The first time they die is when their athletic career ends, & then they die again, when they finally take their last breath & leave this Earth.

When an athlete's career ends, they must ask themselves the perpetual question every athlete before them has asked, & every athlete after them will ask – "What do I do now?"

I had to ask myself this question, & it took me a *long* time to answer it, because it took me a *long* time to comprehend the fact that I was not going to play Major League Baseball.

I had plans, & they fell through. I *hopelessly* wanted to play Major League Baseball, & it did not happen. I prepared throughout my entire career for an opportunity to play professionally, & that opportunity never came to fruition. The way my baseball career ended was exactly the opposite of how I wanted it to end. There was nothing I could do about it… & it *literally* drove me insane.

Maybe, I was delusional in thinking that I could play Major League Baseball… but, I honestly *believed* that I could. I thought I *deserved* at least a chance to prove that I could play.

I devoted so much time, focus, & energy to the game of baseball. I threw an innumerable amount of pitches in games, practices & bullpens. I ran an immeasurable number of sprints. I did a ridiculous amount of towel & dowel drills. I fielded so many ground balls & practiced bunt coverage, after bunt coverage, after bunt coverage. I won *a lot* of games; more than most pitchers *ever* will. I struck out a countless number of hitters, including some current Major League hitters. I played with & against a lot of great players & coaches at a *very high* level. I earned *a lot* of awards. I was the Pitcher of the Year. I was an All-American. I was an All-Star in one of the best collegiate summer league in the country; the Northwoods League. Why would I *not* get a chance to play professionally?

To make matters worse, *a lot* of the players who I was playing with & against in the Northwoods League, who I thought I was more talented than, more driven than, & definitely worked harder than, were getting opportunities to play professionally, that I was not even coming close to getting. I did not understand why... I do, now.

During the Major League Baseball Draft that summer following my senior year, I texted Coach Vo & asked him if Robby, J-Do, & I had a chance of getting picked up in the Draft, & all he responded with was, "I do not know. We will see."

Throughout the Draft, I held on to the belief – actually, I clung on to it like my life depended on it - that I was going to get a phone call, & I was going to be selected in the Draft. The final round of the draft came, & I prayed, "God, please give me a chance... All I want is a *chance*." Then, when the final pick of the draft came, I closed my eyes, & I repeated "*please*, God!" over & over again, until I finally opened my eyes, & I saw that I was not the last pick of the Draft. Then, the bitter reality of not being drafted sunk in.

My heart was broken, *but* it was not the last heartbreak, nor the worst heartbreak baseball would eventually give me.

Baseball was my life. Actually... it was so much more than that. I *worshipped* it like it was a god, on a daily basis.

Being a baseball player was my identity, & now, my identity was lost. It was all I knew, & it was all I wanted to know.

YOU ARE *MORE*

There is a hidden message in this book. The letters of all the drop caps at the beginning of each chapter, starting at "Chapter 1 – You Should Quit," spell out "I AM MORE THAN AN ATHLETE."

That is exactly what you are; *more*. You are more than an athlete. You are more than a coach. You are more than a parent. You are more than a husband, or a wife. You are more than a child. You are more than a sibling. You are more than a friend, or a teammate. You are more than what you do. You are more than what people say you are. You are even more than who you *believe* you are.

You may think your glory days are behind you, but they are not. Your best days are ahead of you. Your best game is ahead of you. You would not be alive, if that was not true. It took me a very long time to realize this truth. I could not see myself as more than a baseball player. I could not see a future without baseball. Because of baseball, I had purpose & meaning every day. Then, I lost it. I had a north star that gave me direction, but I had the *wrong* north star.

I went through absolute hell to get to where I am now. I wanted to end it all, *twice*. To be honest, I am surprised I am still here, & I am even more surprised that I was able to write this book.

For the first time in a long time, I *finally* want to be alive, & I finally look forward to waking up in the morning.

As ordinary & insignificant as I thought I was, I also had this undying thought in the back of my mind that there was something *greater* for me. Throughout my childhood, I never felt like I belonged. I never felt like I fit in. I always thought that there was something else for me. The moment I was introduced to baseball, I was *convinced* that, that something else was baseball... but, it was not. It was something even *greater*, but it took me a while to figure what it was.

No one should have to go through what I went through after my baseball career ended, but I am glad that I did.
There is purpose in *every* pain. There is beauty in *every* struggle.

I believe I went through what I went through not for myself, but to help someone else who is going through, or will go through the same thing. Now, I believe sports are a platform, *not* a calling, & I am using this platform I have been given to share my story; to share my struggle. Now, I am the voice I wish I heard when I was playing – the voice I wish told me that I am *more* than an athlete, & the voice I wish let me know that there is something greater for me other than baseball.

LIFE AFTER SPORTS

For all athletes, the transition from athlete to civilian is inevitable. According to NCAA.org, out of all the athletes who play high school sports (roughly, seven-million athletes), *two-percent* of them will play in college (there are roughly 460,000 athletes in the NCAA; this does not include the NJCAA, or the NAIA). *Fewer* than two-percent of the two-percent playing collegiate sports will play professionally. The other ninety-eight-percent of college athletes are left on their own to figure out what is next, which, is a disheartening reality for *all* athletes who have spent their *entire* lives dedicating themselves to their sport.

For the vast majority of these athletes, they spend the rest of their lives thinking about what was & what could have been. They believe the lie that they have been told, that "they are only as good as their last at-bat." They think that because they do not receive trophies anymore, or do not get their names glorified in the headlines anymore, that their lives no longer matter. They think that because they no longer have a championship to pursue, that there is no more direction, significance, or meaning to their lives. They think that because they do not play sports anymore, that they no longer have coaches, or teammates to guide & support them. I know this, because I *was* one of these athletes that believed all these *lies.*

Sadly, most of these athletes who believe these lies have resorted to drug- & alcohol-abuse to cope with the pain, regret, & loneliness that they feel. Some of them have even gone as far as ending their own lives through drug overdose, or suicide. This has quickly become a *very serious* issue, & it is too often overlooked & neglected.

The greatest misconception of athletes is that they are not *real* people, with *real* problems. We think that because they have made a lot of money, & have every resource imaginable available to them any time they want them, that they do not struggle. We think that because they are constantly receiving praise & recognition, that they could not possibly be lonely. Because they are far more physically-gifted than most of us, we hold them up on this pedestal, & expect them to be perfect *all the time*. Then, when they make a mistake, or one of them has the courage to announce that they are struggling with mental health issues, or one of them ends their life, we are shocked, & some of us, are disappointed. Yet, hardly any of us does anything about it.

This misconception, this absence of empathy & compassion for athletes, this lack of action to help these athletes, this deceptive glorification of these athletes, gives me *immense* discontentment. It also gives me purpose.

I believe in a future where *every* athlete understands that sports do not define who they are. They are *not* athletes; they have been gifted with athletic-ability. I wake up *every* morning & try to further this message & make this future come true.

Do not get this message twisted: I do not have a problem with sports; I believe *every* child should play a sport, because sports teach *many* important life lessons. I have a problem with false identification. I do not think that athletes should not dedicate themselves to their sport; I believe that every one of us has a responsibility to maximize the gifts we have been given. I think athletes need to understand that dedicating themselves to their sports is setting themselves up for success in whatever endeavor they do after they are done playing.

For the rest of my life, I am going to do my best to make sure no other athlete goes through what I went through in my life after baseball. I am going to try my hardest to teach every athlete that they have an advantage over everyone else. The advantage is: everything they have learned to be successful in their sport, is everything they need to know to be successful in life - *It all applies*. They just need to change their focus, & I am going to help them change their focus.

THE BEST IS YET TO COME

It is not about the destination; it is about the journey. What a journey I have been on for the last six years of my life.

Baseball was not only my life, but it was my *escape*. It was my escape from my parents. It was my escape from the harsh realities of my life & my childhood. It was my escape from all the awful things that were happening in the house I grew up in. When I was on the mound, I felt freedom, & I felt peace. I had no anxieties. I had no worries. I had no shame. I had no depression. I had no suicidal thoughts. It was just me, the mound, & the baseball in my hand.

Then, my escape was taken away from me. I could no longer run out onto the mound, & away from my problems. I had to face them head on. I had no idea just how many problems there were, nor how *terrible* these problems were. For far too long, I tried to fight them by myself, & I came *very close* to giving it all up... *twice*; Christmas break my senior year was not the last time I tried to kill myself.

From the moment my baseball career ended to right now, as you read this, I have dealt with more heartache than anyone should ever have to deal with. I have experienced more pain than *anyone* should ever experience. I was in some *very* dark places that *no one* should ever be in. I was lost. I was very lonely. I *hated* myself. I felt trapped, like I was imprisoned. I had *zero* hope; I could not see the light at the end of the tunnel. I did not believe that it was going to get better. Then... over time, it *did* get better; *immeasurably* better than I could have ever asked for, or imagined.

I had a mentor come back into life, & ultimately, save my life. He also helped me discover my divine purpose & develop my *true* gifts. I was introduced to some wonderful people, who helped me get back up on my feet. I was welcomed into a *home*, where I was re-introduced to our amazing, faithful God, & He *finally* freed me from my bondage. He also revealed to me the *truth* about who I am. I will talk about all of this, *in detail*, in my next book, *Extra Innings*, coming in 2018.

"I believe in a future where *every* athlete understands that sports *do not* define who they are. Sports are a platform, *not* a calling."

"*Everything* you have learned to be successful in your sport, is everything you need to know to be successful in life - *It all applies.*"

@RileyTincher | #PitchingAgainstMyself

LETTER TO ALL LEADERS

Dear Leaders – Parents & Coaches alike,

I hope you picked up on the reoccurring theme in this book – I remembered *every* good & *bad* thing my coaches & parents did & said to me. *I am not the only one.*

I hope this book opened your eyes to the impact you *all* have on every single one of your children, & athletes.

There is a naiveté amongst all of you that children & young adults have no clue what is going on around them, & that they are oblivious to the problems of the world. Much worse, there is a belief amongst all of you that children do not have real problems themselves, & that the things that bother all of you, cannot bother them, because "they do not know what the real world is like."

I hope this book *destroyed* that belief.

Everything you do, & *everything* you say does not just affect you. They affect everyone around you; especially, the children & young adults around you. The choices you make every single moment, have a consequence, & a ripple effect. Too often, we are unaware of who that ripple effect reaches, & impacts.

Do not be ignorant to the fact that *you* are the main example for your children & your athletes will follow.

Every problem that you have, they *will* have. If you struggle with drug addiction, or alcoholism, they are going to struggle with it, as well. If you are constantly concerned about what others they think of you, they will be concerned with it, as well. If you are always worried about money, they will be worried about it too. If you are fearful of the future, they will be fearful of it too. If you struggle with confidence, & speak negatively to yourself, they will struggle with confidence, & speak negatively to themselves too. If you are not disciplined, they will not be disciplined. If you lie, they will lie. If you cheat, they will cheat. If you are unfaithful, they will be unfaithful. If you compromise, they will compromise. It is not a matter of *"if,"* it is a matter of *"when."*

They see *everything* you do. They see you handle relationships. They see you deal with hardships. They see you carry out the Gospel. It is not about you, anymore. It *never* was.

Coaches – I have heard way too many horror stories of terrible, selfish coaching. I have mentored way too many athletes who have trauma from the awful things their coaches have said & done to them. Athletes do not quit their sports, they quit their coaches.

Your job title is not as important as you think it is, but your *true* job responsibility is much more significant to your athletes than you think it is. The numbers on the scoreboard, & adding wins to the win-loss column are *not* what you are after; they are a byproduct of what you should truly be focusing on, & developing.

For some of your athletes, you have more influence on them, than their parents have on them; that was the case for me.

You should be more concerned with what your athletes do *after* their athletic career, than what they do while they are playing. Their athletic career is a miniscule amount of time compared to the time they have after their athletic career, but what they take away from it, & more importantly, what they take away from *you*, stays with them for the rest of their life. How you teach them to lead, is how they will lead their families. How you teach them to deal with failure & adversity, is how they will deal with failure & adversity in "real-life." What you enforce & encourage molds their behavior & beliefs in the future.

It is not about you, but it starts with you. Everything rises & falls on leadership. Where you go, the team will follow. Becoming a better leader *should* be your number one priority, because your future depends on it. If you become a better leader, *everything* around you will become better. *Everything!*

You need to realize that your athletes do not work for you; you work for them. It is not your team; it is *their* team. You do not lead the team; you lead the athletes who lead the team. You do not win the games; they win the games.

I do not care about how much you know. I do not care about how many years you have coached. I do not care about how much you have accomplished. None of that matters, until your athletes know you *truly* care about them – not about what they do for you as athletes, but about who they are as human beings.

It is amazing what your athletes will do for you when they know you *genuinely* appreciate them & *truly* care about them. Care is not something that can be faked. Your athletes are not stupid. They will know when you are being genuine, & when you are not.

I cannot imagine the pressure you are feeling to win games, & win championships, but that is not the real reason why you decided to become a coach. You must never forget that your responsibilities go *far beyond* winning games, & that your influence reaches *far more* people than you think it does. The greatest coaches of all time – Mike Krzyzewski, John Wooden, Nick Saban, etc. – understand their *true* responsibility, they tailor their priorities, their standards, & their actions around it, & they win *a lot* of games because of it.

Parents - Your kids will have a lot of different coaches, a lot of different teachers & professors, a lot of different managers & bosses, but they will only have *one* dad, & only *one* mom.

You may not have planned on becoming parents, but that is exactly what happened the moment your child was born.

Your child needs you at your best. You cannot waiver; your child is depending on you. You do not have to be perfect, but you have to be *present*, & it is nearly impossible to be present when you have a whole bunch of "stuff" going on.

If you have serious issues, *you need to seek help immediately*, because these issues will not go away on their own, & eventually, they *will* get passed on to your child.

The time that you have with your children, you will *never* get back; you will not get a second chance at parenting. You cannot spend enough time with them; there is no such thing as spending too much time with your child. At the end of the day, time is all they want from you. They will not remember the things you bought for them. They will remember the memories - good & bad - they had with you.

Your child is going to learn everything from *you*.

Your child needs to know how much you love them, *unconditionally*. Your child needs to know how *significant* they are. Your child needs to know how *valuable* they are. Your child needs to know how much you *care* about them… no matter the circumstance. Your child needs to know how *proud* of them you are.

When you take pictures of them, & post them to social media, *only* after they win games, or accomplish something, you are sending a message to them (whether you intend to, or not), that you are *only* proud of them when they achieve something.

When you only show up to "important" events & games, you are sending a message to them (whether you intend to, or not) that you do not think anything else they do is significant.

When you project your fears, your lack of faith, & your failed dreams on them, you are not protecting them (like, you think you are), you are holding them back from being who they are called to be (not, who *you* think they are called to be), & ultimately, you are hindering your future relationship with them.

You are supposed to be their reason to keep going, not their reason for giving up. You are supposed to be their biggest supporter, & greatest encourager, not their first taste of how cruel this world can be.

You may have had a rough childhood. You may not have had the best examples of parenting. You may be under a lot of stress right now, at home & at work. Your children may drive you crazy, & they may be the cause of a lot of your anxiety. You may be completely overwhelmed by the demands of being a parent. However, *none* of these are excuses for not being the best parent you can be, & none of them take away the fact that you have a choice to make (we all do), every moment of every day. You must choose to break the cycle. You must choose to be the parent you always wish you had.

You may think you cannot be used by God, but that is a *lie*.

With *love,*
The boy who never felt like he was good enough,
& The boy who wishes he did not come second to alcohol.

"Parents - Your kids will have a lot of different coaches, & a lot of different leaders in their life, but they will only have *one* dad, & only *one* mom."

"Coaches - It is amazing what your athletes will do for you when they *know* you *genuinely* appreciate them & *truly* care about them."

@RileyTincher | #PitchingAgainstMyself

ACKNOWLEDGEMENTS

GIVE THANKS

I firmly & whole-heartedly disagree with the glorification & the illusion of the "self-made man." I, & everyone else on this Earth did not get to where we are today on our own, nor will we ever get to where we want to go on our own, either.

I am *never* going to pretend that I did this on my own.

There are so many people (too many to count) that helped me & guided me through my baseball career. From coaches, to parents, to teachers & professors, to teammates & friends, to fans, to people who did not believe in me – they all played an important, fundamental role in my growth not only as a baseball player, & athlete, but also, as a man, a leader, & a Christian.

There were also *a lot* of people who helped me, encouraged me, & enlightened me through the entire process of writing this book.

These are some (not all) of those people:

Dad & Mom – I hope you read this book with an open-heart & an open-mind. If I could go back through my childhood, I would not change a thing. All the good, & all the bad things that happened made me who I am today. I am so grateful that you both did the best you could, the best way you knew how to. I know things between us have not been ideal, but please know I still *love* you, & I always will.

Dr. John Saurino – You are, by far, *the greatest* father I know. You have the most faith I have *ever* seen. I am forever in debt to you for the generosity & love you have constantly given to me. Thank you for showing me the *real* Jesus Christ. Thank you for teaching me how to believe - simple, but not easy. Thank you for encouraging me to get out of my own way. Thank you for helping me fix my eye on Jesus.

The Saurino Family – Thank you for always treating me like I am a Saurino. You came into my life when I *desperately* needed you. There has never been a time I have left your *home*, or left your presence, & did not thank & praise God for bringing you all into my life.

The Launch Pad - Nate, Steve, & Seth – This book would not be done without you guys, & your constant support. You all have completely changed the trajectory of my life. Thank you for giving me a safe place to go to, to vent, cry, rejoice, & be vulnerable. Thank you for holding me accountable to such a high standard. Thank you for being on my team; you are *the greatest* teammates I have ever had.

Jonathan Hood – You are *the best* friend I have *ever* had. Getting to know you, & your amazing family the last couple of years has been an absolute pleasure. You are the perfect example of "never judge a book by its cover." I have never met someone who listens as great as you do. Thank you is not enough for your generosity, your *loyalty*, & for understanding me more than I understand myself.

Dr. Stephanie Christner – No amount of words could ever describe how *grateful* I am for you. You have believed in me & my dream from day one – even when people told you not to. Because of you, I am able to wake up every morning & live out my purpose. I could *never* repay you for how much you have done for me. For the first time in my life, I *truly* believe the best is yet to come, & that is because of *you*.

Coach Darin Everson – You are *the best* coach I ever had. Thank you for not giving up on me, when *everyone* else did. Thank you for believing in me, when no one else did. Thank you for helping me get back up there. Thank you for always making me do one pushup for being left-handed. Because of you, I was given opportunities that I could have only dreamed of receiving.

Coach Mark Diercks – Thank you for pushing me harder & farther than I could ever have pushed myself. Thank you for volunteering your most valuable resource – your time – *for free*, to showing me what I am capable of. Thank you for igniting my competitive spirit.

Coach John Vodenlich – Quite frankly, I would not be alive today, if it was not for you. You are so much more than a coach to me. You taught me how to be a leader. You taught me how to be a father. You taught me that everything I learned to be successful in baseball, is everything I need to know to be successful in life. Thank you for giving me the greatest compliment I have ever been given – that you want your son, Sam, to grow up to be like me. I still do not know what you see in me, but I am so honored & humbled that you do.

Coach David Perchinsky – I will never forget the first conversation we had. Thank you for showing me that I am more than a baseball player. Thank you for telling me to "figure out my life," & pushing me to move forward. Thank you for giving me the greatest recruiting experience of my life. Thank you for encouraging me to go to graduate school, & helping me get into Baylor University.

Coach Ryan Callahan - The conversations we had in the bullpen are some of my most-treasured memories. You have no idea how much you helped me, on & off the field. You have no idea how much you, your advice, & your leadership mean to me. Thank you for teaching me about life, & about peaks & valleys. Thank you for always fighting for me, especially when I did not have the strength to fight for myself.

Coach Travis Hergert – Thank you for *caring* about me. Thank you for giving me a chance, without even seeing me pitch. Thank you for following *every* step of my journey after NIACC. Thank you for inciting me to compete, attack the zone, & pitch with *intent.* Thank you for *never* allowing me to get comfortable. It is not by chance that you are having the success that you are having as a head coach.

My Eighth-Grade Coach & Every Other Coach Who Passed On/Overlooked Me – Thank you for putting *the biggest* chip on my shoulder. Because of you, I was an All-American, the Pitcher of the Year, & an All-Star in one of the best collegiate summer leagues in the country. Your doubt ignited a fire in me that could not be contained. I *loved* proving you all wrong.

Thank you, God.

Because of You, I am made new. Because of You, I am completely different from who I once was. Because of You, I am a walking *miracle*. Thank you for your Word. Thank you for your Son, Jesus Christ. Thank you for giving me *constant* guidance through the Holy Spirit. Thank you for giving me grace, even though I do not deserve it. Thank you for always doing *immeasurably* more for me than I could ever ask for, or imagine. Thank you for showing me that *all* things are possible through You. Thank you for showing me that *everything* I was looking for was already inside of me. Thank you for teaching me who I truly am. Thank you for showing me that I *belonged* here.

I cannot wait to sit on Your lap, on Your throne, in Your Kingdom.

ABOUT THE AUTHOR

Riley Tincher is a coach, an author, & a speaker. He is also the creator & program director of Coachability, which is a mentorship program for all athletes, at all levels (youth, high school, collegiate, professional, & Olympic), all throughout the country. This program teaches athletes the principles needed to be successful in sports, & in life.

Photograph by Allie Klawitter

Riley specializes in leadership development, & identification - which, is our *true* identity; who God says we are. There is an identity crisis among the vast majority of athletes; especially, among elite-level athletes. It has become a *very* serious issue, that Riley has personally gone through & has overcome, & now, he is helping numerous other athletes overcome it, as well. He believes in a future where *every* athlete understands that sports do not define who they are; it is something they have been gifted to do. Sports are a platform, not a calling.

Riley also mentors coaches, by helping them develop coaching philosophies, build championship cultures, & maximize their leadership potential. He also helps them realize that their responsibilities go *far* beyond winning games, because he understands, first-hand, the impact coaches have on their athlete's lives. Often times, coaches have more influence over an athlete's life than that athlete's parents have over them. The problem is, the majority of coaches do not understand this, & quite frankly, they misuse & abuse the influence they have, without realizing the life-long effect this has on their athletes. Riley believes in a future where *every* coach, at *every* level, fully-comprehends the power & impact their influence has on *all* of their athletes; especially, in life after sports.

Riley enjoys traveling the country, & spreading the message of: *everyone* needs a team, *everyone* needs a coach, & *everyone* needs to be coachable. His authentic, passionate, & engaging talks have influenced & impacted several leaders, coaches, & teams in sports, business, healthcare, education, & churches. Riley speaks on a variety of topics, including: leadership, legacy, purpose, perseverance, teamwork, culture, preparation, introspection, identification, & much more. Each speech he delivers is customized to fit the needs of the audience.

Riley hosts a weekly Facebook Live video series called Coachability. Each episode includes topics on leadership, identification, personal growth & development, & more. Coachability airs every Tuesday night at 8:00 PM CST on his Facebook Page – Facebook.com/RileyBTincher

Riley also hosts the Coaching The Coach Leadership Podcast that is released on the 1st & 3rd Monday of every month on iTunes, Spotify, & Soundcloud. The purpose of the podcast is to help you become the leader you are called to be, by providing wisdom through teaching & interviews.

Up until recently, Riley has been best known for his historic, record-breaking collegiate baseball career. He was a two-time All-American, the Midwest Region Pitcher of the Year, the Wisconsin Intercollegiate Athletic Conference (WIAC) Pitcher of the Year, a two-time First-Team All-Region pitcher, a two-time First-Team All-WIAC pitcher, a "Max Sparger Award" recipient (awarded to the top academic student-athlete in the WIAC), & an All-Star in the prestigious Northwoods League. Riley also holds several school, conference, region, & NCAA records. Among all of the accolades & awards Riley has received, he believes *the* greatest accomplishment of his career was being voted Captain of his team by his teammates, his senior year.

Photograph by Lisa Van Horn

66612919R00235

Made in the USA
Lexington, KY
19 August 2017